MALTA
DIARY OF A
WAR

1940 – 1945

MICHAEL GALEA

BDL Publishing

(+356) 2138 0351

www.bdlbooks.com

First edition, 1992
Second edition, 1994
This edition, 2016

Proofreading: Louis J. Scerri

Malta Diary of a War
1940 – 1945
Michael Galea

ISBN: 978-99957-46-63-6

Printed by Gutenberg Press, Ħal Tarxien

'Malta is a little island with a great history. The record of the Maltese people throughout that long history is a record of constancy and fortitude. It is with those qualities, matchlessly displayed, that they are now confronting the dark power of the Axis. But it is not given to them, any more than it is to other peoples, to maintain resolute defence without suffering or to escape loss in achieving victory.'

Winston S. Churchill

Contents

Malta the target. Walled in to the north and south by enemy territory, and to the west by Vichy controlled Tunisia. Malta was isolated by nearly 1000 miles of sea from Gibraltar and over 800 fom Alexandria, in 1941 the nearest Allied land bases. Enemy minefields in the Sicilian Narrows and against the island hemmed the approaches. Encircling Axis air fleets in Italy, Sardinia, Sicily and Africa seemed to imprison her.

Introduction

In his essay on 'Diaries', William Ralph Inge enumerates several motives for writing a diary, such as: 'the writer is tempted by a big cheque ... others have a grievance, and wish posterity to know why they were elbowed out of office ,... others again have left memoirs which they intended or hoped would be published after their deaths, and in which they have inserted as much venom as they knew how, conscious that they themselves will not be able to be called to account ... sometimes prompted by sheer vanity.' Writing in 1922, Inge continues: 'We have already half-forgotten our hopes and fears at various periods during the war [1914–18], and we have wholly forgotten our state of mind in July, 1914. When we look back at our diaries (if we keep them) during any crisis of our lives, we shall have some surprises. We have come to tell the story differently to ourselves. We pride ourselves on our foresight, though what happened was a mere stroke of luck, and we narrowly escaped some disastrous decision.'

However, I must readily confess from the outset, this diary falls under none of these classifications. For one thing, this isn't essentially a personal diary. On the other hand, the leading motive behind it is to provide a lasting tribute to the garrison and the civilian population of Malta who have either fallen victim during or survived the epic siege of World War Two.

The reader already knows from the title that this is a Diary of War.

The Maltese Islands are a small archipelago of some six islands and islets in the centre and on the crossroads of the Mediterranean. The total area is 246 km2, approximately equivalent to that of the Isle of Wight. Malta, the major island, consists of a series of low

The Maltese Islands.

hills, and its coastline provides numerous harbours, bays, creeks, and rocky coves. The distance between Malta and the nearest point in Sicily is 93 km. The distance from the nearest point on the North African mainland is 288 km. Gibraltar lies 1,826 km to the west and Alexandria is 1,510 km to the east.

On the background of its geographical and strategic position, Malta played its role first as a most vital outpost of defence, and later as an advanced base for attack; submarines, ships, and aircraft operating from Malta dealt blow after blow on the enemy. From a besieged island, Malta became a besieging driving force; from a defensive base it became an offensive platform intercepting Axis convoys plying between Sicily and Africa. Malta's leading and decisive role in the struggle for the Mediterranean is retold and illustrated in this book.

This diary endeavours to give a graphic day-to-day description of events of the wartime ordeal as experienced by the peoples of the Maltese Islands. It gives the inside story of the war as the Maltese people lived and survived it. This is not a story on Malta written by an outsider, but a story of a war as seen by those who were in it. It is indeed the Malta Story, the war as seen from the Malta front. And Malta was indeed in the forefront.

The diary is written and compiled strictly from the scanty information available at the time the events described therein actually took place. The contents therefore appear severely trimmed in accordance with the information made available from time to time under conditions of siege. Other information may well have been purposely inflated and stilted to boost morale amongst a suffering nation on the verge of surrender. Such information may have been justifiably enough incomplete for security reasons, or intentionally inaccurate in order to mislead the foe. The members of the general public were not allowed to know more than was necessary as regards defence – and obviously as a security measure or because it was not desirable to permit certain information to leave Malta.

It is with this background and within the context of such circumstances, conditions, and limitations that the diary must be read and understood.

Many books on World War Two have been published since the cessation of hostilities and these include diaries in the form of autobiographies and memoirs. But whereas these books were published in the post-war years and are perhaps more elaborately written, this diary-book is contemporary to the events themselves, at a time when, information made available to the public, was more cautious, and at times deliberately vague. Post-war books look at the war events in retrospect, whereas this diary uses the present tense, that is, as the war proceeded from its commencement up to its conclusion. Details which can be found in post-war books were often not available when the war and the blitz were still raging.

Official news bulletins and public notices were often ruthlessly censored before release. It could be that at times the meagre information made public was strongly worded against the enemy and also not devoid of a touch of propaganda. But, of course, this language is understandable only with the background of the war conditions then prevailing.

Useful and important information could be gleaned and obtained from very few sources; these included valuable information in the form of official circulars issued and addressed to government departments and other public establishments, as well as from public notices released from time to time from the Lieutenant Governor's Office, public speeches and official communiqués. The debates of the Council of Government, the *Malta Government Gazette* and contemporary newspapers (mainly the *Times of Malta*, the *Sunday Times of Malta*, *Il-Berqa*, and *Lehen is-Sewwa*) constitute another important source of information.

As a result of its strategic position at the time, Malta was to play a leading role in the Mediterranean struggle for power between the Allied Nations and the Axis Powers. No wonder that Malta was the Mecca for the Supreme Command of the Allied Forces in the battle for the Middle Sea. All this goes to show the large and significant contribution the little island gallantly offered to the Allied cause against heavy odds.

This book includes the most salient events and occurrences of World War Two that took place in Malta, without failing to put these events in their international context and perspective better to assess and appreciate their significance on a global scale. These events include Italy's declaration of war and its repercussions on Malta (June 1940), the arrival of the Luftwaffe in Malta's skies (January 1941), the Italian E-boat attack on the Grand Harbour (July 1941), the award of the George Cross to the Maltese Nation (April 1942), the famous *Santa Marija* Convoy (August 1942), the Royal Visit of George VI (June 1943), the visit by Churchill (November 1943), the presentation of the Scroll to the People of Malta by President Roosevelt (December 1943), the presentation of the Sword of Honour to Governor Gort (March 1944), the Victory celebrations (August 1945) – to mention just a few.

The illustrations in this book are strictly contemporaneous and none is dated after 1945. The illustrations coincide with the time and place of the events described or referred to in the diary proper. The book is profusely illustrated as the pictures help as visual material to understand better the text. The photos have been carefully selected and are therefore all the more significant and representative.

The population figures for Malta and Gozo during the war years read as follows:

	1940	1941	1942	1943	1944	1945
Male	132,981	133,145	131,833	133,468	137,044	141,182
Female	137,774	138,214	137,257	138,653	142,143	145,414

The intensive blitzkrieg on Malta is to be understood if these figures are kept in mind. Because of these demographic figures, it is generally believed that, with the exception of Germany, the Maltese Islands had a much higher percentage rate of casualties/deaths through enemy action than Britain and, therefore, probably greater than in any other country. No doubt, without the rock shelters the blitz in Malta would have had a more disastrous and catastrophic effect.

A part of the diary, that is, from June 1940 to mid-May 1942 was first published in instalments in *The Armed Forces of Malta Journal* (No. 28 – October 1977; No. 29 – April 1978; No. 30 – October 1978; No. 31 – April 1979; No. 32 – October 1979) but, unfortunately due to *force majeure*, it had to stop as the *Journal* ceased publication. This book comprises that part which was published (but has now been revised) together with the rest of the original manuscript which is appearing in print for the first time.

Michael Galea

Explanatory Note

Casualties in the context of this diary mean 'deaths' - killed through enemy action; the number enclosed in brackets after the names of the casualties refers to their respective ages.

AD 1940

Mon 10 Jun

Mussolini joins Hitler's war. His declaration was made at 6 p.m. today at Palazzo Venezia in Rome – 7 p.m. Malta time. A state of war exists between Italy and the Allies. Italy's declaration of war is received in Malta with calm.

HE Lieutenant-General William George Sheddon Dobbie in a broadcast to the people of Malta and Gozo expresses his trust in the people to maintain the utmost calm and trust in God; this is the greatest contribution which the civilian people can make to the common good and towards the defence of our island home.

Tue 11 Jun

Editorial headed 'We are at War' in today's *Daily Malta Chronicle*:

'Sig. Mussolini last evening threw in his hand with Hitler and placed the Italian nation in pledge and forfeit against the Allies in the present war. For the first time since the Napoleonic campaign, we in Malta find ourselves a focal point in a struggle which our fellow-members of the British Empire have undertaken. We can do no greater service to ourselves and our Commonwealth brethren

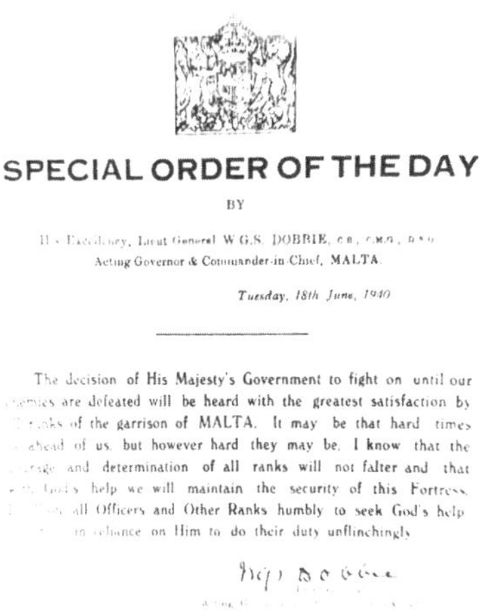

SPECIAL ORDER OF THE DAY

BY

His Excellency, Lieut General W.G.S. DOBBIE, C.B., C.M.G., D.S.O.
Acting Governor & Commander-in-Chief, MALTA.

Tuesday, 18th June, 1940

The decision of His Majesty's Government to fight on until our [illegible]mies are defeated will be heard with the greatest satisfaction by [illegible] ranks of the garrison of MALTA. It may be that hard times [illegible] ahead of us but however hard they may be, I know that the [illegible] and determination of all ranks will not falter and that [illegible] God's help we will maintain the security of this Fortress. [illegible] all Officers and Other Ranks humbly to seek God's help [illegible] in reliance on Him to do their duty unflinchingly.

General Dobbie's stirring call.

A wartime poster of Governor Sir William Dobbie.

than to stand firm and calm, and accept the facts of the new situation with cold and unyielding determination. We must fight ... Our province from this moment on is that of being a front-line unit in the general battle with forces that threatened to destroy free Europe ... You are now a vanguard of the war. The position which Malta holds today in the sphere of European activity lays certain demands upon the individual. A few days ago we mentioned that Italy's problem is where to strike. She will strike, and may even gain initial advances. But at bedrock, the problem remains with her, and will be her downfall, for the only point at which she can concentrate is the French frontier, a move that is counter-balanced by her vulnerability in every other sphere. She can strike, but she can be heavily struck. That latter is our task. Let us get on with it. Italy has thrown down the glove. We, Malta and the Empire, pick it up.'

The very first air-raid warning in Malta is sounded at 6.25 a.m. Anti-aircraft batteries open fire against two formations of seven and three hostile aircraft respectively. These formations approach the Grand Harbour, Valletta, from the SE, flying over Kalafrana and Ħal Far. Bombs are dropped on Ħal Far aerodrome.

More bombs are dropped between Fort Bengħajsa and Birżebbuġa. The attack lasts about half an hour.

Almost immediately a second raid commences. The aircraft follow the same course at first but then make for Corradino, Portes des Bombes, Pietà Creek, Sa Maison, and the new hospital of St Luke. However, the hospital still continues to be used in the present emergency.

At Portes des Bombes the Government Water and Electricity Dept. shed is damaged by two bombs, one of which kills two Maltese workmen. Meanwhile, one plane carries out a low flying attack on Fort St Elmo which is manned by the lst Heavy Regt., Royal Malta Artillery (RMA). Two of the three bombs dropped on St Elmo hit the Cavalier and kill six RMA men – Bdr Joseph Galea, Gnr Michel'Angelo Saliba, Gnr Richard Micallef, Gnr Carmel Cordina, Gnr Paul Debono, and Boy Philip Busuttil. These are the very first military casualties of the war in Malta.

Pamphlets in Maltese promoting anti-Axis propoganda in the series *Kollezzjoni Safra* (Yellow Collection).

Other bombs hit the new hospital of St Luke and destroy a house nearby, while yet another wrecks a house at Msida killing a man and his wife.

Another raid takes place at sunset: Marsa, Cospicua, Gżira, and Sliema suffer their first casualties.

In the evening the air-raid alarm is sounded at 7.25 p.m. Twenty-five Italian aircraft take part in the raid, operating in formations of five. These formations approach the island from various directions and a number of heavy bombs are dropped, some of them in salvoes of three at a time. In this raid material damage is caused at Żabbar, Tarxien, and Verdala Barracks (Cospicua). Bombs also fall in the sea off Fort Ricasoli and in the Grand Harbour and at the Turkish Cemetery, Marsa. Except for superficial damage to Forts St Elmo and Ricasoli, military objectives remain untouched.

At Sliema, the Modem Imperial hotel and Parall.el Street are hit. At Gżira, Ponsonby Street is also hit. At Cospicua, St Theresa's Convent is damaged, as well as a school being used as a hospital.

In all there have been eight raids or raid alarms throughout the day with the following civilian casualties:[1] Birkirkara: Carmelo Galea (40); Cospicua: Joseph Ancilleri (–), Maria Fenech (6), Doris Galea (5 months); Gżira: Michael Camenzuli (39), Lilian Doublet (7), Mary Doublet (46), Giuliano Micallef (65), Giovanni Trapani (48), Rosina Vassallo (33); Mqabba: Giuseppe Ellul (36); Msida: Paolo Galea (37).

The Lieutenant Governor, E. St. J. Jackson in a Proclamation says that now that war has broken out with Italy, 'we humbly trust in the guidance and protection of Divine Providence and in assured confidence of the cordial support and tried fidelity and determination of the people of Malta.' Malta's reaction to Italy's declaration of war against the Allies is expressed in the people's fierce determination to get to work. In Valletta crowds collect at various points. Opposite the Police Station in Kingsway, a large crowd watch members of the Italian community being taken in for detention at the Internment Camp. Italian shipping in Maltese waters has been seized.

1 The names of the civilian casualties mentioned in this diary are exclusively of those who were killed through enemy action.

It is notified for public information that, as from today until further notice, curfew will start from 8.30 p.m. This early curfew has been rendered imperative owing to the spread of war in the Mediterranean, so as to give the greatest possible facility to the defence forces of the island to move without interference on the public thoroughfares.

The bus service will terminate at 7 p.m. daily until further notice.

Because of the very heavy traffic on the switchboards, owing to the needs of defence, telephone subscribers are earnestly requested not to use the telephone except for urgent and important calls. The public is also requested to limit the number of private calls and conversation on the telephone; such calls should be as brief as possible and, under no circumstances, should the duration of the call be allowed to exceed three minutes.

The *Società–Economico–Agraria del Gruppo di Malta*[2] announces that the show, which the Society holds annually at the Boschetto Gardens on 28 and 29 June, has this year been postponed *sine die* owing to abnormal times.

Sir Arturo Mercieca, Kt., MA, LL.D. has tendered his resignation of the offices of Chief Justice and President of the Court of Appeal.

People removing the debris at Gżira discover two children in a room beneath the debris. They do not have a scratch, but are very hungry! Wed 12 Jun

Today's editorial of the *Daily Malta Chronicle* is dedicated to the 'First Day':

'Yesterday war came to Malta. We had a succession of air visits from the Italian Air Force. One real fact on which one can pride ourselves emerged. The Maltese were grand. The authorities have already paid tribute to the manner in which the civilian population behaved. Let us keep that headline before us in whatever the future may hold, that copper-plate unconsciousness and the calm bravery. We have earned the trust that can be laid in us. We are facing a large

2 The agricultural show was held for the first time on the feast of St Peter and St Paul (*Mnarja*) at Boschetto Gardens in 1854 during the time of Governor Sir William Reid.

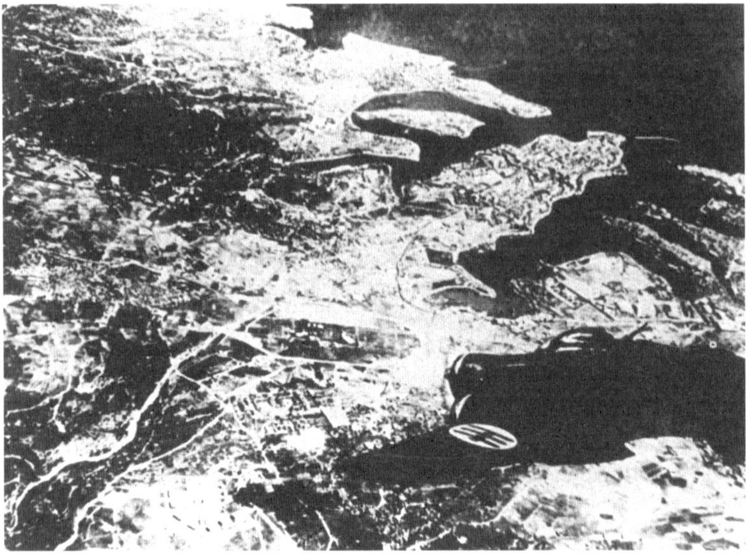

An SM 79 of the Regia Aeronautica on a bombing run over Malta.

task and a heavy one, but we face it now in full confidence in our own quiet ability. Yesterday our first casualties of the War shed their lives on their own little island, defending their homes and their people, the gallant ranks of the Royal Malta Artillery. They have left us a pledge to carry on. We will not let them down. And for today and tomorrow, God's blessing go

Italian Cants during a bombing sweep of Grand Harbour.

with you while you are living up to this new one-day old tradition they have left.'

A single reconnaissance aircraft flew over the island. Bombers followed later, causing seventeen casualties: *Cospicua*: Antonia Fenech (28), Francesco Fenech (33), Saviour Fenech (8), Lorenzo Calafato (35), Carmelo Camilleri (9), Romeo Pace (35), Concetta Scicluna (24); *Gżira*: Arthur Brooks (18), John Gatt (24); *Paola*: Giuseppa Camilleri (24); *Pietà*: Antonia Farrugia (25), Antonio Farrugia (5), Joseph Farrugia (4), Josephine Mangion (4); *Sliema*: M'Assunta Borg (48), Victor German (17); *Żabbar*: Joseph Facciol (23).

Several persons are convicted under the Black Out Regulations for having left light in their residences, the reflection of which could be visible either from the air or from the sea.

Fri 14 Jun

Low clouds today favoured the enemy. The first air-raid warning this morning is caused by two Italian aircraft, possibly an Ala Littoria transport with a military escort. They came to within eight miles off Delimara from the North, circled Filfla to fix their position, and flew on southwards.

In the 12.30 p.m. raid an enemy bomber drops bombs in the Kalafrana area.

There is another air-raid alarm when an enemy plane attacks Kalafrana slipway. Bombs are dropped. The air-raid warning is again sounded. Bombs are haphazardly dropped near a camp north of Mellieħa. Today's casualties: *Cospicua*: Giuseppa Scicluna (24), 2 males and 1 female unidentified.

As from today the *Daily Malta Chronicle* appears in four pages instead of eight (War Edition).

Fri 14 Jun

An air-raid alarm is sounded at 8.35 a.m. Two enemy bombers drop high-explosive bombs on the Grand Harbour, Fort St Angelo, and also on the beach of Ta' Xbiex. From the Marsa end of the Grand Harbour the enemy raiders appear to fly in a straight line over St John's Co-Cathedral, the Public Library, and the Palace. A bomb is dropped just opposite the Co Cathedral but does not explode.

Today's casualties: *Birżebbuġa*: Anġlu Farrugia (50); *Cospicua*: Emanuel Gauci (50); *Gżira*: Elvira Micallef (23), 2 females (unidentified).

Refugee Settlement Centres are established in the villages of Malta in order to deal with the problem that has arisen with regard to the exodus of people from the cities and towns.

Sat 15 Jun

One air-raid. One person killed at *Ħamrun*: Antonio Borg (26).

HMS *Calypso* is sunk by an Italian U-boat. One officer and 38 ratings are missing and feared lost. The sinking has occurred in the Mediterranean. However, all Maltese ratings have been reported safe.

Sun 16 Jun

Today is the first Sunday since the commencement of hostilities with Italy. First alarm is sounded: three formations of enemy aircraft, totalling 13 aircraft, flying in line astern from the East to the West, are sighted. Several bombs are dropped in the neighbourhood of Kalafrana. The third formation of enemy aeroplanes are Macchi 200

Leaders of the Siġġiewi group of the Malta Volunteer Defence Force. *(Sunday Times of Malta)*

fighters. During the early afternoon the 'wailing' sends pedestrians scurrying to shelter. Five bombs are dropped in the neighbourhood of Mosta. Civilian casualties: *Cospicua*: Emanuel Spiteri (65); *Żejtun*: Salvatore Mifsud (56).

Gen. Dobbie visits six centres of the Malta Volunteer Defence Force: Żejtun, Żebbuġ, Birkirkara, Naxxar, Mosta, and Rabat.

The Malta Relief Fund is started to afford relief to those who are suffering in Malta from the hardship of war.

Mon 17 Jun

The first air-raid is the earliest we have had so far: at 6.15 a.m. In this raid about seven enemy aircraft in two flights, consisting of five bombers and two fighters, drop several bombs in central Malta.

There were more raid alarms throughout the day.

Thu 20 June

Malta experiences its first night air-raid. Some of the churches could be heard from Valletta pealing the 'all clear'.

Casualty: *Naxxar*: Felice Farrugia (47).

Fri 21 Jun

Four more raids. Bombs fall on Marfa and in Gozo.

Sat 22 Jun

All ranks, except Officers and Warrant Officers, are prohibited from entering bars or wine shops, except between the hours of 1500 and 1900. All ranks are forbidden to accept drinks from civilians.

A circular released from the Lieutenant Governor's Office requests Heads of Government Departments to draw up a list of employees serving in their departments, who have absented themselves from duty since 11 June 1940, continuously or otherwise, and who have failed to explain satisfactorily the reason for their absences.

Sun 23 Jun

Enemy attacks over Malta. A two-engine monoplane crashes, and two of its seven men forming the crew make the descent by parachute into the sea; they are picked up and are now prisoners of war in Malta.

The Parabolic Acoustic Mirror, known to the Maltese as *Il-Widna* (the ear) at Ta' San Pietru valley beneath the Victoria Lines, helped to detect aircraft over Sicily. The 'Mirror' preceded the advent of radar.

Mon 24 Jun

Feast of St John the Baptist

Gen. Charles de Gaulle has set up a French National Committee in London, which has been recognized by His Majesty's Government. The British Government has withdrawn recognition of the Bordeaux Government as it is no longer the government of an independent country.

Wed 26 Jun

Frequent and severe air-raids during which several bombs are dropped in inhabited areas. Casualties: *Birkirkara:* David Castles (62), Arthur Farrugia (40); *Gżira*: Joseph Farrugia (31); *Ħamrun*: Joseph Cordina (22), George Zammit (32); *Marsa*: Karmni Frendo (29), Filomena Pace (60), eight charred bodies (unidentified) collected from Marsa Cross Road; *Mqabba*: Anġla Ghigo (55), Giulio Ghigo (25), Emanuel Ghigo (18), Carmela Saliba (30), Giuseppa Saliba (3), Polly Saliba (6), one male (unidentified); *Paola*: Francis Caruana (54), Raffaele Cini (55), George Howard (35); Qormi: Gianni Borg (25), Grazio Cassar (26), PC 284 Calcedonio Saliba (25); *Valletta:* Francesco

Farrugia (50), Domenico Galea (28); *Vittoriosa:* Paul Saliba (7), *Żejtun:* Lorenzo Caruana (35). Locality not indicated: Emanuel Cassar (53), Dockyard Policeman Albert Pell (20).

Farmers and other owners of animals are informed that there is at present a shortage of imported animal foodstuffs which is likely to continue for some time. Under these circumstances, all owners of animals are requested to make greater use of locally grown foodstuffs in order to make imported ones last as long as possible. At the same time the increase of locally grown fodder is to be stimulated by making water available to farmers wishing to grow green crops such as maize millet and mangolds.

Enemy air attacks are repulsed by heavy anti-aircraft fire from our defences. The twenty-eighth air raid occurs at 9.15 p.m. and for the first time it takes place in pitch darkness. Casualties: *Cospicua:* Carmelo Fiteni (40); *Marsa:* Giuseppe Gatt (2), Giorgio Gatt (7); *Tarxien:* Angiolina Orland (30). Thu 27 Jun

Lt.-Gen Dobbie broadcasts to the people warning against rumour mongers.

Heads of Departments are requested by the Lieutenant Governor to supply information on any event concerning the activities of their department which may be of public interest, with particular reference to anything which is of a character calculated to support public morale and to encourage the maintenance of normal life in the island.

Two formations, each of three bombers, are seen approaching the island. During the air battle that ensues one of the enemy planes, badly damaged, is seen to dive into a low cloud, emitting clouds of smoke from its tail. Sat 29 Jun

A circular issued by the Archbishop's Curia dispenses the Faithful from the law of Fasting and Abstinence.

More raids and one casualty at *Birkirkara:* Joseph Genovese (21), an evacuee from Sliema. Sun 30 Jun

It is officially confirmed that while flying over Tobruk during an enemy bombardment, an aircraft piloted by Marshal Balbo, Governor-General of Libya, fell in flames. Balbo and all members of his crew perished.

Owing to the need to conserve supplies of motor spirit while maintaining adequate public passenger and supply services, no private motor or hired car (other than taxi-cars) are allowed on the road after midnight, unless provided with a special permit, showing that it is on approved service.

Wed 3 Jul

More raids by Italian Savoia Marchetti 79 bombers.[3]

The last issue of *The Daily Malta Chronicle* is published today. Editorial comment: 'Unpleasant duties sometimes fall to the lot of newspapermen. Few can equal that which circumstances force us to perform today. For almost 53 years,[4] the *Malta Chronicle and the Imperial Services Gazette* ... served the public of Malta. Since the declaration of war by Mussolini, the proprietors have continued publication with extreme difficulty. Every effort conceivable has been made by both them and the management to avoid a suspension. That now seems inevitable. At the very least, the Daily Malta Chronicle from today ceases publication in its present form. During the war of 1914–18, this paper never missed an edition, and that the present step

Ready to combat any gas attack!

3 Standard long-range bombers of the Regia Aeronautica; bomb load: 2205 lbs; maximum speed: 260 mph.

4 The first issue of this local newspaper had appeared in 1887.

is forced upon us in this phase of a new struggle with the old enemy ... While we may not be with you in the concluding stages of this struggle, we were never more confident that we shall join you again in celebrating a hard-won but certain victory. With you, we have passed through some bright and some very black days. Today is not the worst. In our little island we are solidly united and bent on a single goal, victory over the traitor who professes brotherhood with us and bombs our homes.'

There is a heavy raid and several bombs are dropped haphazardly on the central and north-eastern parts of the island. Casualty: *Naxxar*: Michael Falzon (70). Sat 6 Jul

A supply of the most recent type of civilian respirators is available for issue from Police Stations.

Frequent air-raids with much indiscriminate bombing. Casualties: *Kalkara*: Vincent Borg (2), Ċettina Borg (3), Giuseppina Borg (4), George Borg (5), Irene Borg (8 months), Maggie Borg (10), Melania Borg (42); *Qormi:* Amante Abela (30); *Tarxien*: Joseph Garcia (14). Sun 7 Jul

The air-raid alarm is sounded following the approach of several formations of enemy planes. Wed 10 Jul

There are exciting moments when an enemy plane is brought down and bursts to smithereens, followed by a hunt for souvenirs.

Casualties: *Qormi*: Modesta Cassar (37); *Żabbar*: Angelico Pulis (45).

HM the King awards the Distinguished Flying Cross to Flight Lieutenant George Burgess for his courage in the air defence of Malta. Sat 13 Jul

Air-raids, gunfire and much searchlight activity. Sun 14 Jul

Mon 15 Jul **More bomb-proof shelters** are opened in Valletta: that in Queen's Square has additional entrances in Old Theatre Street and Merchants Street. New tunnels are opened at Portes des Bombes.

Sun 21 Jul **More air assaults.** More air battles.

Tue 23 Jul **The first number** of *Information Service Bulletin* (bilingual: Maltese/ English) is issued by the Information Office. Its aim is to promote anti Italian feelings among the population.

Tue 30 Jul **At the Cathedral** Church of Gozo a monument to the memory of Archbishop Pietro Pace is solemnly inaugurated. Mgr Michele Gonzi delivers the speech to mark the occasion. The monument is the work of Maltese sculptor Antonio Sciortino.

Ancient catacombs converted into air raids shelters.

INFORMATION SERVICE
BULLETIN

No. 1 MAĦRUĠ MILL-INFORMATION OFFICE, MALTA 23.7.40

Il-Bidu

Il-Mediterran

Il-Futur

The first issue of the *Information Service Bulletin* dated 23 July 1940, and published by the Information Office, Malta.

1940 – The Valletta Air Raid Precaution Squad photographed at its headquarters, The Old Lyceum, Merchants Street.

Sitting of the Council of Government. During the sitting, HE the Officer Administering the Government reads a letter which the Clerk of House had received from the Nationalist Leader Dr Enrico Mizzi who excused his absence on the grounds (a) that he had been ill for a considerable time, so ill that during an aerial bombardment which seriously hit Fort San Salvatore, where he was being confined, he was obliged to remain in bed, on which splinters fell, and (b) that he had been forced to absent himself by reasons of *force majeure*. He also complained that notices of sittings have been handed to him late.

Tue 13 Aug

All remaining street names in Valletta, Cospicua, Senglea, and Vittoriosa written in Italian are changed into English.

Thu 15 Aug

Strong formations of enemy bombers escorted by fighters continue to raid the island.

Thu 22 Aug

Lord Gerald Strickland passes peacefully away at his residence, Villa Bologna in Lija. Throughout his brief illness he was surrounded by his family and assisted by Fr Seraphin Zarb, OP and Fr Michael Balzan, Parish Priest of Attard, who administered the Last Sacraments.

Fri 23 Aug

Reconnaissance flights by enemy planes.

Sun 1 Sep

'Piazza Maggiore' at Żurrieq is renamed 'Churchill Square'.

Tue 3 Sep

The first convoy with essential commodities for Malta is safely brought into harbour.

At about 6 a.m. this morning an Italian motor boat approached Malta and was at once engaged by Naval patrol vessels and shore batteries. The motor boat turned back to base.

The 4th Heavy Battery, Royal Malta Artillery, of the 1st Heavy Regiment Royal Malta Artillery, is formed.

A group of Boys of the Royal Malta Artillery.

Thu 5 Sep

Enemy planes approach the island in formation. A terrible barrage of anti aircraft fire is unleashed against them. At times the enemy dive down to elude the fire of our fighters. A dogfight takes place over Gozo. Bus passengers are machine-gunned.

Sat 7 Sep

A strong formation of enemy aircraft raid the island. Damage to naval property is reported.

Casualties: *Valletta:* Mary Pisani (27), Carmelo Pisani (5), Lorenza Pisani (3) and Joseph Pisani (1).

Lord Lloyd, the Secretary of State for the Colonies, broadcasts a special Message to Malta from London on the eve of Malta's National Day. In his clarion call to the Maltese people, he said: 'The old Maltese spirit rises again, and with hearts steeled they cherish the sacred soil of Malta, defying all who would attack their island.'

Sun 8 Sep

Malta's National Day.

Lieutenant General Dobbie in a broadcast to the people of Malta and Gozo said: 'Important as the fortress of Malta has always been on account of its geographical position and the facilities provided, yet it is now more important than ever and suddenly finds itself in the very forefront of the battle.'

Tue 17 Sep

More air-raids. More bombs. An enemy plane, shot down at L-Iskorvit near Zammitello Palace, between Ġnejna and Mġarr, burns itself out; its pilot is taken into custody by the Military Authorities.

Sun 22 Sep

More bombs dropped. Several houses destroyed. Casualty: Paul Magri (16) at Luqa.

Lord Beaverbrook, Minister for Aircraft Production, in a message to Malta said: 'The world needs no proof of your people's devotion to our common cause, but it will never forget their valour and constancy in these days of crisis.'

Mon 23 Sep

Ħal Far cleared of all unexploded bombs.

Thu 26 Sep

Malta is featured in the *Times* of London. The Article, written by the paper's Naval Correspondent, says: 'Malta as a fortress is, perhaps, stronger than it ever was, and it would be a bold enemy who would attempt its reduction and capture. But it is one of the most thickly populated places in the world, and thus an attractive target to an enemy who counts terrorism among his weapons ... Malta stands or falls by sea power, and the spirit of its people, while Britain holds command of the sea, the prowess of the garrison on land and the staunchness of the people are assured of constant support, which is all they need to beat off any foe.'

Sat 28 Sep

The Scout Company of 2nd Battalion, The King's Own Malta Regiment (KOMR) parade on the Palace Square, Valletta, for inspection by Lt.-Gen Dobbie.

Addressing the Scout Company, after the inspection, Dobbie reminded these soldiers of the Old Scout motto: 'Be Prepared' and told them that he could find no better words of advice for them!

Tue 1 Oct

The latest Royal Air Force Casualty List gives the name of Aircraftman J.E. Mangion, born in Malta, mother living in Senglea, as 'killed on active service'.

At the Council of Government sitting, HE the President said: 'Before we start working, I thought it might interest Hon. Members to know that one of our warships has sunk an enemy submarine.' This news is received with cheers from the House and the strangers.

Tue 8 Oct

In the pale light of an early moon, two enemy planes approach the island.

They are rapidly picked up by the searchlights which blaze into the skies in dozens. Within a short time the enemy is engaged by our fighters. One enemy plane is shot down. As the machine is hit, there appears a great sheet of flame, which is seen crashing downwards like a gigantic shooting star, accompanied by a terrific roar.

Sat 12 Oct

The Naval Authorities in Malta announce that during the course of an operation in the Eastern Mediterranean, a convoy consisting of four large merchant ships carrying essential commodities for Malta was successfully brought into port. Throughout the day units of the Fleet entered and left the harbour after refuelling.

Mr Anthony Eden, the Secretary of State for War, passes through Malta on his way to Egypt. During his brief stay on the island Mr Eden, accompanied by Lt.-Gen Dobbie, makes a tour of the defences and visits a number of units, both those from the United Kingdom and those raised in Malta.

Tue 15 Oct

Access is prohibited to the Addolorata Cemetery, except to priests and persons forming part of a funeral cortege. This measure, at a time when it is customary for so many people to visit and tend the graves of their dead, has been introduced because the Addolorata Cemetery has been hit more than once by bombs and lies in an area which has been repeatedly attacked from the air. It is therefore expedient to prevent the gathering of large numbers of people in this exposed spot where the shelter available is very limited.

Thu 17 Oct

More air-raids. Casualty: *Żabbar*: Saviour Brincat (-).

Thu 31 Oct

Mrs Carolina Caruana, formerly of Paola, attains the venerable age of 100 years. She recalls when her late husband drove the carriage of the late King Edward VII, when His Majesty had visited Malta. She had been presented to His Majesty and she still retains a gold medal which the late King presented to her husband as a souvenir of the day when he drove him into Valletta.

Sun 3 Nov

The inhabitants of Qormi are awakened soon after midnight by the loud drone of a low-flying Royal Air Force plane. In an attempt to clear the village, the plane crashes on two houses on the outskirts (Don Mario Street). Fredu Agius and his wife Dolores, both aged 40 years, are trapped in the debris and killed.

More raids, more bombs, and more houses damaged.

The public is warned against sending postcards abroad showing views of Malta which may be useful to the enemy. Such postcards are withheld by the censors, without their senders being notified. Fri 8 Nov

Mr Neville Chamberlain, Prime Minister of Great Britain from 1937 to May 1940, dies at his country home in Hampshire. Sun 10 Nov

The Naval Authorities in Malta announce that during the course of an operation in the Mediterranean a convoy consisting of five merchant vessels, carrying essential commodities for Malta was successfully brought in. In addition, Military reinforcements have also been disembarked. Tue 12 Nov

Shortly before sunset a formation of enemy aircraft fly over the island from the north and make a low attack on Luqa aerodrome. Our ground defences heartily engage the enemy. Sun 24 Nov

No motor bicycles and cyclettes are allowed on the road without a special permit issued by the Director of Transport.

A typical war scene in Malta.

Life in the rock-cut shelters.

Thur 28 Nov

More raids. Enemy aircraft approach the island and anti-aircraft batteries engage them heavily. The afternoon raid is pressed home vigorously. Bombs are dropped near Kalkara Gate and Żabbar. An air of excitement in Valletta. There are rumours that ships have been sighted on the horizon. Just when the ships are clearly seen approaching, an early afternoon alert is sounded and an air battle ensues.

As soon as the church bells have sounded the 'all clear', hundreds of people dash to the Upper and Lower Barrakka and the bastions which embrace the harbour, in good time to welcome the convoy as it steams in port. The 'boys of Senglea' cheer wildly, as they sing and shout a welcome to the first ships, which have just passed the Customs House. The crowds clap and wave handkerchiefs.

One-hundred-and-ninety-one alerts have been sounded since the beginning of the war with Italy.

Governor Dobbie delivers a lecture at the British Institute on 'Land Invasion Past and Present'.

The Naval Authorities in Malta issue a communiqué saying that during the course of an operation in the Mediterranean two convoys, consisting of six large merchant vessels, have been safely brought in. Fri 29 Nov

The new church of St Gregory at Sliema is inaugurated today, the feast of St Andrew the Apostle. The church is blessed by the Vicar General, Mgr Canon Paul Galea. His Grace the Archbishop Mgr Dom Maurus Caruana, OSB consecrates the High Altar. Sat 30 Nov

Winston Churchill celebrates his 66th birthday at No. 10, Downing Street 'by getting on with the war'.

A Press Release states that, to date, we have lost 4 aircraft to the enemy's 24 (confirmed) and another 25 (probables). Sun 1 Dec

Marshal Badoglio, who in 1922, when Mussolini marched on Rome, had urged the King to give him three battalions to oppose the march, is relieved at his own request of his office as Chief of General Staff of the Italian Armed Forces, by Royal Decree. General Ugo Cavallero is appointed as his successor. Sat 7 Dec

Paul Mifsud, 44, is sentenced to death for having murdered Lippa and Karmena Agius, both of Żebbuġ, on 15 July 1940, and wounded Police Sergeant Toni Attard, Constable Moses Buttigieg, and Karmenu Agius. Thu 12 Dec

Formations of enemy aircraft over Malta. They are engaged by anti-aircraft defences. Bombs are dropped. Damage to civilian property. Sat 14 Dec

The following Advert is published in today's issue of the *Sunday Times of Malta*: 'Wanted - Motor boats. Small fast motor boats are required for Naval Service. Any person owning such a boat and willing to sell it is requested to forward particulars forthwith to the Admiral Superintendent, HM Dockyard.' Sun 15 Dec

Mon 16 Dec **As from today** the Rediffusion offices are transferred from 28, South Street to 'Vincenti Buildings', 121, Brittanica Street, Valletta.

Thu 19 Dec **Air Commodore F.H.M.** Maynard, AFC, lectures on 'The Air Weapon in War' at the British Institute.

Fri 20 Dec **Several alerts. A** Savoia Marchetti S79 is shot down in flames off Fort Tigné.

Mon 23 Dec **The Naval Authorities** in Malta announce that during the course of an operation in the Mediterranean another convoy of six merchant vessels carrying essential commodities for Malta has been safely brought in.

Tue 24 Dec **Special Order of** the Day by HE the Governor, Lt.-Gen Sir William Dobbie: 'I wish all ranks and their families in Malta a Happy Christmas.'

Pope Pius XII in his Christmas broadcast mentions five Precepts for Christian Victory: 'We must strive first for victory over hatred, for grave damage is inflicted upon the human soul by lack of the love of Christ. Secondly, victory over lack of trust in international cooperation. Thirdly, victory over the grim principle that force stands for right - that is a return of morality among the nations. Fourthly, victory over economic divergences. Fifthly, victory over egotism.'

Tue 31 Dec **Enemy bombers over** Malta. Bombs are dropped causing damage to Government property.

AD 1941

January – April

There is a further call for application for appointments as interpreters in Prisoners-of-War camps in India. Tue 7 Jan

Lord Baden Powell, the 83-year-old Chief Scout, dies at Nyeri, Kenya. During the 1890s, His Lordship, then a Major, had served in Malta as Assistant Military Secretary. Wed 8 Jan

This morning the enemy carry out a fighter attack on one of our airfields. Twelve to fifteen aircraft in three formations, from the North East take part; one formation flies low and machine-guns our ground forces. Anti-aircraft fire intense. Our fighters, who were up on patrol, engage the enemy and shoot down four which crash into the sea. Two Italian pilots are seen to bale out and one is picked up badly wounded and is brought back to Malta. More raids in the afternoon. Thu 9 Jan

The number of enemy aircraft shot down over Malta to date is 40 confirmed, 25 probables.

Eleven Maltese officers left Malta for Egypt on the captured Italian ship *Rodi*. The officers were Capts. J. Chapelle, H.W. Micallef, J. Gatt, H.A. Jackson, J. Inglott, G.F. Stivala, J. Ellis, W.E. Said, P. Zammit, J.R. Speranza, and J.L. Muscat and are *en route* to India where they will be joining the staff of the Italian POW camps as Interpreter Officers.

HE Cardinal A. Hinsley, Archbishop of Westminster, in a private letter addressed to Mr Joseph Bonello of Birkirkara, writes: 'May God keep you all in safety and grant us peace through justice and charity. We are confident that the courage of the people of Malta will do very much to secure victory and lasting peace.' Fri 10 Jan

This morning an enemy aircraft flies very high over the Eastern part of the island. No bombs were dropped but it is noted that the enemy plane carried the markings of a Red Cross in a white circle. The same method has been adopted over Britain for reconnaissance purposes; such planes are now fired upon by the Royal Air Force and Anti-Aircraft Batteries. Wed 15 Jan

Aircraft carrier HMS *Illustrious* enters Grand Harbour.

An all-night air-raid alarm – a record for its duration. The drone of planes has been overheard for some time and could be frequently heard from various parts of Malta. This notwithstanding, night shifts on essential work continue their work undisturbed.

Sicily is now for all practical purposes German territory, according to reports received in diplomatic circles in Washington. It has been heavily occupied by German troops and technicians.

Thu 16 Jan

Massey Anderson, Reuters correspondent aboard the British aircraft carrier *Illustrious,* cables: 'The *Illustrious,* battle-scarred but triumphant, made port today, after fighting off waves of German dive bombers at intervals for seven hours in the Straits of Sicily. Goering's Luftwaffe had swooped out of the sky in its first Mediterranean action and had given her one of the severest poundings ever delivered from the air against a single ship.'

But although the *Illustrious* has survived all efforts to sink her and has managed to enter harbour under her own steam, the Germans do not seem disposed to allow her any respite from her recent ordeal! They have organized formidable air strikes to try and sink her in our harbour.

The first raid against HMS *Illustrious* this afternoon is intense in character and includes dive-bombing. The enemy formations are engaged by our fighters and by anti-aircraft guns.

Later in the afternoon, a second heavy raid takes place. During the night raid, heavy damage is caused to property. Referring to today's raids, official reports say that ten enemy aircraft have been brought down. Our fighters have shot down four Junkers 88s[1] and one Junkers 87[2] and also seriously damaged three more Junkers 87s. The guns shot down five bombers.

The War Correspondent in Malta reports: 'The first time I saw dive bombing in earnest. I saw the enemy bombers dive almost straight down from a cloud, dropping bombs. The enemy's dive-bombing tactics were spectacular. Seeing it done at close quarters, I could not repress a feeling of admiration for the enemy pilots!'

Extensive damage has been inflicted on property. In Valletta a block of flats has been hit. The ancient, historical parish church of St Lawrence, at Vittoriosa has been badly shaken.[3] German mines, bombs, and air torpedoes razed the Chapter Hall and the Vestry to the ground. Glass windows were smashed. Among the many precious treasures declared lost beyond repair, there are: (a) a full-size painting of St Lawrence (*c*.1400), painted on wood. This was the altar-piece of the old church of Vittoriosa before the advent of the Order of St John; (b) an Icon in Byzantine style representing Our Lady of the Wayside which has been brought over to Malta from Rhodes by the Knights in 1530; (c) a painting of Our Lady of Protection (*c*.1452), once the altar-piece of the old chapel of Fort St Angelo; (d) an altar-piece of Saints Cosmas and Damian by Filippo Paladini (*c*.1544); (e) an oval painting of the Death of Christ, and a life-size portrait of Pope Pius VI by Antoine Favray (1766–98). Behind the church of St Lawrence workmen are digging in the debris in search of survivors.

---

1 The JU-88 was the most versatile aircraft in the *Luftwaffe* armoury, serving as level bomber and dive bombers. Bomb load 5510 lb; max speed 292 mph.

2 JU-87 : the famous and legendary gull-winged Stuka dive bomber ('The terror of Europe') was the main weapon of the *Luftwaffe* against RAF fighter bases. Bomb load one 1102 lb, four I 10 lb bombs, max speed 217 mph.

3 This church served as the Conventual Church of the Knights of St John from 1530, the year of their arrival in Malta, up to 1571, when the Order transferred its headquarters to Valletta. St Lawrence Church was severely damaged in the earthquake of 1693.

Luftwaffe's check.

The parish church of Our Lady of Victory, at Senglea, suffered still more destruction. A direct hit exploded in the aisle to the right of the High Altar. Gaping holes and cracks in the walls are evident in several places. The statue of Our Lady of Victory has, however, been spared.[4]

Casualties: *Floriana*: Robert Grech (21); *Ħamrun*: Pawlu Gauci (25); *Marsa*: Duminku Vassallo (15); *Qormi:* Carmelo Sammut (42); *Senglea*: Elicio Briccio (70), Nicola Buhagiar (70), Emanuel Caruana (50), Giovanna Cassar (20), Rita Cassar (17), Tessie Cassar (9), Tonina Farrel (27), William Farrel (38), Mary Farrugia (8), Jane Gatt (64), Vincenza Grima (50), Angiolina Kamm (50), Michael Mallia (65), Rosina Remigio (35), Revd Prof. J. Theuma (28), Carmela Teuma (30), Bice Teuma (5), Emily Teuma (21), Evelyn Vella (19); *Valletta*: Vincent Cachia (38), Mary Healey (66), Carmela Mamo (44), Teresa Mamo (80), Mary Rapinett (6), Sunta Rapinett (43), Emanuel Spiteri (48); *Vittoriosa:* Mary Cardona (-), Erminia D'Agostino (12), Joe

4 This statue was removed to safety to the parish church of Birkirkara on 20 January 1941.

D'Agostino (11), Josephine D'Agostino (41), Laurence D'Agostino (-), Sosa Darmanin (50), Alfonso Degabriele (67), Joseph Degabriele (21), Lorenzo Degabriele (56) sexton of the church of St Lawrence, Francis Falzon (16), Anna Galea (9), Carmela Gatt (-), Cettina Gatt (-), Dolores Gatt (24), Laurence Gatt (-), Mary Gatt (23), Lorenza German (11), Anthony Hili (-), Emanuel Mallia (-), Francis Mallia (-), Laurence Mallia (55), Lora Mallia (-), Albert Mizzi (-), Anthony Mizzi (-), Francis Mizzi (32), Lorenza Pisani (32), 11 Vincent Pisani (-), Lorenzo Zarb (434); Zejtun: Albert Brignoli (51); Unidentified: 6 females and 9 males.

Goering's Luftwaffe has come to Malta.

Demolition squads and volunteers for rescue work are urgently needed.

More heavy air-raids. Casualty: *Tarxien*: John Calleja (32). Fri 17 Jan

Morning air-raids. This afternoon three enemy raids are carried out in rapid succession. In the first raid many enemy formations Sat 18 Jan

Senglea – the parish church receives a direct hit.

In the foreground, part of Senglea destroyed by bombing.

attack the island in continuous waves for over an hour. Dive-bombing attacks by over 80 bombers are carried out against Luqa and Hal Far airfields where many bombs are dropped. For a time Luqa became unserviceable. Our fighters shot down seven of the enemy, and the Gunners, four. A second raid consisting of a formation flies over at a considerable height on reconnaissance.

A third air-raid is carried out by two enemy formations who, on this occasion, confine themselves to looking for survivors far out at sea.

Throughout the day the Royal Malta Artillery carries out firing practice from the Ħaġar Qim area.

The Governor, the Archbishop, and the Lieutenant Governor separately visit Senglea and Vittoriosa.

Determined efforts are made to intensify and expedite rescue work on those areas badly hit by enemy bombs. The work of clearing debris in Old Mint Street, Valletta by the King's Own Malta Regiment continues late into the night. Particularly at Vittoriosa and Senglea, the Governor calls in the help of the Military, and details the Royal

Engineers, the Royal Malta Artillery, and the King's Own Malta Regiment together with members of the Public Works Department and the Air Raids Precautions (ARP) personnel, to clear the debris from the bomb-battered areas. Several persons are rescued.

Commenting on the Nazi air bid in the Mediterranean and the significance of changed German tactics, Reuters correspondent in London reports: 'The German air force in seeking to aid Italy by gaining control over the Central Mediterranean waters, has made further attacks on the British Naval base at Malta.' Sun 19 Jan

Today's issue of the *Sunday Times* of London carries an article by the Air Correspondent, who writes: 'Malta appears likely to face the fiercest attacks of its stormy career within the next few weeks.'

Frequent and intensive air attacks by large formations of German planes continue. Several alarms accompanied by dive-bombing attacks on the Grand Harbour contrasted with the high calibre guns blazing at them. In the Grand Harbour hell seemed let loose as the *Luftwaffe* made yet one more desperate effort to destroy HMS *Illustrious.*

What had survived of the church of Our Lady of Victory at Senglea after recent bombing has now been reduced to a mass of wreckage by another direct hit.

A direct hit has also been reported on the priory of the Dominican Fathers at Vittoriosa. A complete wreck. Among the treasures now declared a complete loss is an old wooden Icon representing the Nativity of Our Lady which, since the Great Siege of 1565, used to be carried in solemn procession on 8 September of each year.

Extensive damage to property around the Dockyard perimeter. Casualties: 2 males and 5 females unidentified. Figures regarding enemy aircraft losses between last Thursday and today: 39 certainly destroyed, 5 probables, 9 damaged.

Anecdote – A mother had sent her son to fetch the Sunday joint from the community kitchen. An 'alert' was sounded as the youngster was returning home. The family had retired to a shelter. Anxious to join his parents, the boy placed the dish on the doorstep and he too retired to the shelter. But it was just bad luck: the mongrels, out on the 'scrounge' went away with the Sunday joint ...

Mon 20 Jan

Only slight air activity. A Ju-88 carried out reconnaissance over the Grand Harbour from a height of 23,000 feet and at night some indiscriminate bombing. Casualty: *Żabbar*: Joseph Attard (33).

Tue 21 Jan

Lectures at the Royal University of Malta are suspended until further notice.

The Director of Education, Dr Albert V. Laferla, issues instructions to the effect that all Government schools in Malta (but not in Gozo) are to be closed for a fortnight from today, while the members of the teaching staff are to place themselves at the disposal of the Protection Officers for six hours a day.

Message from Winston Churchill, Britain's Prime Minister, to the Officer Administering the Government of Malta: 'I send you on behalf of the War Cabinet, heartfelt congratulations upon the magnificent and ever memorable defence which your heroic

Valletta – Kingsway after the bombing.

Aftermath of the blitz.

garrison and citizens, assisted by the Navy and above all, by the Royal Air Force, are making against the Italian and German attacks. The eyes of all Britain, and indeed, of the whole British Empire, are watching Malta in her struggle day by day, and we are sure that success, as well as glory, will reward your efforts.'

Two raids. Indiscriminate bombing.

The Governor broadcasts to the People: 'We are living in stirring times, and Malta, like other parts of the British Empire, is taking its share in the momentous happenings.'

Thu 3 Jan

The main altar-piece and the statue of the Immaculate Conception of the parish church of Cospicua are taken to the church of Birkirkara for safe custody. Similarly the statue of St Laurence of the parish church of Vittoriosa and other precious items are transferred to the nunnery of the Benedictine Sisters at Mdina.

Tobruk falls to Allied forces.

Sat 25 Jan

During the night, an Italian flying boat Cant Z 501 landed near Comino. Having lost his whereabouts but thinking he was close to his base, the pilot requested a searchlight to be exposed to guide him in his descent. Just at that moment one of our searchlights happened to be turned on and the aircraft landed straight into our hands! The crew of four is now in Malta as prisoners-of-war.

Thu 30 Jan

Today begins the case before His Majesty's Criminal Court of Appeal of seven persons charged, *inter alia,* with having attempted to conspire against His Majesty's Government in favour of His Majesty's enemy. The Court is composed of His Honour the Chief Justice, Dr George Borg, MBE, LL.D., Mr Justice Prof. Dr E. Ganado, LL.D., and Mr Justice Dr William Harding, B. Litt, LL.D. The accused are Harry Briffa (21) of Msida, Dino Borg (18) of Pietà, Oliviero Xerri (19) of Gżira, Charles Schranz (22) of Sliema, Anthony Xerri (21) of Żabbar, Joseph Depasquale (23) of Vittoriosa, and Louis Gatt (19) of Vittoriosa. Counsel for Defence are: for Dino Borg and Oliviero Xerri, Dr A. Magri, LL.D; for Harry Briffa, Prof. Dr C. Mifsud Bonnici, LL.D., and Dr A. Mercieca, LL.D.; for Charles Schranz, Dr J.

Bofors crew guarding Grand Harbour. *(Imperial War Museum)*

Flores, LL.D.; and for Anthony Xerri, Joseph Depasquale, and Louis Gatt, Prof. Dr C. Mifsud Bonnici, LL.D. Prosecuting for the Crown is Dr J. Reynaud, LL.D., Crown Counsel. The accused are charged with having between l June and 8 November 1940 bound themselves into a society in these islands with the intention of helping Germany and Italy, so that, by means of propaganda, there may be formed in these islands a large organization of Fifth Columnists.

A night-long alarm — one of the longest! A magnificent display of searchlights. At one moment a 'sneak' raider is seen dashing through the searchlights. Lost for a split second, it is quickly picked up again and the guns belch flame. Fri 31 Jan

The case before His Majesty's Criminal Court against the seven persons charged with conspiracy is concluded today. The Court did not find the accused guilty of conspiracy with aggravating circumstances, but it found five of the accused, Harry Briffa, Dino Borg, Oliviero Psaila alias Xerri, Joseph Depasquale, and Louis Gatt, guilty of 'single conspiracy'. The Court sentenced Harry Briffa, Joseph Depasquale, and Louis Gatt to three years' imprisonment with hard labour, and Dino Borg and Oliviero Psaila to four

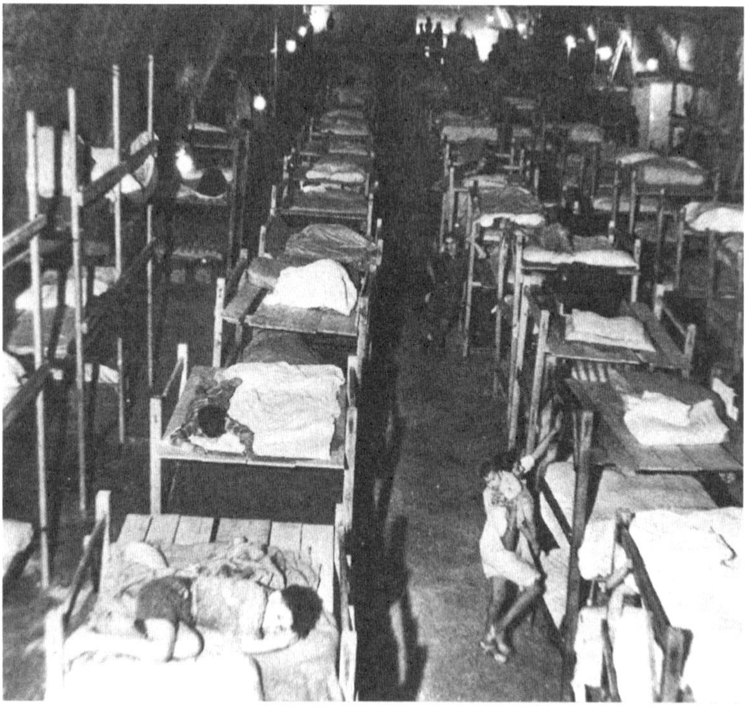

Valletta – The Old Railway Tunnel is converted into a public shelter.

years' hard labour. Charles Schranz was condemned to one year's imprisonment with hard labour and Anthony Xerri to 18 months' hard labour.

Lady Dobbie pays a visit to the Valletta Railway tunnel Shelter. This is one of the shelters which have been inhabited by evacuees since the outbreak of war. On the first day of the war with Italy a female refugee had given birth to twins in this shelter.

Mon 3 Feb

Addressing the parish priests at the traditional Candlemas ceremony, the Governor said: 'This war is different to most wars in the past. They have been mainly concerned with the armed forces of the belligerent nations, and the civil population has been affected only indirectly. But in this war the civil population has to share the hazards of war with the armed forces, and the outcome of the war is greatly affected by the way in which the civil population faces the ordeal. It is thus of the greatest importance to help the people to maintain their courage and their determination without faltering, and everyone who can assist in this great task is performing a service of incalculable value. And who are better fitted for such a duty than you, reverend gentlemen, and your brother clergy? That is why I am glad to know that I can rely on you to do this, and in fact I am confident that you are already doing it.'

More enemy raids. Low flying dusk attacks. Official figures say that civilians killed by enemy action during the month of January 1941 total 63. Since the entry of Italy into war the total number of civilians killed is 132, while 218 persons were admitted to hospital, of whom 26 subsequently died of their injuries. Tue 4 Feb

Lt.-Gen Dobbie broadcasts to the People: 'All sections of the community must know the part they have to play so that, when and if the time comes, they may be able to play it with determination, intelligence, and courage.'

The enemy carry out diving attacks on airfields. Thu 6 Feb

More air-raid alerts – reconnaissance flights. Fri 7 Feb

Casualty: Carmela Vella (14) in a rural room near *Buskett*.

A succession of air-raids. Damage to the Leprosy hospital, St Vincent de Paule hospital, and to civilian property. Sat 8 Feb

Casualty: *Sliema*: Francis Grech (17) Malta Auxiliary Corps.

Official reports state total number of aircraft shot down over Malta to date: 85 confirmed, 24 probables, 33 damaged. Sun 9 Feb

More raids. More anti-aircraft barrages. Wed 12 Feb

Valletta under fire.

Scenes of Valletta after the blitz.

Fri 14 Feb

More raids.

Casualties: *Valletta:* Giuseppa Aquilina (64), Speranza Borg (80), Filippo Camilleri (60), Susanna Mercieca (85), Rużar Spagnol (14).

Sun 16 Feb

Several enemy air-raids throughout the night. No bombs dropped, though enemy aircraft are known to have laid mines not far from the harbour entrances.

Tue 18 Feb

A press release issued from the Lieutenant Governor's Office informs the public that if, at any time, the electric sirens should fail to function, the airraid warning will be given instead by the firing of three maroons or petards in succession, accompanied in some cases by the sounding of hand sirens.

Wed 19 Feb

CONSCRIPTION is introduced in Malta as from today.

Sun 23 Feb

The British Admiralty announces a danger area in the Central Mediterranean with Malta as the hub of the minefield.

Conscription.

Tue 25 Feb

A succession of alerts. Two Dorniers shot down.

Wed 26 Feb

A midday heavy attack by dive-bombers and an escort of fighters on airfields. The enemy is met by our fighters and a heavy anti-aircraft barrage. This is one of the most determined and sustained attack.

Later in the afternoon a Red Cross seaplane, accompanied by a number of enemy aircraft fly around the island apparently in search of this morning's enemy aircraft. Another enemy attempt to penetrate the defence. Dive-bombers approach and attack in heavy waves. After what appears to be a preliminary skirmish with our fighters, the Malta barrage opens fire. The first wave appears to dive the lowest. They approach at a high altitude, then break up and dive singly. The barrage concentrates over the enemy's objective. To reach it with any chance of getting close hits, the bombers, diving almost vertically, have to dash at high speed right into a veritable inferno of fire and bursting shells. They seem to release four bombs at a time. Clouds of smoke rise from the bursting bombs and from those enemy aircraft which dive straight to earth. Just as one wave of attackers appears to have been dealt with, another follow in quick succession, mostly from the same direction as the first wave.

Casualty: *Gudja*: Anġlu Caruana (84).

Thu 27 Feb

Naval Authorities announce that a Gozo boat struck a mine and sank. Of the crew of eleven, six have been landed in Malta and one of them is seriously wounded. The others are missing.

Gozo boats are warned that they must keep at least one mile from the shore when proceeding between Malta and Gozo.

More heavy attacks from the sky and more destruction on land.

Casualties: *Valletta*: Carmelo Attard (50); *Gozo* (*Nadur*): Tony Cauchi (29), *Victoria*: Franġisk Vella (29).

Lt.-Gen Dobbie broadcasts to the people: 'The coming months may bring situations which will require our biggest possible efforts, and we may need to use all our resources of all kinds to cope with the problem. We must be as strong as possible in order to ensure that all attacks are decisively beaten off, should they be attempted. The

Enemy aircraft shot down in flames.

Government must, therefore, be in a position to utilize the resources of Malta (including the manpower) to the best advantage, and it is for that reason that conscription of manpower is being brought into being. These are the reasons why it is being introduced. I have ordered it in order to enable me to carry out my responsibility for the security of these Islands.'

Fri 28 Feb

Deliberate and indiscriminate dropping of parachute-mines. Anti-aircraft gunfire explodes one mine before it reaches the ground. Very considerable damage in Valletta. Casualty: *Valletta*: Anthony Zammit (19).

From 150 to 200 have been rendered homeless in Valletta. Some 40 families are directly affected. Most of the homeless were temporarily accommodated during the day in St Francis Convent in Kingsway, Valletta. The mines themselves are clearly devised for the purpose they achieve: as they drop by parachute at a reduced speed, they do not sink deep into earth and thus their blast effect extends over a wider area. One crater, about 25 feet across, was only some 5 feet deep. This particular mine damaged also the church of Our

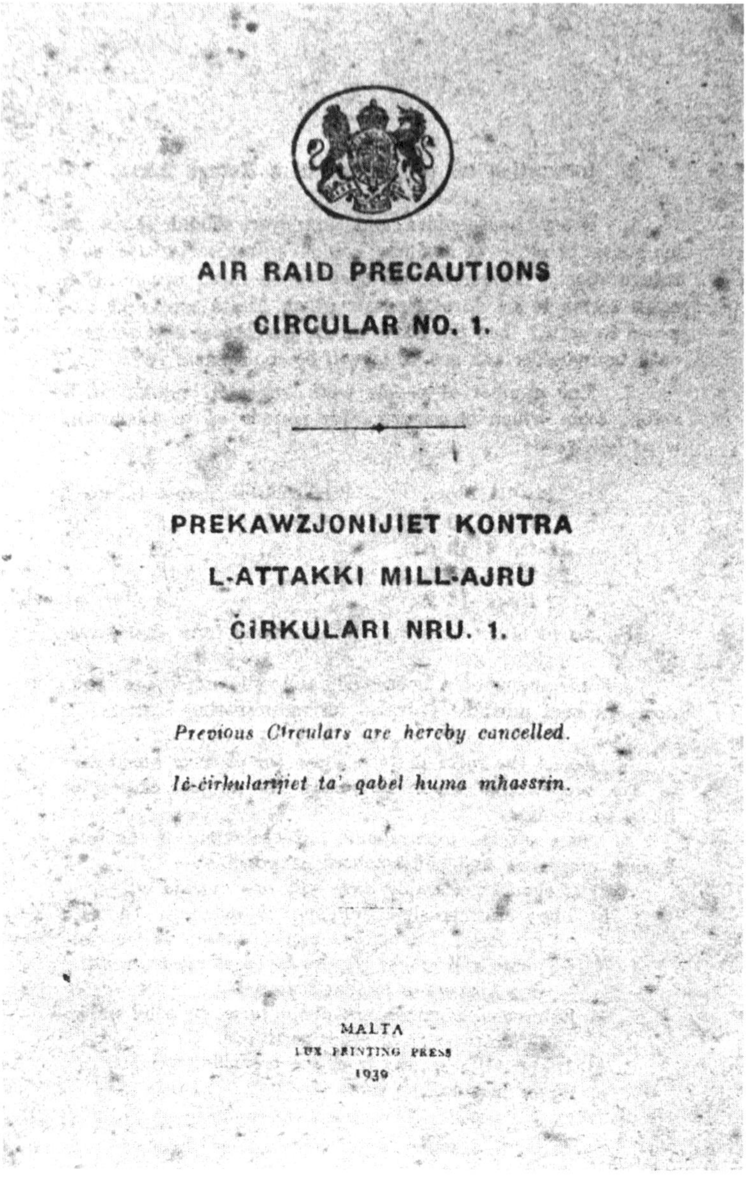

AIR RAID PRECAUTIONS

CIRCULAR NO. 1.

PREKAWZJONIJIET KONTRA

L-ATTAKKI MILL-AJRU

ĊIRKULARI NRU. 1.

Previous Circulars are hereby cancelled.

Iċ-ċirkularijiet ta' qabel huma mħassrin.

MALTA

LUX PRINTING PRESS

1939

Circular No. 1 issued by the Government regarding Air Raid Precautions.

Lady of Pilar.[5] It blew in the massive front door, broke all glassware and woodwork, and a holy painting above the high altar fell to the ground.

At the adjacent convent, also seriously damaged, all the nuns are safe in their shelter, although they received a severe shock like all the neighbourhood.

The Auberge d'Aragon has been severely damaged. It suffered the full force of the blast. The roof crashed in at several places. A boys' school closes and the children are sent home, as structurally the building was too severely shaken.

Morale in Valletta remains unshaken. It seems that Hitler's *Nervenblitz* has failed to shatter the nerves of the people of the city.

Following the recent indiscriminate bombing, slogans reading 'Bomb Rome' have appeared on the walls of ruined buildings!

Early this morning the enemy carry out a reconnaissance flight. Sat 1 Mar

Later today, a small formation of bombers escorted by fighters drops bombs in several places and are engaged by anti-aircraft defences.

The Naval Authorities have announced that, during mine-sweeping operations in Grand Harbour yesterday, mines were exploded. The minesweeper, although damaged, was taken to safety by a tug boat. One of the crew is missing and nine are injured.

More raids throughout the day. Sun 2 Mar

Today's edition of the *Malta Government Gazette* notifies 'that His Majesty the King has been graciously pleased to approve of the award of the George Medal to 1st-class Police Constable, No. 347, Carmel Camilleri, of the Malta Police, for gallantry and devotion to duty on the occasion described hereunder: Mon 3 Mar

'In the early morning of the 4th November 1940, a Royal Air Force aircraft crashed on a house at Qormi, and the front portion of the machine

5 This church was erected in 1670 and belonged to the Knights of the Langue of Aragon. Its roof fell down during the earthquake of 1693.

fell ·into a 40 ft shaft at the bottom of a deep quarry beyond the house. Moans were heard coming from the shaft, from which flames were spouting, and an injured airman was observed supporting himself under the vertical edge of the shaft. A wire rope was lowered which the airman grasped, but after being drawn up a few feet he could not maintain his hold and fell back into the shaft. PC Camilleri, who had been one of the first on the scene, immediately volunteered to go down for him, in spite of the flames from the burning aircraft and in disregard of danger from the possible explosion of heavy-calibre bombs, and was lowered into the shaft. The rope slipped and he fell to the bottom, fortunately without serious injury. A third rope was lowered to which PC Camilleri tied the injured airman who was then hauled up. The rope was again lowered for Camilleri, who was brought up with no injuries beyond slight burns.'

Wed 5 Mar

Heavy air battles over Malta.

One big black four-engined enemy bomber is first hit by tracer bullets and then tackled by one of our fighters; it is last seen enveloped in black smoke.

There are several dogfights, and the sound of machine-gun is heard as our fighters engage some of the enemy beyond the area covered by the barrage.

This evening a large formation of enemy aircraft drops a number of bombs. The raiders consisted of Domiers, Junkers, and Messerschmitts.

Thu 6 Mar

In the dull light of a growing moon and a sparsely clouded sky, a long air raid warning is sounded. Display of searchlights, burst of gunfire, and the glare of red light as of bursting explosives.

Several enemy bombers succeed in carrying out individual attacks. Two enemy fighters attack one of our flying-boat bases, causing damage to an aircraft.

Lt.-Gen. Dobbie, C-in-C of the Fortress, writes to Air Officer Commanding, Air Vice-Marshal F. Maynard, AFC, and to General Officer Commanding Troops, Maj. Gen. J.P. Scobell, CB, CMG, DSO: 'The air battles fought in the Maltese sky since January 16, when the

Luftwaffe made its first appearance en masse over our island have been decisive ones.'

Early this morning enemy aircraft come over on a machine-gunning spree. During this raid a German Junkers bomber crashed in Gozo and is burnt out; its crew of four being killed. The plane hit rock and on impact its wings flew asunder and rested on the top of the hills some 200 ft away from the scene of the crash. One of the enemy pilots is found dead with an open parachute alongside. Two other pilots are found at the bottom of the ravine, below the hills. Before the plane crashed it flew low over a road and crashed into the rock about 50 feet above the roadway. Sun 9 Mar

Following the bombing of Valletta, dozens of horse-driven carts came into the city from all over the island and the shifting of furniture was quickly achieved. In the evening the Police barbed wired the damaged areas to prevent pilfering, and a local curfew is now enforced with Police patrolling the areas affected.

Midday. Three enemy formations approach from different directions. Mon 10 Mar

Several Messerschmitt 110s[6] attack and machine-gun sea-plane bases, causing damage.

At night. Large number of enemy aircraft over Malta. One enemy plane making a perfect target, disappears just as a mass of flame seems to fall from the spot where the plane is last seen as a tiny dot in the middle of the searchlights.

Casualty: *Cospicua*: PC 291 Francis Camilleri (21).

More bombing. Tue 11 Mar

Casualties: *Sliema*: Giorgina Borg (22), Giovanni Borg (24), Giuseppe Borg (13), Gunner RMA Saverio Borg (20), Emanuel Buttigieg (40), Toninu Buttigieg (309), Dorothy Churcher (4), George Churcher (6 wks), James Churcher (50), James Henry Churcher

6 Messerschmitt 1 10, fighter; it lacked manoeuvrability; armament: two 20 mm cannons, four 7.9 mm machine-guns, one free-mounted 7.9 mm gun; max. speed 349 mph.

After the initial bombing, people begin to evacuate Valletta. The horse and cart are the only means by which households chattels can be moved – petrol being strictly rationed.

(9), Andrea Degiovanni (43), Annie Farrugia (67), Alex Grech (15), Annie Grech (11), Mary Grech (18), Teresa Grech (3), Anġlu Saliba (16), Beneditt Scicluna (17), John Scicluna (44), Żarenu Scicluna (50), Dolores Zahra (60).

Addressing the House of Commons, when presenting_ the Air Estimates, the Air Minister Sir Archibald Sinclair, disclosed: 'I am glad to have this opportunity of paying a tribute to the gallantry and efficiency of the defenders of the island [of Malta] (Cheers) and to the courage and high morale which the civil population has displayed throughout.' (Cheers).

Sat 15 Mar **More bombs are** dropped by Junkers on airfields.

This afternoon a mine explodes in the harbour and blows up a Gozo boat. The casualties are three dead, six seriously and four slightly wounded.

Casualties: *Gozo*: (*Għajnsielem*): Carmelo Costa (35), Salvu Grech (50); *Nadur*: Salvu Rapa (74); *Xewkija*: Manuel Borg (46).

The shelters belonging to the Allied Malta Newspapers Limited are closed to the public and reserved for the use of personnel of the newspapers – the staff number 75. Thirteen thousand copies of the local *Times* are printed daily.

Thu 20 Mar

Government announces its intention to prepare schemes to provide with official assistance for compensation for damage to property and personal injury resulting from enemy action.

Sat 22 Mar

More bombing.

Casualty: *Żabbar*: Francis Cassar (14).

Sun 23 Mar

This afternoon enemy bombers and fighters attack the island. Several engagements take place between the enemy and our fighters. One enemy aircraft shot down. Night attacks. Bombs dropped. Reports say that from 10 to 12 enemy aircraft have been shot down. Today's were amongst the most spectacular raids so far.

A blitzed area of Valletta.

Valletta – Queen Victoria's statue survives the bombing.

Casualty: *Dingli*: Giuseppe Zahra (27).

The public is asked to refrain from removing parts and equipment from enemy aircraft before the Military or the police arrive at the place where the aircraft has crashed. Such parts and equipment may furnish useful information to the Authorities.

This evening formations of Junkers 88s escorted by Messerschmitt 109s[7] drop bombs in the Grand Harbour. Mon 24 Mar

The Naval Authorities announce that during a periodical sweep by the Fleet in the Mediterranean a convoy of four merchant vessels were safely escorted to Malta bringing essential commodities for local use. Tue 25 Mar

During the day the enemy carried out two heavy dive-bombing attacks on the Grand Harbour causing some casualties to Service personnel and damage to property. There were moments of anxiety when a lighter moored to one of the ships was hit and went up in pieces. Boxes and pieces of wood could be seen floating in the area.

Marshal Rodolfo Graziani, Italian Commander-in-Chief in Africa, has resigned at his own request. He is succeeded by General Italo Gariboldi.

Today's issue of the *Times of Malta* publishes the following poem entitled 'Civilians in War Time' written by Maurice Caruana Curran:

We who have seen the sun obscured
By War's black pinioned eagles in full flight,
We walk in the shadow of death,
Our eyes are stones flung into dark chasms.
In our embattled streets we look
Like frail, mute, hunted things,
But our hearts have wings
That soar into the light.

7 The ME-109 was known to *Luftwaffe* pilots as the 'Emil' fighter/bomber; armament: two 7.9 mm machine-guns and two 20 mm cannons; max speed 357 mph.

Mooring vessel *Moor* in Grand Harbour.

Sat 29 Mar

Two forced landings by our aircraft while on patrol. During the night, enemy raids. Bombs dropped in several localities.

Casualty: *Rabat*: Anthony Grech (51).

Thu 3 Apr

An Italian S 79 bomber, escorted by C.R. 42 fighters,[8] attempts an unsuccessful machine-gun attack on an RAF launch 40 miles off the island. Later a formation of JU 87 dive bombers, escorted by a number of Messerschmitt109 fighters, drop bombs in the vicinity of two minesweeping trawlers of Filfla but obtain no hits.

Mon 7 Apr

As from today, sugar, matches, soap and coffee are to be rationed.

Tue 8 Apr

Naval Authorities in Malta announce that the mooring lighter *Moor* was sunk by enemy action in the Grand Harbour this evening. At the time she had a crew of twelve and a working party of seventeen on board; only one (Toni Mercieca from Marsa) was rescued.

8 Fiat CR-42: single-seater biplane; armament: two 12.7 mm machine-guns; max speed: 261 mph.

Several people witnessed the tragedy of the sinking of the *Moor* when she struck a mine. The explosion shook the surrounding buildings over a wide area. As people rushed to balconies, terraces, or to the bastions, they caught a glimpse of the ship turning over on her side and swiftly sinking.

Immediately a ferry boat and several Naval Dockyard and Air Force pinances, together with · many dghajsas, approached the scene of the disaster; but all the men had perished except for the sole survivor who was picked up from the sea.

Casualties: Giuseppi Mazzelli, Emanuel Darmanin, Manwel Hatchings, Mikiel Aquilina, Ġeraldu Vella, Wiġi Bezzina, Anġlu Vella, Karmnu Zammit, Duminku Flores, Wenzu Grima, Pawlu Vella, Pietru Calleja, Toni Bonnici, Ġorġ Zahra, Wenzu Tabone, Ċikku Degabriele, Karmnu Zammit, Giuseppe Bartolo, Ċensu Xerri, Ġenju Spiteri, Rafel Cauchi, Spiru D'Emmanuele, Ċensu Camilleri, Giuseppe Calleja, Manwel Psaila, Ġanni Mizzi, Gianmarì Xerri, Giuseppe Brincat.

No traffic is allowed to move outside town or village areas during curfew, unless appropriately routed by Fortress Headquarters.

HE the Officer Administering the Government issues instructions referable to the Malta Volunteer Defence Force in order to augment the local defences by providing static defence of localities and protection of vulnerable points and by giving timely notice of enemy movement to superior military organizations.

Casualty: *Għaxaq***:** Carmela Dimech (22). Wed 9 Apr

This morning large formations of enemy fighter patrols are active all around the island. For the first time in the history of the Church in Malta, the bells of the churches ring on Good Friday. Bells have never been rung between the chanting of the *Gloria* during Mass on Maundy Thursday until the *Gloria* on the following Saturday. Today they rang to give the 'All Clear' signal after the enemy raids. Fri 11 Apr

During the night several enemy aircraft, believed to be Junkers 87s, drop bombs in various localities.

Casualties: *Għargħur*: Rosaria Mifsud (8); *Mġarr*: Giuseppe Borg (44), Maria Vella (36), Salvu Vella (60); *Siġġiewi*: Michael Angelo Sammut (46).

Since the commencement of hostilities the enemy has suffered the following aircraft casualties: 132 destroyed, 44 probably destroyed, and 58 damaged.

Our fighter losses for the same period: 29 fighters.

Sun 13 Apr

This day is marked by the sounding in Malta of the 500th 'alert'. More bombs dropped.

In the Vatican City, Pope Pius XII in his Easter Message says:

> *'Would that all belligerents who have human hearts would feel pity for the sufferings of the civil population, for unarmed women and children, for the sick and aged, often exposed to greater dangers of war than the soldiers at the front. We supplicate all belligerents to refrain from using even more deadly instruments of war.'*

Senglea – after the bombing.

Mon 14 Apr

A large formation of enemy aircraft, mostly Junkers 87s and 88s, attack in waves at spaced intervals.

Tue 15 Apr

More raids. Casualty: *Mosta*: Carmela Cassar (29).

Wed 16 Apr

More raids. More bombs.

Sat 19 Apr

Still more raids.

Casualties: *Msida*: Nicola Cassar (40), Michael Sammut (40), Ġanna Zammit (60), Ġiuseppe Zammit (65).

Sun 20 Apr

Today marks the 52nd birthday of Adolf Hitler, who was born at Braunau am Inn, near Innsbruck, Austria.

In the middle of the morning a small formation of Italian S 79 bombers, escorted by Italian CR 42 fighters and a few Messerschmitt 109s come over the island. Bombs are dropped on the eastern districts.

Casualty: *Msida*: Lukarda Vassallo (70).

Mon 21 Apr

In today's issue of the *Times of Malta* an appeal is made for pullovers for homeless children.

The night blitz over Malta continues. A parachute mine falls on civilian property in the immediate vicinity of a large shelter in which there were hundreds of people. The blast raised clouds of dust in the shelter.

Casualty: *Żejtun*: Anna Spiteri (21).

Tue 22 Apr

A large number of German Messerschmitts and Junkers drop bombs. During the early part of the night there is a heavy raid by a large number of enemy aircraft identified as Junkers 88 and Heinkel 111s[9] who use flares in order to identify their objects. Many bombs and mines are dropped. Considerable damage.

Casualty: *Valletta*: Vincent Schembri (60).

9 13. The Heinkel 11 l was the standard level bomber of the *Luftwaffe*; bomb load: 5510 lb; max. speed: 258 mph.

Postage Labels for overseas mail. Stamp-Labels bearing the White Ensign and the RAF Colours were issued in recognition of the services rendered by the Royal Navy and the Royal Air Force in connection with the conveyance of mails to and from Malta.

Sat 26 Apr

Casualty: *Msida*: Toni Sammut (33).

Sun 27 Apr

Casualty: *Valletta*: Toni Caruana (35).

The Post Office has issued for overseas mail stamp-labels bearing the White ensign and the RAF Colours and the inscription: 'Malta is grateful to the Royal Navy and the Royal Air Force for the safe arrival of this letter.'

Mon 28 Apr

Casualty: *Marsa*: Giuseppe Dimech (10).

Tue 29 Apr

More bombs.

Casualties: *Senglea*: Carmela Degiorgio (34), Mary Zarb (7); *Valletta*: Rochani Tikamdas (48); *Żebbuġ*: Fra Bonaventura Attard (21), Fra Hilarion Borg (22), Żarenu Cachia (42), Kunċett Grech (54), Philip Grech (24), Fra Marċellinu Pisani (22); 1 female (unidentified).

Wed 30 Apr

Heavy raids over Malta. Main targets: the Grand Harbour and Valletta.

Malta experiences its heaviest night raid when a large number of enemy aircraft drop mines and bombs. This is followed by a second wave. Fierce anti-aircraft barrages are put up at the raiders and searchlights hold them on many occasions.

St John's Co-Cathedral has been seriously damaged. It narrowly misses total annihilation. The Oratory and paintings by Mattia Preti suffer most. The Vestry is also heavily damaged, while the main door has been blasted and destroyed. The Museum attached to the Cathedral has also been damaged, though the exhibits had been transferred elsewhere in good time. The two belfry towers have been damaged.

The church of the Greek Orthodox community has been destroyed. The Holy Sacrament is taken from the ruins of the church to the Catholic parish church of Our Lady of Porto Salvo (St Dominic's Priory).[10]

The Exchange and its adjacent two banks are irreparably damaged. The St George's Overseas League Club is blasted. Shops and business premises over a wide area have suffered heavily. A direct hit by a mine on the *Circolo Giovine Malta*.15 One other building which has been destroyed in Valletta is Flores College. 16 The Law Courts are again damaged heavily. Kingsway Main Gate is blocked by rock and debris caused by a direct hit on the entrance to a shelter.

Casualties: *Senglea*: Agnes Ashmoor (9), Iris Ashmoor (11), Tommy Ashmoor (4), Charles Zarb (13), Edward Zarb (12); Valletta: Carmela Caruana (71), Ċensa Macgil (33), Edwige Zarb Cousin (5).

10 Although the Greek Orthodox-Schismatic Church is not in communion with Rome, its priests are properly consecrated, because there is a direct and undisturbed episcopal succession since the time of Apostles. One hundred and thirty years ago the Greek Orthodox church in Valletta caught fire and the Dominican Fathers on that occasion carried the Holy Sacrament to their conventual church.

AD 1941

May – August

Thu 1 May

Casualty: *Marsa*: **Joseph** Vassallo (39).

The public is informed of mines laid in the wire surrounding Ħal Far Aerodrome. Persons tampering with or endeavouring to get through the wire do so at their own risk.

The *Circolo Giovine Malta* was founded in 1901.

Flores College was founded in 1874.

Fri 2 May

A number of enemy unexploded bombs are found in Valletta. More raids. More bombs. More destruction.

The Times of London in today's editorial entitled 'Malta's Ordeal' says: 'The most exposed position in the British Empire is Malta.'

Sun 4 May

Severe damage is caused to St Publius Church, the parish church of the suburb of Floriana. The church is severely damaged; its front door, glass windows, and organ have been completely destroyed. The clock is blasted, and the iron hands point at 9.40; by some

Valletta – Bombed houses in the vicinity of St John church.

The parish church of Floriana after an air-raid.

strange freak, its bells are still defiantly chiming the time every 15 minutes. The statue of the patron, St Publius, is safe in its niche, well embedded behind an anti-blast wall and sandbags.

Government urges that rock shelters constructed by Government be enlarged by private voluntary enterprise, so that persons may provide themselves with more comfortable accommodation. Tue 6 May

Casualties: *Birkirkara*: Joseph Calleja (40); *Gudja*: Spiru Brincat (74); *Tarxien*: Ċensu Falzon (56).

Government complains of the scarcity of lorries for the removal of debris blocking roads and streets. Wed 7 May

More raids are carried out by ME 109s and Heinkel ll l s. A big four engined Dornier is believed to have been shot down.

As from today the Archbishop's Curia has been transferred to Cini's Institute, Ħamrun.

Casualties: *Luqa*: Carmelo Gatt (51); *Mosta*: Salvu Galea (82).

During the month of April the number of civilian deaths as a result of enemy action was 62. In addition 56 persons received serious injuries, and 56 persons received treatment for injuries of a minor character. Thu 8 May

More raids. A small formation of Junkers attack shipping off the Grand Harbour notwithstanding the bad weather. Fri 9 May

Explosions at St Lucia Street and Kingsway, Valletta. Sat 10 May

The Episcopal Seminary in Floriana is to be used for the holding of sittings and for the transaction of other business of His Majesty Superior Courts of Justice. The lower part of the Auberge de France with entrance from Old Bakery Street, Valletta, is to be used for the holding of sitting and for the transaction of other business of the Courts of Magistrates of Judicial Police for the Island of Malta.

Floriana – St Anne Street.

Since the destruction of the Law Courts, the salvage of Court Records and documents has been proceeding briskly.

Sun 11 May **Enemy fighters –** ME 109s – make a machine-gun attack on one of our seaplane bases, where one of our aircraft is set on fire. More bombs on Valletta. Casualties: *Żejtun*: Dolores Degabriele (5 days), Joseph Degabriele (2), Bernarda Mifsud (33).

On the initiative of Archbishop Maurus Caruana, the Miraculous Crucifix which dates back to 1637 is taken from the church of the Franciscan Minors of St Mary of Jesus (*Ta' Ġiezu*) to the church of St Anthony at Mġarr, Gozo, for safety reasons.

Mon 12 May **It is reported** from London that Rudolf Hess, Hitler's deputy, has landed in Scotland.

Casualty: *Valletta Railway Tunnel*: Ġeraldu Camilleri (33).

Tue 13 May

More raids on airfields.

Casualty: *Ħamrun*: Adorata Scicluna (60).

Wed 14 May

Valletta scene. Valletta is being quickly restored. The Coloseum Theatre, which has been damaged, is scheduled to re-open next week. Likewise the Manoel Theatre is expected to make its post-blitz inauguration.

Notwithstanding the incessant air-raids, all Government Departments remain in Valletta and Floriana.

The popular flower shops and similarly the cafes and other business establishments are carrying on business from improvised stands.

A notice released from the Lieutenant Governor's office says: 'Arrangements have recently been made for the removal to places of safety of pictures and other objects of artistic or historical importance from St John's Co-Cathedral, the Palace, the Museum, and the Public Library. The manuscripts of the Public Library have been placed in two small rooms in the basement of the Library.

During the night a small number of raiders come over in separate waves; bombs are dropped.

Thu 15 May

It is notified that Empire Day (May 24) and the King's Birthday (June 11) shall not, this year, be kept as public holidays.

Casualties: *Valletta*: Anthony Cremona (52), Paul Vella (75); *Żabbar*: Anna Psaila (82).

Fri 16 May

During the early hours of this morning a small number of enemy aircraft crossed the island. Bombs are dropped and Bofors guns heavily engaged .

Casualties: *Żejtun*: Carmel Attard (15); *Żurrieq*: John Abdilla (16).

Air Vice-Marshal F. Maynard AFC, Air Officer Commanding RAF Mediterranean, in a broadcast says: 'We have been and still are in the process of obtaining more up-to-date types of aircraft both for offence and defence, and I am confident we shall thereby continue to give a good account of ourselves.'

Tue 20 May

More fairly heavy raids accompanied by aerial combats. The convents of St Francis and that of St Augustine both in Valletta receive direct hits.

One side of La Valette Band Club[1] collapsed as did the shipping offices of Messrs Vadalà and Brizzi's musical establishment and adjacent buildings – all in Kingsway. The Rediffusion Offices received a direct hit and an unexploded bomb is believed to be lying beneath the debris. The Rediffusion has immediately moved a few yards downstreet to Britannica Street, comer with Old Bakery Street.

This morning the Governor visited the bombed areas.

Casualties: *Valletta*: Joseph Gauci (16), Alphonse Herrera (80), Charles Lewis (17), Emanuel Pantalleresco (70), Giuseppa F. Ullo (75); *Żabbar*: John Bonnici (17).

The Colonial Office announces that His Majesty the King has approved the appointment of Major-General (temporary Lt.-Gen) Sir William George Sheddon Dobbie, KCB, CMG, DSO as Governor and Commander in-Chief of Malta. Sir William has been administering the Government of Malta since he assumed command of the troops in April 1940 immediately before Gen. Sir Charles Bonham Carter left the island.

Fri 23 May

The Governor sends to the Secretary of State for the Colonies the following report on the situation in Malta: 'The outstanding features of the last month has been the frequent occurrences of night raids by about forty bombers dropping parachute flares and mines as well as bombs. Damage both from mines and bombs has been widespread, but has been greatest in Valletta. St John's Co-Cathedral has been damaged and the Law Courts and Banks destroyed. A mine fell on the Civil Hospital and the hundred patients who had not already been removed were carried out in the night without one casualty. There has also been extensive damage to dwelling houses and shops. The main street and several others are blocked with great quantities of stone from destroyed buildings and will take a long time to clear with our limited resources. The extensive damage to their principal city, which was founded immediately after the Great Siege of 1565

1 La Valette Band Club was founded in October 1874.

1565 and 1941: undaunted. *(Sunday Times of Malta)*

and has stood unchanged since the time of the knights, has been a profound shock to Maltese sentiment and the damage of several large churches, including the Co-Cathedral of St John, has given deep offence. Added to that, but separate from it, is the material loss caused to a large number of individuals by the destruction of property and business which it has taken them many years to acquire. Nevertheless the reaction of the people is deserving of the highest praise. They have hardened in anger towards the enemy and are facing their own individual calamities with cheerfulness and fortitude.

With the first light after the destruction of their homes and shops, they are busily engaged with hammers and boards patching up damage where they can and rescuing their stock and possessions from among the debris to make another start. As one of them recently said after the destruction of his home, "We will endure anything, except the rule of these barbarians and savages." The homeless are received by others, especially among the poorer classes with the most remarkable hospitability and people in the undamaged areas have been living for nearly a year with comparative cheerfulness, in conditions of close overcrowding and consequent discomfort. The great majority are, I am sure, quite unshaken in their belief in final

Blitzed Valletta.

victory and the Prime Minister's recent statement that Malta, with Egypt and Gibraltar, will be defended with the full strength of the Empire meant very much to people here.'

Commencing from today, there will be special film shows at 10 a.m. at the Coloseum Theatre for the troops. Sat 24 May

There is a shortage of restaurants as, in the recent big blitz over Valletta, the more popular restaurants were demolished.

More raids. Casualty: *Naxxar*: Francis Mifsud (38). Sun 25 May

A communiqué issued by the Admiralty in London announces that the German battleship *Bismarck* has been sunk after a dramatic 1750–mile chase. The Bismarck was one of the newest and most powerful enemy battleships. Wed 28 May

More raids. More bombs dropped. Sat 31 May

This afternoon the premises of the former Courts of Justice, already badly damaged by the blast of an enemy mine, collapses. Large blocks of masonry have blocked up Kingsway. The collapse of the Law Courts building (erstwhile the Auberge d'Auvergne) was apparently caused by the concussion of an explosion in the Tigné area.

At an informal gathering at Captain Caruana's Bar in Kingsway, a number of Squadron Leader Burgess's, DFC friends in Malta meet to bid him Godspeed and good luck before leaving the island. Major Briffa de Piro presented him with a cigarette case in recognition of his magnificent work in the air defence of Malta.

During the second raid this afternoon, enemy aircraft are reported near Malta; a troop carrier JU 52 is shot down into the sea. Tue 3 Jun

The names of signposts are being obliterated since the information displayed thereon could be of value to enemy parachutists, should they succeed in landing in any part of the island.

Sat 7 Jun

More night raids by Heinkel 111s.

Sun 8 Jun

Casualty: *Marsaxlokk*: **Grezzju** Fenech (28).

Mon 9 Jun

Our fighters shoot down a Savoia Marchetti 79 bomber which crashes into the sea.

Casualty: *Mellieħa*: Ġanni Vella (14).

Wed 11 Jun

This morning one Savoia Marchetti 79 comes over on reconnaissance escorted by five Messerschmitt 109s. AA defences are engaged heavily and our Hurricanes on patrol chase away the enemy planes. Since Italy entered the war, Malta has had 694 alerts. The number of enemy aircraft destroyed to date by fighters and AA defences combined is: 155 shot down confirmed; 60 badly damaged unconfirmed.

The Lieutenant-Governor, Sir Edward Jackson, in a broadcast says: 'The people of Malta have lost much during the last twelve months: lives that have left an emptiness never to be filled, material things that were the fruit of years of labour, religious and historic buildings that meant much in people's thoughts.'

Thu 12 June

This morning a strong enemy force flew in. After being engaged by accurate AA fire the formation is broken up and the enemy is engaged by our fighters. More raids follow throughout the day.

Casualties: *Mosta*: Mary Barberi (74). According to unofficial statistics, to date: civilian killed – 295; serious casualties – 310; houses demolished or badly damaged – 2,341.

Sun 15 Jun

Casualty: *Tarxien*: Francis Abela (22).

Mon 16 Jun

Casualty: *Marsa*: Wiġi Farrugia (42).

In the afternoon a force of enemy fighters fly in. Three of them separate from the formation and are intercepted by our Hurricanes. A Macchi 200 fighter[2] is shot down. More raids follow. Wed 18 Jun

The news reaches Malta of the death, in London, of the Dowager Lady Plumer, the widow of (later Field-Marshal) Viscount Plumer who, as Governor of Malta (1919–1924), inaugurated Self-Government in these islands in 1921. Sat 21 Jun

An S79 Italian bomber, escorted by a large number of Macchi 200s, comes over this morning. Three Macchis are shot down. Wed 25 Jun

During the air alarm this morning a large formation of enemy aircraft attempting to round the island are intercepted and driven off by our fighters. One enemy fighter is shot down into the sea and the body of one dead Italian pilot is recovered. Fri 4 Jul

Casualties: *Ħamrun*: Carmelo Azzopardi (24), Walter Azzopardi (16), Anthony Burlò (33), Carmelo Burlò (55), Lorenza Burlò (56), Carmelo Criminale (21), Francis Criminale (47), Mary Criminale (12), Paul Criminale (17), Ines Micallef (13), Francis Sant (56), Aldo Serra (10), Joseph Woodhouse (18).

More bombs dropped. Casualties: *Ħamrun*: Carmelina Serra (5), Ines Serra (14), Nello Serra (13). Sun 5 Jul

According to a Notice issued from the Lieutenant-Governor's Office, action will be taken against civilians found wearing military clothing illicitly obtained.

More bombing. Casualties: *Paola*: Carmela Attard (22), Elisa Borg (28), Anthony Cappello (–), Joseph Cappello (–), Salvatore Cappello (–), Karlu Cassar (68), Toni Coleiro (30), Publio Cini (52), Salvu Galea (42), Mary Grima (3), Salvu Tanti (70), Victor Tanti (2), Giuseppe Zerafa (33), Mary Zerafa (15), remains of a 'corpse Mon 7 Jul

2 The Macchi C-200 was one of the best Italian aircraft of the war; armament: two 12.7 mm machine-guns; max. speed 312 mph.

presumed to belong to Paul Zerafa (22); one male (unidentified and disfigured).

The Governor authorizes the further issue of legal tender paper currency of the following denominations: Notes of 2s. 6d., 10s., and £1.

Tue 8 Jul

More raids, more bombs. Several enemy aircraft cross the coast. Searchlights and AA guns engaged. One bomber Fiat B.R. 20[3] is caught by searchlights and shot down in flames into the sea. Our fighters intercept a formation of enemy fighters Macchi 200s and some seaplanes.

Casualty: *Paola*: Tona Spiteri (24).

Thu 10 Jul

It is notified that gaps have been opened in the barbed wire entanglements along the shores at the following places for the convenience of bathers: Armier, St Paul's Bay (Skoll tal-Għażżenin), Baħar iċ-Ċagħaq, St George's Bay, St Julian's Bay (Central Aquatic and Neptune's sites), Fond Għadir, Sliema (Sliema Point), Marsascala (Daħla Tawwalija near salt pans), Marsaxlokk, Birżebbuġa, Wied iż-Żurrieq, and Għar Lapsi. The public are warned to use only these gaps to gain access to or from the water, and are reminded that certain sections of the entanglements contain booby traps and explosives which are highly dangerous and that any attempt to go through the barbed wire, except at the gaps indicated by the notice boards (*Ħawnhekk tista' tgħum* – Bathing is allowed here), may have very serious consequences.

During the night a few enemy aircraft attack. Searchlights exposes them and some bombs are dropped on outlying districts.

Fri 11 Jul

In the afternoon a large formation of enemy aircraft, about forty Macchi 200 fighters, attack but are split up by our fighters. A small formation, however, carries out a low-flying attack which causes damage to military installations, including Luqa airfield. In engagements which follow three Macchi 200s are shot down into the sea.

3 The Fiat BR-20 Cicogna was one of Italy's heaviest bombers; bomb load: 3300 lb; max speed 267 mph.

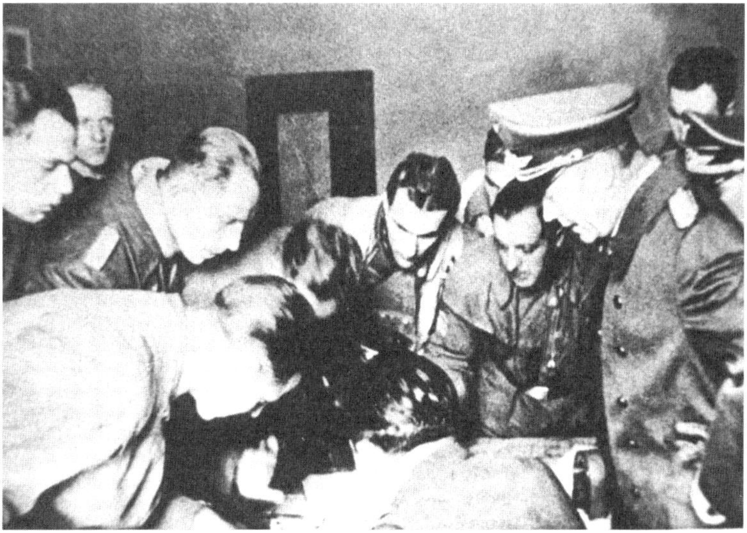

Luftwaffe officers study intelligence pictures of Malta.

More raids. Casualties: *Ħamrun*: Carmel Grima (44), Emanuel Sultana (40), Paolina Verzin (70); *Marsa*: Antonietta Debattista (26), John Debattista (61), Leli Sammut (16), Joseph Spiteri (15), Albert Woodward (37). Sat 12 Jul

More air attacks – for the last month no longer by the *Luftwaffe* (recalled to the Russian front) but by the *Regia Aeronautica*. The country people call the 'Macchi' – '*Makku*' – fry: young fishes fresh from the spawn. Asked what the news of the day was, one old Maltese fisherman said: '*Xejn; resaq ftit Makku, imma qabdu l-Urugan*' –'Nothing much; some fry approached, but they were caught by the Hurricane'! Sun 13 Jul

Two mines are exploded today between the hours of 9.45 a.m. and 11.45 a.m. off the Breakwater Viaduct and Tigné Sparbuoy respectively. Tue 15 Jul

In the afternoon minesweeping takes place off the coast between St Elmo and St George's Bay. During sweeping operations, the minesweepers fly a large red flag over two black balls.

More raids accompanied by the dropping of bombs throughout the day.

Thu 17 Jul

This morning a large number of enemy fighters accompanied a reconnaissance aircraft over Malta.

The public is reminded of anti-tank and anti-personnel mines laid in various parts of the island. Notices proclaiming the danger areas are displayed.

Fri 18 Jul

More raids. More damage to property. Casualty: *Attard*: Giovanna Fenech (50).

Fri 25 Jul

Two 'recce' planes and a large number of fighters came over in the early hours of this morning and one of the most spectacular of all the air combats witnessed in Malta's skies ensued. A shot-down Macchi 200 crashed in Kingsway and ended in a cloud of thick dust. The pilot baled out but was killed. One other Italian pilot is picked up alive.

Appeal by Kalafrana RAF Station for donations of deck chairs or easy chairs for use by pilots and aircraft crew during periods of rest.

Sat 26 Jul

The Naval Authorities in Malta have issued a communiqué on this morning's Italian attack against the Grand Harbour: 'Italian Light Forces consisting of E-boats of various sizes, attempted to breach the defences of Malta at about dawn on 26 July. As has been customary throughout this war all the defences, many of which are manned by local units of this Fortress Island of Malta, were ready and waiting for any form of attack. At about 4.30 a.m., 26 July, the searchlights were switched on and the battle began during which a large explosion was heard in the vicinity of the Breakwater Viaduct near St Elmo. For a few minutes the illuminated area off the entrance of Grand Harbour was criss-crossed by a devastating fire which was visible to the naked eye. The tracer bullets were a 'regular Brock's' benefit. The firing soon ceased but it was obvious from the explosions in the illuminated area that the guns had found their targets and many of the enemy boats had been sunk and that the attack had failed. As daylight approached it was easier to see those of the enemy who had escaped the guns or had not come under their fire, and our fighter planes took up the attack and soon accounted for the remainder. It is very difficult to ascertain which boats fell to the shore defences, and which to the Air, but there seems no reason to believe that a single boat escaped back to Sicily. Several prisoners were taken. Thus ended in complete disaster the enemy's first attempt to break through the defences of Malta.'

T.W.H. in the *Times of Malta* gives an eyewitness account of the battle: 'The shock of an explosion and the sound of gunfire immediately after the sounding of the signal of "All Clear" at the end of an early alert, sent hundreds of people in Valletta, Sliema, and Floriana rushing, not to public rock shelters, but to bastions and shore fronts. In the hazy mist of the hour before dawn, these spectators were treated to an unforgettable spectacle of Malta's shore defences in action. I was one of those who pelted hard for a coign of vantage. When I got there, jostled, and jostling many others who had spent the last few hours in shelter, the "show" was on. And what a show! The foreshore of the forts guarding the Grand Harbour was illuminated in a ghostly manner, the morning mist wreathing and swirling through a floodlit expanse, while overhead the stars still shone bright though the sky was paling in the East. Through the mist, from the massive walls, that had kept watch and ward for centuries, belched flame. From three directions, came lightning streaks of flame, that were tracer bullets. All concentrated on one point and where they converged was a microscopic spot of rushing wave – an Enemy Boat or E-Boat, attempting to sneak through Malta's defences to attack the Harbours of Valletta. The effect of concentrated fire was stupendous. Hundreds of pounds of lead must have smashed into the EBoats simultaneously. It blew up with a roar. A large black column of water spouted up. That was the first of many 'kills' which the gunners manning our shore defences made during this fantastic, fast-moving, episode off the Breakwater. One of the attacking craft, luckier than the rest, managed to get within torpedo range of the Breakwater and let loose. The missile hit and exploded against the

St Elmo viaduct, causing some damage. But attempts to force the boom-defence were remorselessly halted before they had time to materialize. The rapid and accurate fire from the Forts proved far too effective. Many of the E-Boats were struck and went up in the air without trace of any survivors. Overhead the whine of shell fire was mingled with the roar of aircraft-engines as RAF fighters dived and zoomed down to add their quota to the defence of the Grand Harbour. The excitement of the hundreds of people on the bastions overlooking the Harbour and Breakwater was contagious. It seemed to have caught hold of the men behind the guns, for they fired l.ike madmen – but ever such accurate madmen. The stream of liquid fire pouring from the light guns seemed attracted as by a magnet to the low lying hulls of the enemy MAAR's, the equivalent to our MTBs practically hidden behind the bow-wave set up by their speed. Out at sea there was occasional glare of a horizon lit by more distant gunfire. And there came the dull boom of distant firing ... Dawn broke and all was peaceful.'

Sun 27 Jul **More raids over** Malta throughout the day. A joint Admiralty, War Office and Air Ministry communiqué released in London gives further information concerning the attack on Valletta Harbour: 'Shortly before 5 a.m. local time E-Boats appeared off the harbour entrance, and the fixed defences manned by the military garrison immediately engaged them. One E-Boat was hit and blew up, while four more were destroyed by gunfire. It then appeared that the E-Boats were acting as a cover for smaller torpedo carrying craft, which attempted to break into the harbour. These were heavily engaged by gunfire from the shore defences, eight being blown up or sunk. None succeeded in entering the harbour. RAF fighters pursued the remaining E-Boats, while they were attempting to extricate themselves, sinking four more and damaging others. The British fighters then encountered enemy aircraft endeavouring to give air support to the retreating enemy E-Boats. Three enemy aircraft were shot down into the sea, while one RAF fighter was lost, but the pilot saved. Reports so far received indicate that the assault on the harbour was attempted by eight torpedo-carrying craft, all of which were destroyed. The view that none of the assaulting force survived is confirmed by a special Italian communiqué issued on

Breakwater footbridge damaged by Italian E-boats.;

Saturday night. This merely referred to explosions seen by escorting forces from a distance to seaward.'

Reuters from Rome reports: 'Italy's E-Boats raid on Malta was made after the news had been received that the remaining ships of the British Convoy, attacked for three days and nights in the Mediterranean, had taken refuge there. The presence of the convoy was detected on Friday (25th). Immediately the Italian Navy decided to attack with these tiny but powerful craft on which the designers have worked in silence for many years – one of the most precious secrets of the Italian war machine. The men chosen for the attack knew that retreat was impossible – they must either be killed or taken prisoner. None flinched before his task, despite the formidable nature of the British defences. The violation of Malta will go down in history as one of the most remarkable exploits of this war.'

More raids. HAA barrage in action. Mon 28 Jul

The film *The Great Dictator*, written and directed by Charlie Chaplin, starts showing at the Manoel Theatre. Chaplin plays the dual role of Hynkel, Dictator of Tomania, and that of a Jewish Barber. The film has been acclaimed as one of the greatest comedies.

A telegram from the Chief of the Imperial General Staff, Sir John Dill, to the C-in-C Malta, Lt.-Gen Sir William Dobbie: 'Please convey my congratulations to all ranks of the Royal Malta Artillery, manning Wed 30 Jul the fixed defences, on their great success in breaking up the determined enemy sea-borne attack on the Grand Harbour. The action of these gunners has excited universal admiration here in the United Kingdom. The skill and the determination shown by them will act as a strong deterrent to future enemy attack by sea.'

War Commentary from London by Lieut-Cdr Woodruff, RN: 'Malta had been bombed from the air for over a year. Yet it fought on with such determination that Ansaldo,[4] in a broadcast to the Italians, has described the island as a gigantic aircraft carrier moored at the foot of Italy.'

Fri 1 Aug

More raids (so far over 800 alerts).

Civilian casualties as a result of enemy action for July: Killed or died of injuries 39; seriously injured 20.

Sun 3 Aug

During a night raid, bombs dropped from Italian aircraft hit and destroyed the sacristy of the parish church of Our Lady of the Sacred Heart at Sliema.

Mon 4 Aug

Feast of St Dominic. This evening, the first religious procession since the outbreak of war is conducted by the Dominican Fathers. As the procession left the church, looking down Merchants Street could be seen the ruins of a demolished school and part of the ancient hospital of the Knights. The procession turned to the right into St Dominic Street, past the ruins of houses just across the street from the church. Then it went up Kingsway, half bombed by enemy action, into Bishop Street, and past Frederick Street, where families have been recently entombed in a well-shelter, all to be saved. Then again down Merchants Street, past the ruined Greek Church, which had received a direct hit. The procession was touching for its very simplicity.

Tue 5 Aug

During this afternoon's sitting of the Council of Government, the Governor reads a message from Winston Churchill: 'Now that the

4 Giovanni Ansaldo was editor of Ciano's paper, *Il Telegrafo* of Leghorn.

One of many German aircraft shot down in Malta's skies.

convoys have reached you safely with all the stores and reinforcements, I take occasion to congratulate you on the firm and steadfast manner in which you and your devoted garrison and citizens have maintained Malta inviolate against all attacks for more than a year and to express my confidence that with the help of God our cause will continue to prosper and that the contribution of Malta to the final victory will add a noble chapter to the famous story of the island.'

Intense enemy raids. Three bombers shot down. Wed 6 Aug

Raids continue. One raider is seen to burst into flames and crashing into the sea. Thu 7 Aug

It is reported from Rome that Bruno Mussolini, the Duce's younger son, was killed in an aircraft crash near Pisa.

Vice-Admiral Sir Wilbraham Ford, KBE, CB, broadcasts a talk about the Merchant Navy. He dwelt on the epic story of a Malta convoy. 'Here in Malta we know only too well what it feels like to have bombs raining down on our devoted heads, but we do not have to risk a long swim of 150 miles or to be marooned in an open boat in mid-Atlantic with little food or water and maybe two Wed 13 Aug thousand miles to go before reaching safety, if ever they do. That is what our merchant seaman face. All power to them.'

Thu 14 Aug

A raid is sounded. Incendiaries dropped.

Sat 16 Aug

More raids. More bombs dropped. Casualty: *Ħamrun*: Carmelo Pisani (29).

Tue 19 Aug

Casualties: *Żejtun*: Joseph Cutajar (19), Consiglia Farrugia (48).

Thu 21 Aug

Casualty: *Sliema*: Annunziata Borg (60).

Fri 22 Aug

A telegram is received by the Air Officer Commanding RAF Mediterranean, Air Vice-Marshal H.L. Lloyd, MC, DFC, ADC, from the Secretary of State for Air, Sir Archibald Sinclair: 'Heartiest congratulations to you and all ranks of squadrons operating under your command on the magnificent success of air operations from Malta. The brilliant defence of the island by Hurricanes, the audacious attacks of Beaufighters on enemy air bases, the steady and deadly slogging of the Wellingtons at the enemy's ports; the daring and dexterous reconnaissances of the Marylands, culminating in the tremendous onslaughts of Blenheims and Fleet Air Arm Swordfish on Axis shipping in the Mediterranean are watched with immense admiration by your comrades in the RAF and by our fellow-countrymen at home. You are draining the enemy's strength in the Mediterranean. Good luck to you and good hunting.'

Sun 24 Aug

It is notified that 8 September this year will not be kept as a public holiday and on that day all Government offices shall be kept open.

It is revealed today that during last September, Tonin Chiodi, a member of the Fascist Grand Council died in an aerial battle over Malta. Chiodi was well-known as an aircraft builder.

Tue 26 Aug

More raids. More incendiaries dropped.

Notice issued from Lieutenant Governor's Office: 'All householders are reminded that temporary fittings or structures of an inflammable nature should be removed from housetops to minimize the chance of fires taking a hold as a result of falling incendiary bombs.'

Air attacks. Casualties: *Naxxar*. Andrea Vella (7), Carmela Vella (11), Carmelo Vella (4), Maria Vella (14), Marianna Vella (42), Teresa Vella (3). Thu 28 Aug

It is revealed that Germany's growing need for soldiers has necessitated the calling-up of German priests studying in Italy; these will be required to serve, not as priests, but as ordinary soldiers. Fri 29 Aug

Today's issue of the *London Gazette* notifies the award of the British Empire Medal to Mr Joseph Gauci. In the middle of a spate of raids Mr Gauci, an Admiralty diver at Malta Dockyard, was called to an urgent job to examine the hull of a damaged ship. He knew that more bombers might be over at any minute and he knew that he was in the target area. The diving boat's crew knew that if he was under water when the bombs would begin to fall there was little chance that they could bring him to the surface. And only men who work under water know what sudden pressure caused by an explosion can do. Joseph Gauci put on his diving gear and went down. He did his job ... and the ship sailed.

AD 1941

September – December

This morning a large formation of Macchi 200s approaches and is engaged by RAF fighters. In the ensuing combat six enemy fighters are shot down. During the night a succession of raids take place with enemy raiders operating singly. Bombs are dropped.

Thu 4 Sep

It is learnt that Italy has lost her 'Goering', Lieut. Carlo Romagnoli, in an air battle over Malta today.

Governor Dobbie, in a letter to the Heads of the Three Services calls for strict economy in the consumption of water. The water supply situation in Malta is becoming extremely difficult, unless rain falls in considerable quantities early in September. This year the difficulties have been increased by the presence of an abnormally large number of troops and by the losses of water suffered through enemy action earlier in the year. Restrictions on the use of water both by the civil population and by the Services have been in force for a considerable time.

Sat 6 Sep

More dogfights over Malta.

Sun 7 Sep

Valletta – policemen supervising the distribution of water.

Mon 8 Sep

During last night three alarms sounded. A number of bombs dropped. One enemy heavy bomber (Cant. Z1007) is shot down and five of its crew are taken prisoners. Casualty: *Ħamrun*: Anthony Farrugia (18).

Wed 10 Sep

Casualties: *Rabat*: Emanuel Bartoli (55), Carmelo Borg (61).

Fri 12 Sep

Early night: few enemy aircraft drop bombs. AA barrages put up. Shooting down of two BR 20s.

The Times of London pays a stirring tribute to Malta: 'To and fro round the globe roll the tides of war and the place that is at one moment in the forefront of the thickest battle is allowed a few months later to sink into a complete lull. But there is never any respite for the devoted Island of Malta.'

Sun 5 Oct

Casualty: *Żurrieq*: Nina Camilleri (24).

Wed 8 Oct

Casualty: *Balzan*: Susanna Galea (41).

Tue 14 Oct

At dawn, enemy low-level bombing attack. Among the Hurricanes that pounced on them was one piloted by a 19-year-old DFC, a pilot of the Malta Night Fighter Unit, David Barnwell, third son of the famous aircraft designer, Capt. Frank Barnwell. A listener in the Fighter Control at RAF Headquarters in Malta picked the young pilot's final dramatic signal: 'Baling out – coming down in the sea.' The pilot has been declared killed. Capt. Frank Barnwell is the designer of the Blenheim and Beaufort aircraft of this war and of the famous Bristol fighter of World War One. Capt. Barnwell was killed in a plane crash three years ago. His two elder sons have also lost their lives whilst serving in the RAF.

There is a call for smart active men for enlistment as Special Reserve Constables in the Malta Police Corps.

Fri 17 Oct

Intensive raids continue.

Issue of paper currency: Notes of 2s. 6d.; 5s.; 10s.; and £1.

Transporting belongings salvaged from blitzed homes.

More raids. Casualties: *Burmarrad*: Carmela Bonnici (44), Ċikka Bonnici (6), Ċikku Bonnici (50), Giuseppe Bonnici (16), Leli Bonnici (4). Sat 18 Oct

Casualty: *Gozo* (*Nadur*): Ġanni Pisani (49). Fri 24 Oct

Chatties (*patalotti*) are available for sale at 4s. 6d. each at the Protection Offices of the Central Region – Birkirkara, Żebbuġ, Siġġiewi, Rabat, Mdina, Dingli, and Qormi.

Notice released from the Lieutenant Governor's office: 'It is desirable that the gas-masks which have been issued to the public should be tested from time to time in order to ensure that they fit correctly and have not deteriorated. The Air-Raid Precautions Office is therefore arranging for a mobile gas chamber to visit all important centres in Malta in order to give an opportunity to the public to test their respirators. The chamber will contain a concentration of tear gas which is harmless, but which is a useful medium for testing gas Tue 28 Oct masks. This notice should not be interpreted as an indication that Government considers that the use of gas by the enemy is imminent.'

Fri 31 Oct **Night raids and** bombing. Enemy plane (Cant. Z 1007) shot down.

Sat 1 Nov **In the early** hours of this morning an earthquake is felt throughout Malta.

Air-Raids. Casualties: *Marsa*: Peter Bonett (52); *Valletta*: Caterina Agius (50), Edward Borg (16), Paul Camilleri (15).

Mon 3 Nov **The Governor sets** up a special committee, for the purposes of visiting and supervising the internment camps composed of the following persons: G.N. Nunn (Chairman), Lieut.-Col B. Ede, OBE, J.E. Axisa, MBE, F.G. Gollcher, and P. Calleja Gera (Secretary).

Sat 8 Nov **Heavy raids and** bombing.

1941 – The Valletta Air Raid Precaution Squad.

Casualty: *Birkirkara*: Giuseppe Parnis (26). Sun 9 Nov

Casualties: *Birkirkara*: John Parnis (17); Ġżira: Carmelo Xuereb (23). Mon 10 Nov

Mrs Inez Galea has been appointed member of the Visiting Committee of Internment Camps pertaining to the Camp for Women Internees. Thu 13 Nov

On the occasion of the opening of the third Session of the Council of Government, the Governor delivered a speech to the Hon. Members. *Inter alia,* he said: 'For nearly eighteen months Malta has been in the forefront of the battle and has stood firm against the attacks of the enemy. The steadfastness of the garrison and the fortitude of the people have won the admiration of the whole free world. Never in her history, neither under the knights, nor when Napoleon's forces were driven out, has the star of Malta shone more brightly. We have maintained ourselves up to now, and, with God's help, we shall continue to do so ... Here, in the centre of the Mediterranean, Malta remains a target for the enemy's bombers and a thorn daily more venomous, in the enemy's side. We have known heavy bombing raids and returned them with interest ... Malta has had 972 airraids, of which 350 have been bombing raids. Three-hundred-and-forty-four people have been killed and 685 injured seriously enough to be detained in hospital, 2,552 houses have been destroyed or seriously damaged. The casualties are heavy for so small an island, but the widespread provision of shelters has prevented them from being much heavier. People have had to leave their homes in large numbers to seek accommodation in safer parts of the island, but everywhere they have found families to receive them or arrangements have been made by the Government to house them. Transport has necessarily been much restricted and private cars have been taken from the roads almost entirely. But nobody who has to travel for work or business has been prevented from doing so, and people can still move about for pleasure and relaxation. Some foodstuffs have been scarce and most have gone up in price, but price increases have been checked and there has been no general shortage ... Some people have been thrown out of work by Tue 25 Nov reductions in particular trades, and sections of the commercial community have suffered through loss of business, but the volume of employment has increased very greatly and everyone fit to work can find work to do. The health of the people has been well maintained in spite of war conditions … When Malta was first confronted with conditions of active war, new departments of the Government had to be set up and existing departments expanded … The Police, the Air Raid Precautions Service, and the Emergency Medical Service had to be rapidly expanded and none of them has ever failed to respond to the calls which have been made upon it … In January, as a result of the German bombing attacks, a service was established for the rescue of people trapped in damaged buildings, the demolition of these buildings and the clearance of sites and roads. This has since been rapidly extended and has operated with conspicuous success under conditions which have always been arduous and often dangerous. The service has a number of fine pieces of rescue work to its credit. More recently an organization has been formed by the Public Works Department for the repair of buildings damaged by blast. The fire brigades of the Government and the three Services have been fully co-ordinated and have proved their worth in a recent serious fire. The conscription of manpower has been proceeding since the beginning of the year. Men from the age of 19 to 20 have been called up for military service, and 3,872 men have been attested for the Forces. The registration of manpower for compulsory labour service has now been started, with a view to promoting the efficiency of those large forces of labour which are employed on shelter construction and essential defence works and increasing the speed with which these works are carried to completion. Since Italy came into war, we have had to establish in every town and village an organization to maintain contact between the Government and the people. The distribution of relief, the care and accommodation of refugees, the administration of rationing and the preparations for a possible attempt to capture the islands have been only some of the functions which the organization has performed … We are thus not merely spectators of these great happenings. We have a place in the struggle and a share of responsibility for the course of events. The burden of this responsibility is heavy, but, with the help of God, we shall know how to bear it until victory is won.'

Malta extends its front. During November bombers operating from the island dropped more than a million pounds of high-explosive and incendiary bombs on enemy targets. The total becomes more impressive when it is considered that weather permitted full-scale operations on an aggregate of less then three-quarters of the month. The figures are taken from operations by heavy, medium, and Hurricane bombers and include bombs dropped by naval aircraft but not torpedoes or mines. The bulk of the total is supplied by the heavy bombers which flew a quarter of a million miles to reach their targets. These included Naples, Brindisi, and Messina, and, towards the latter part of the month, efforts were concentrated on Tripoli, Benghazi, and other North African targets, thus providing powerful support for the successful operations by our land forces in Libya. In many of these raids as much as 30 tons of bombs were dropped in one operation. A great part has been played in this month's offensive effort by the medium bombers which have harried and sunk the enemy's shipping in the Mediterranean and carried out daring low-flying strafes on his transport on the coastal roads of Tripolitania. Naval aircraft, besides attacking the enemy convoys, have also carried out numerous successful blitzes on Sicilian aerodromes. During the month the Malta sirens have sounded more than 70 times, bringing the island's total air alarms to 1,000 since the beginning of the war. Sun 30 Nov

8.30 a.m. The removal and demolition of bombs is carried out at the Opera House. Tue 2 Dec

At the second sitting of the third Session of the Council of Government, the Governor, President of the Council, says: 'During the last 24 hours our forces, naval and air, based on Malta have had considerable success. As you know, it is important to stop supplies, especially petrol, getting into Libya. In the last 24 hours, between them the naval and air forces have sunk a destroyer, a tanker with 11,000 tons of petrol, and a large merchant ship. The sinking of the tanker was the joint work of the two Services; the others were the work of the Royal Navy, which was assisted by air reconnaissance. On land, on the road, the Air Forces have in the last 24 hours destroyed at least 9 petrol lorries where they were left in flames and a great number of other vehicles have been damaged.'

The King awards special honour to Squadron Leader Powell Sheddon who, as the leader of the Night Fighters at Malta, has played an outstanding part in the protection of the island from night bombers.

Helpers are needed for the knitting of comforts for the RAF serving in Malta.

Wed 3 Dec

The Postmaster General notifies that as letters bearing propaganda labels addressed to certain foreign countries may be mishandled or stopped during transit or in the country of destination, it has been found necessary to limit the use of 'V' labels issued by the Post Office to mail matter for Empire Countries, Egypt, and the United States of America. 'V' labels may be freely used on correspondence intended for local delivery.

Thu 4 Dec

Air-raids increasing.

Fri 5 Dec

Casualties: *Żabbar*: **Clementa** Pullicino (48); *Żurrieq*: Toni Farrugia (49).

Mon 8 Dec

Air-raids continued with increased intensity during the last three days.

Malta-based low-flying Blenheims demolish the barracks at Homs (Tripoli) and carry out heavy bombardments over Naples.

The United States of America declares war on Japan following yesterday's attack on her naval base at Pearl Harbour by the Japanese.

Tue 9 Dec

A notice released from the Lieutenant Governor's office says: 'In view of the strict rationing of kerosene, the Government has made arrangements for the manufacture of certain number of chatties (*patalotti*) in the Dockyard.'

Wed 10 Dec

Incessant enemy attacks over Malta. Fortress Order: 'A number of Maltese volunteers are required for training as Pilots and Observers in the RAF. The number at present is six. Candidates will be not more than 26 years of age and applications are not confined to officers. All ranks are eligible to volunteer.'

Fri 12 Dec

More raids. More bombs dropped.

Mon 15 Dec

Six alerts sounded during last night and early this morning.

Tue 16 Dec

The air-raids continue.

Lieut.-Gen. Dobbie reviews the war situation in a broadcast: 'It is gratifying to consider that the forces based on Malta have been able to make some contribution to our success in that theatre (Libya] by attacking and constantly cutting the Axis life line between Italy and Libya. We have greatly admired the great work done by the Royal Navy, the Fleet Air Arm, and the Royal Air Force, and are quite sure other, and, perhaps greater, feats of arms are still to come.'

Valletta – queueing for kerosene.

An exhibition of the toys which men of the Royal Artillery and Royal Malta Artillery have made for distribution to children at Christmastide is held at the Auberge de Castile.

Wed 17 Dec

The air-raids still continue.

In a stirring broadcast to the people of Malta, Air Vice-Marshal Lloyd says: 'Reconnaissance for shipping in the open sea and in ports is our main task. The enemy has an army in Libya. It must be fed and maintained with all the material of war. This is almost entirely a matter of sea transport. The ports of entry into Libya are Benghazi, Tripoli, and Derna. The enemy shipping from Naples goes either west of Sicily and down the Tunisian coast, or through the Straits of Messina, along the Greek coast, down to Benghazi and along the coast of Tripoli. Shipping from Taranto and Brindisi also travels down the Greek coast. In fact, the enemy shipping now keeps away from Malta. They have every reason for doing so.'

Looking for victims under the debris.

Fri 19 Dec

At 10.43 a.m. three enemy dive bombers (JU 88) escorted by Italian Macchi fighters attempted to attack airfields and shipping in harbour; they are engaged by our Hurricane fighters. One bomber is damaged and a second shot down over Gozo. One of the crew is dead and two others have been taken prisoners.

Sat 20 Dec

This morning two formations of enemy bombers escorted by fighters cross the island dropping several bombs.

Casualty: *Żabbar*: Anthony Lia (76).

Sun 21 Dec

Casualties: *Cospicua*: Salvu Cutajar (55); *Ħamrun*: Carmelo Cassar (8); *Żabbar*: Joseph Galea (20), Anthony Psaila (16).

Mon 22 Dec

Casualties: *Gżira*: Lina Griscti (8); *Marsa*: Carmelo Briffa (13).

Tue 23 Dec

Casualty: *Żejtun*: Carmelo Attard (16).

Wed 24 Dec

This morning more raids are carried out by a small force of enemy bombers escorted by a large force of fighters. Bombs dropped. During this raid AA guns have engaged the enemy.

Casualties: *Gżira*: Toni Abdilla (28); *Ħamrun*: Samuel Cauchi (55); Qormi: Vincent Cachia (65); *Rabat*: Carmelo Borg (40); *Sliema*: Carmelo Muscat (17); *Valletta*: Antonia Frendo (19); *Gozo* (*Victoria*): Carmela Borg (23).

Fri 26 Dec

Casualty: *Żurrieq*: Francis Camilleri (12).

Sat 27 Dec

Still more raids, still more bombs.

There were 104 alerts during this month; 64 during the night and 40 during the day. Casualties: *Għaxaq*: Carmelo Abela (3 months), Ġanni Abela (33), Teresa Abela (1½), Vincenza Abela (26), Michelina Busuttil (47).

Sun 28 Dec

In the early part of today AA defences claim to have destroyed one enemy bomber. A second bomber is shot down in flames into the sea. Heavy raids continue.

The Postmaster General announces that the following surface mails have been lost by enemy action: Letters, parcels, and printed paper posted for Malta between 17 and 19 May. It has been notified in Mideast General Orders that mails posted in the United Kingdom from 25 August to 5 September have been lost by enemy action. *The Times* of 14 December 1941 notified that parcels for Malta posted on 23 June 1941 have been lost at sea through hostile action.

Mon 29 Dec

Heavy raids continue. Casualties: *Ħamrun*: Gaetano Scicluna (18); *Luqa*: Saver Demicoli (15); *Siġġiewi*: Nicholas Schembri (50); *Żejtun*: Carmel Mercieca (64); *Gozo* (Għajnsielem): Paolo Azzopardi (52), Felic Bigeni (32), Marcel Teuma (51).

Tue 30 Dec

Casualties: *Marsascala*: Lawrence Cachia (24); *Gozo* (*S. Leonardo*): Joseph Muscat (35).

Wed 31 Dec

Although units of the German Air Force in Sicily have made almost hourly attempts during the last twelve hours to paralyse RAF squadrons operating from Malta, our heavy and medium bombers relentlessly continue to hammer Axis forces retreating into Tripolitania. To keep these aircraft operating, Malta's fighter squadrons and AA batteries are waging war day and night, a ceaseless war against the raiding Junkers 88 dive bombers and their yellow-nosed Messerschmitt escorts. Since this phase of the Battle of the Mediterranean opened on 19 December, with its 52 days and 47 night raids, RAF Hurricane fighters have so far destroyed 7 JU 88s and two fighters.

AD 1942

January – April

Thu 1 Jan

The New Year is ushered in with frequent alerts. Bombs dropped.

In a New Year Message, the Lieutenant Governor, E. St. J. Jackson, says that no one can foretell how events will develop, but the war has again flared up in the Mediterranean and it seems certain that 1942 also will be a hard year. Continued effort and determination is needed to carry us through the year.

Fri 2 Jan

Incessant raids; the enemy is heavily engaged by AA artillery and barrages. Considerable damage caused to property.

Casualties: *Gżira*: Josephine Abdilla (32), Josephine Azzopardi (30), George Debono (32), Saver Debono (24), John Filletti (34), Mary Filletti (22), Anġlu Mallia (43), Stella Micallef (13), Violet Micallef (13), Albert Mifsud (10), Alfred Mifsud (2), Blanche Mifsud (14), Joseph Mifsud (13), Mary Mifsud (36), Tancred Mifsud (15), Winnie Mifsud (4), Giorgia Schembri (56), Carmela Spiteri (10), Benedetta Spiteri (15), Freddie Spiteri (7 months), Emanuel Spiteri (2), Domenico Spiteri (10), Domenico Spiteri (50), Josephine Spiteri (5), Mary Spiteri (12), Vincenza Spiteri (3); *Mosta*: Carmel Mifsud (55), Carmel Muscat (58); *Żejtun*: Carmelo Bonnici (50). Remains of an unidentified corpse, probably Giuseppe Debono (65).

The SS *Georgette Marie*, a schooner, was machine-gunned by an enemy air raider. The vessel which, besides food and goods for Gozo, also carried passengers, caught fire. The master, Marcel Theuma, of Għajnsielem, Gozo, rushed to the bridge, took the helm and succeeded in heading the vessel towards St George's trenches. The enemy then returned to the attack and the gallant Theuma was struck by a bullet and mortally wounded. The burning vessel, however, was beached and soldiers in the vicinity quickly rushed to the rescue of the survivors. The casualties included one passenger missing, a second passenger killed, and a seaman, Pawlu, killed. The wounded Master was carried to St Patrick's Hospital where he succumbed to his injuries.

Sat 3 Jan

Between breakfast and tea time there were five alerts. The attacks lasted several hours.

Night raids over Malta – tracers, searchlights, shells and flares light up the sky.

Casualties: *Birkirkara*: Raphael Caruana (69), Louis Di Mauro (59); *Siġġiewi*: Luqa Saliba (27); *Gozo* (*Nadur*): Carmelo Gatt (2), Ġanni Meilak (28).

Sun 4 Jan

Civilian casualties for December 1941: Killed or died of injuries – 29; Seriously injured – 68; Minor injuries – 85. Notwithstanding determined efforts by the *Luftwaffe*, operating from Sicily to put the island's airfields out of action, RAF heavy bombers from Malta carried out raids on Naples and Tripoli. The railway station at Naples, which was damaged by our bombers during intensive raids last month, was again hit by high-explosive bombs and fires were started round an air-frame factory. Tripoli, now visited almost nightly by our Wellingtons, suffers heavily.

Mon 5 Jan

German Stukas have been carrying out a non-stop attack on Malta's airfields during the last 36 hours.

Casualties: *Birkirkara*: Elena Cachia (38), Toninu Cachia (8).

NOTICE: A demolition charge of 7 lbs of TNT is fitted to German aircraft. This could easily be discharged accidentally by the uninitiated. All guns of crashed aircraft are invariably loaded and are liable to fire if any part of the structure is interfered with. All public and Service personnel are warned that no part of crashed aircraft, whether friendly or enemy, must be touched until the arrival of RAF technical officers, unless it is to remove the bodies of the crew.

Incessant air-raids. During the last three weeks the *Luftwaffe* has given Malta a systematic pounding. Tue 6 Jan

Some of our aircraft have been destroyed on the ground.

Orders are issued restricting the use of boats and the ferry service plying between Malta and Gozo, owing to the increasing air attacks.

Malta-based Wellingtons continue bombing Sicily and Libya. Wed 7 Jan

Casualty: *Dingli*: Anthony Pace (75).

More raids. Casualties: *Luqa*: Mary Camenzuli (78), Joseph Penza (71), Josephine Psaila (24), Teresa Sammut (68), Peter Vella (60). Thu 8 Jan

Reuters from London, quoting a senior military Officer who has returned from Malta, says: 'The lessons of Crete are being applied to Malta, and if the Germans attempt to invade Malta they will pay for it very dearly. The Germans are "stoking up" their air attacks on the fortress a little, with the idea of "neutralizing" the island which has been a nasty thorn in the flesh of the Axis. Without commenting as to whether Malta's air defences are adequate, the Officer is quoted to have said that they are very strong. Maintenance of the island's defences as a whole is a difficult and a dangerous job and demands a rather specialized form of fortress defence. The coastline of the island is comparatively long, and although some of it is impregnable, parts may be called vulnerable. However, the liaison between the Services is first class.' Sat 10 Jan

Sun 11 Jan

As from today, church bells are not being rung as an 'All Clear' signal after air-raids. They will only be rung in the event of an expected general attack.

Casualty: *Luqa*: Rosina Vella (47).

Tue 13 Jan

Non-stop raids over Malta.

Casualties: *Siġġiewi*: Ċensu Farrugia (24), Wiġi Schembri (3).

NEW ORDERS: The 'Alert' signal including the danger of an air-raid shall consist of the sounding of a warbling note on a siren or the firing of three petards.

The 'Raiders Passed' signal indicating that the danger of an air-raid has passed shall consist of the sounding of a steady note on a siren.

The 'General Alarm' indicating the imminent danger of a general attack by the enemy on these islands shall consist of the ringing of church bells.

Underground installations are being constructed for the preservation of objects of antiquarian and historical interest.

Wed 14 Jan

More raids.

Malta-based bombers continue bombing Libya and Naples.

Thu 5 Jan

During the last 24 hours we have had 17 alerts, some accompanied by heavy bombing.

Casualties: *Siġġiewi*: Ġanna Micallef (17); *Żurrieq*: Wiġi Farrugia (22); *Gozo* (*Nadur*): Franġisk Cutajar (48), Rita Galea (15), Joseph Muscat (9).

A Public Notice says that the Officer Commanding Royal Army Service Corps, Malta, may requisition by purchase, or otherwise, such motor cycles as may be necessary for the prosecution of the war.

Fri 16 Jan

Since Italy joined Germany in the war Malta has had 1,285 air alerts. Total enemy aircraft losses to date by the combined Malta defence forces: 54 confirmed; 68 probables; 120 damaged.

Casualty: *Senglea*: Vincent Micallef (48).

A Messerschmitt 109 shot down over Malta.

Sun 18 Jan

Casualty: *Żebbuġ*: Filippo Chircop (68).

Mon 19 Jan

For more than 10 hours last night, wave after wave of RAF Wellington heavy bombers swept in from the sea and blasted the German and Italian air Forces based at Catania. The Luftwaffe have been using Catania for their dive bomber attacks on Malta and as jumping-off place for troop carriers on the way to try and stem the retreat of General Rommel's Afrika Korps in Tripolitania.

Air-raids continue with same intensity and greater frequency.

Casualties: *Lija*: John Fenech (27); Mosta: Luigi Barbara (60), Ines Bugeja (4), Joe Bugeja (7), Karmnu Bugeja (5), Karmnu Bugeja (58), Mariana Bugeja (43), John Caruana (7), Francesca Riolo (71), Sunta Riolo (30), John Spiteri (23), Orazju Schembri (19), Evanġelista Vella (34), John Vincenti (45).

Tue 20 Jan

Nine alerts sounded today.

FRANCIS MELI

The Sunday Times of Malta

FAR EAST "POWDER BARREL" PAGE THREE

No. 1,458 SUNDAY, AUGUST 17, 1941 Price 3d.

MEDITERRANEAN: IMPORTANT BLOWS AT ENEMY SHIPPING

F.A.A. Attacks Tripoli Convoy

SICILIAN HARBOURS HEAVILY BOMBED

YEAR OF WAR IN MIDDLE EAST

Lesson Of Cooperation

4,000-TON TANKER BLOWN UP:

Chinese Circles Forecast Pacific "Show Down"

5,000-TON SUPPLY SHIP SUNK

Severe Fighting From Arctic To Black Sea

HITLER ALL OUT IN RACE AGAINST TIME

TWO AXIS VESSELS INTERCEPTED

19 Fighters Destroyed In Three Daylight Sweeps

THRUSTS AGAINST RUSSIAN INDUSTRY AND COMMUNICATIONS

JAPANESE GOVERNMENT BANS RETURN OF AMERICAN NATIONALS

Russian Bombers Over Berlin

BRITAIN'S GROWING AIR STRENGTH

THE MALTA FRONT

FRIDAY – SATURDAY

Importance of Sea Power in Waging War

STRATEGY THAT DEFEATED NAPOLEON:

A copy of the *Sunday Times of Malta* has burnt edges after the newsprint stores of the Allied Malta Newspapers Ltd received a direct hit in which the paper reels were seared.

Casualties: *Floriana*: Carmelo Grima (37); *Ħamrun*: Carmelo Brincat (54), Wiġi Micallef (55); *Lija*: Luigi Fenech (47); *Mosta*: Edwige Vincenti (37); *Sliema*: Attilio Mamo (45).

Wed 21 Jan

Eleven alerts today. More bombs.

Casualties: *Mosta*: Maria Bugeja (9).

Thu 22 Jan

This evening the alert is sounded when a few enemy bombers and fighters drop several bombs. Our fighters were up and intercepted them, making several attacks on an enemy bomber and four accompanying fighters.

Sat 24 Jan

Raids continue incessantly. A 20,000-ton Italian liner is believed to have been sunk as a result of a determined attack during the night by Malta's heavy bombers and Naval torpedo bombers on a large Axis convoy on its way to Tripoli with reinforcements for Rommel's forces, which are making a desperate bid to stop the 8th British Army advancing upon Tripolitania. It is possible that one other large merchant vessel was also sunk by torpedoes and several damaged by bombs which exploded only a few feet from their sides. Pilots carrying out this daring operation say that some of the units of the powerful naval escort which was protecting the merchant ship from sea and air attack also suffered damage. The convoy was one of the largest yet encountered in the Central Mediterranean.

Casualty: *Mqabba*: Joan Mary Briffa (54).

Sun 25 Jan

More raids. More bombs over Malta.

Copies of the *Sunday Times of Malta* have burnt edges. The paper is part of that salvaged when one of the newsprint stores of the Allied Malta Newspapers Ltd received a direct hit some months ago. The paper reels on top were blown into shreds and, in the blazing fire that resulted, the tops of the reels below were seared.

Mon 26 Jan

Heavy enemy attacks and heavy AA barrage. Five of our fighters shot down. Fortunes of war!

Tue 27 Jan

Incessant, heavy raids continue. As from today air-raid warning signals will be given by the sounding of sirens only. Petards will only by used when the sirens are out of order. Night raids over Malta have ceased abruptly. This is because RAF Wellington heavy bombers have successfully made surprise attacks for nearly two hours on the Sicilian airfields at Catania and Comiso from where the Luftwaffe have been launching many of their raids. At Catania, the Germans were taken so completely unawares that the flare path was alight when the first Wellington arrived and dropped two sticks of high-explosive bombs, one of which straddled the hangars at the north-east end of the airfield. As these bombs exploded, the ground crews quickly doused the landing lights. Bombs did burst in the centre of the runway making it temporarily useless for landing and taking off.

Blenheim medium bombers have again been harassing Rommel's lines of communication between Tripoli and the front. Cruising along the coast road between Homs and Misurata, a Squadron Leader came across six covered lorries and a petrol tanker with a trailer. Diving to 50 feet above the vehicles, the rear gunner of another Blenheim saw the bombs straddle the lorries. One bomb exploded within fifteen yards of the tanker. As the lorries came to a standstill, soldiers scrambled out and raced for cover on either side of the road. All the vehicles were sprayed with machine-gun bullets. A wireless station just outside Homs was also raked with machine-gun fire.

Wed 28 Jan

Afternoon. Hurricanes airborne and engage raiders. One Hurricane shot down. More raids.

Thu 29 Jan

More raids.

Casualties: *Siġġiewi*: Leonardu Attard (57); *Gozo* (*Għajnsielem*): Anġlu Grech (7), Carmela Grech (49), Emilia Grech (17), Ines Grech (16), John Grech (14).

Fri 30 Jan

More raids.

Casualties: *Qrendi*: Joseph Aquilina (38), Mary Rose Aquilina (34).

More raids.

Casualties: St Julian's: Carmelo Manicolo (55); *Żejtun*: Anthony Farrugia (6), Antonia Zahra (6), John Mary Zammit (11), Joseph Zammit (1), Mary Zammit (30).

Internees (political suspects)[1] at Internment Camp, Rabat, are notified of their deportation from Malta to an unknown destination. The relative Area Order No. 40 reads:

> *'A party of detainees – as per list annexed – is being removed from Malta. The departure will not take place for some days but very short notice of the actual date will be given.*
>
> *'Luggage – All luggage to be ready at 5 p.m. on February 7th. Each member of the party will be permitted to take one ordinary-sized cabin trunk and one suitcase. If any person has no cabin trunk he may take two suitcases instead, i.e. a total of three cases. Each box must be labelled clearly with the name and number of its owner.*
>
> *'Clothing – Members of the party are warned that they are being removed to warm climate and that they will therefore be require to take with them a reasonable quantity of clothing suitable for wear in such climate. Clothing such as are worn in Malta during the summer months will be suitable. No clothing will be provided from public funds.*
>
> *'Pocket Money – Each member of the party will be permitted to take not more than £10 (ten pounds) with him as pocket money. No pocket money will be provided from public funds.'*

Members of the party: No. 5 Abela Guido+* – 63 Bencini Alfred+* – 143 Bartolo Salvatore – 142 Bajona Albert+* – 34 Bonello Vincenzo+* – 163 Borg William* – 80 Caruana Vincenzo+* – 141 Casabene John+* – 51 Cortis, Prof. Giulio, LL.D.+* – 52 Cossai Emmanuele+* – 37 Cini Joseph+* – 30 Curmi Frank +* – 46 Chetcuti Charles +* – 138 Farrugia William +* – 56 Farrugia Anthony+* – 91 Farrugia Charles+* – 43 – Formosa Charles+* – 151 Felice Paul+* – 114 Gabell lfar+ – 159 Gatt Salvatore+ – 33 German Daniele+* – 36 Gauci Albert+* – 65 Ganado Herbert, LL.D.+* – 79 Gatt Henry +*

1 These included both Maltese and foreigners who were initially confined in Fort Salvatore but were transferred to Corradino Civil Prisons in July 1940 when the fort was bombed and became uninhabitable. They were finally moved to St Agatha Convent, Rabat.

– 162 Grech Marguerat Joseph +* – 167 Klein Ladlaus+ – 38 Lateo Edgardo+* – 49 Lateo Carmelo+* – 147 Lateo Carmelo Ur)+* – 66 Laudi Orazio+* – 68 Laudi Joseph+* – 67 Laudi Salvatore+* – 4 Laferla Edgar+ – 50 Laferla Alberto, ACE* – 7 Lepre Georges+ – 133 Maitland Woolf Eric+ – Mercieca, Sir Arturo+ – 57 Mizzi Enrico, LL.D.+ – 144 Naudi Joseph W.+* – Pantalleresco, Mgr A.V.+ – 156 Pirrone Umberto+* – 53 Savona Victor+* – 32 Scicluna Joseph+* – 35 Sammut Giovanni, LL.D+* – 37 Saffrette Charles+* – 158 Soler Edgar George+* – 54 Stilon Alberto, LL.D * – Stilon De Piro Alexander, LL.D+*

Governor Sir Wiliam Dobbie calls on the Archbishop, Mgr Caruana, to inform him personally of the decision taken regarding the internees. Mgr Caruana tried to induce Dobbie to reconsider the decision, but the Governor makes it clear that the decision is irrevocable.

Sun 1 Feb

More frequent air attacks.

RAF heavy bombers and continue their successful communications.

Mon 2 Feb

The BBC reports that there were 263 raids on Malta during January.

Wed 4 Feb

Air-raids and AA Barrages.

Casualties: *Mosta*: Joseph Buhagiar (50), Francis Chetcuti (29), Elia Tonna (51), Joseph Tonna (31); *Naxxar*. Bartholomew Buhagiar (80); *St Paul's Bay*: Grazio Galea (42). Civilian casualties for January 1942: killed – 83; seriously injured – 59; slightly injured – 76.

Thu 5 Feb

Air-raids.

Casualties: *Sliema*: Liberata Bugeja (75), Adelaide lncorvaja (6), Edward Pace Bonello (51), Caroline Ethel Yabsley (72).

Fri 6 Feb

During this morning's air-raid, heavy AA artillery destroyed a JU 88 bomber and a ME 109 fighter.

9.30 a.m. – The hearing the case is initiated in His Majesty's Civil Court, First Hall, the Hon. Mr Justice AJ. Montanaro Gauci presiding, of 38 internees,[2] who, *inter alia*, plead that any order issued or about to be issued for their deportation from the island is or would be *ultra vires* the powers of the Governor. Counsel for defence are Dr A. Magri, LL.D. and Dr F.N. Buttigieg, LL.D. The Crown is represented by the Hon. Dr L. Galea, LL.D., Attorney General, and Dr J. Reynaud, LL.D., Senior Crown Counsel. The plaintiffs have summoned Major Walter L. Bonello, Commandant Internment Camp, and the Hon. Sir Edward St. J. Jackson, Lieutenant Governor of Malta, as the representative of the Government of Malta. Plaintiffs plead that 'Area Order' No. 40, notifying them that they are to be deported from Malta is illegal and *ultra vires*, as there is no law authorizing anyone to deport a British subject from Malta, especially if he be a native Maltese, and that the said Order and any other Order which may involve the transfer of plaintiffs to a place outside these islands, be declared null and void for all intents of the Law. The Court adjourns.

Last night, while RAF heavy bombers were blitzing Sirte airfield, naval torpedo bombers were again attacking Axis shipping in the Central Mediterranean. Two merchant ships of 8,000 tons and 3,000 tons respectively, both fully loaded and on their way to North Africa with supplies for Rommel's army were torpedoed. Sun 7 Feb

In the case instituted by the 38 internees who pleaded that any Order issued or which may be issued for their deportation was without legal sanction, the Court's judgement is delivered. The Court (1) Disallows the claim of the prematurity of the cause; (2) Rejects the claim for a declaration of nullity of the Warrants of Internment of the plaintiffs, except for that part which empowers competent Military, Naval, and Air Force authorities the right to prescribe the place of internment, which part of the Warrants the Court declares *ultra vires*, and therefore of no effect; (3) Declares that 'Area Order' No. 40 is not an Order for the transfer or deportation of the plaintiffs, but a mere notice of a decision of the Government and

2 The 38 internees referred to here are those shown with an asterisk (*) against their names in the list appended to Area Order No 40.

a warning, and, therefore, the said Order is not illegal or *ultra vires*, and, therefore, it is not null; (4) Declares that the Government of Malta has not the right, according to Law, to order the deportation of the plaintiffs outside Malta, by transferring them to another country, and, therefore, the Order to plaintiffs to prepare themselves for departure, which implies an Order for their transfer, is illegal, *ultra vires*, and of no effect. In view of the lack of precedent, the Court makes no order with regard to costs.

Mon 9 Feb

Enemy air activity continues with more intensity.

Casualties: *Mosta*: Vincenzo Borg (55), Annetto Mifsud Ellul, A&CE (53), Marietta Pizzuto (50), Salvina Scerri (28); *Qormi*: Carmelo Bonnici (45), Francis Felice (56); *Siġġiewi*: Wistin Baldacchino (58); *Valletta*: Spiro Cefai (43).

Afternoon – Emergency sitting of the Council of Government, Sir Edward Jackson, Leader of the House, seconded by Dr Louis Galea, Attorney General, moved the first reading of a Bill entitled 'An Ordinance to empower the removal from Malta of persons lawfully detained therein'. Parliament empowers Governor to transfer detainees in the interest of the defence of Malta, amidst Nationalist opposition. The two Nationalist Members, Sir Ugo Mifsud and Notary Dr Giorgio Borg Olivier, maintain that, apart from politics and political partisan questions, a most important constitutional question was involved.

Extract from Sir Ugo Mifsud's speech: ' ... I am concerned with the constitutional aspect of this matter. Unfortunately, we have been given very little time to ponder and consider; we were told of this Bill at noon by the Lieut. Governor. When I say 'we', I mean our party [the Nationalist Party], because the Members of the other Party [the Constitutional and Labour Parties] were told yesterday afternoon of what was going to be presented before this House. But the actual text of the Bill was handed to us exactly at 3 p.m. If I had come more prepared, if I had been given the chance of coming more prepared – and, I open a parenthesis, I had hardly time to get some lunch in order to prepare myself a little – I would have shown to this House, with texts and authorities in hand, that the whole Bill is illegal, *ultra vires*. I take my stand first of all from a statement which

Grand Harbour under air attack.

was made by the Lieut. Governor that this is the consequence of a judgement, which was given by our Courts, by the Courts of His Majesty in Malta, which, according to the opinion of the Lieut. Governor, who is a legal man and who has held high and important positions in the Empire, in his legal capacity, has shown a gap, a gap which he has tried to explain. He has limited himself only to the technical reasons which have moved him to present this measure. Sir, that judgement, like many other judgements given in our Courts and sanctioning the Constitutional rights of the people of this island, will stand out as one of the landmarks with regard to what constitutes the right of the citizens. That very same judgement on which the Government today has taken its stand, has enunciated many and many important principles which are the birthright of every British citizen, which are the birthright of every subject, and which are the birthright of us Maltese who, when accepting and asking for the protection of Great Britain, made it a point that our liberties would be respected. We also made it a point to assume and to ask that we would be given the liberties which are enjoyed by free Englishmen – not to say the principles contained in the Magna Carta, and the principles, the unwritten principles, which constitute the unwritten law of England regarding the rights of the citizen. The citizen has rights which are recognized by custom and by usage and which have not and need not ever be incorporated in any written law. These are: the right of liberty; the right not to be condemned except by a judgement of a competent court; the right not to be detained long in arrest; the right not to be extradited out of England. On the occasion of imminent war, or the possibility of imminent war, the Parliament of England, which is omnipotent in the technical sense of the word, that is to say, King, Commons and Lords, passed an Act for the defence and ty of the Realm and of the Empire, and by that Act they imposed limitations on the liberty of the subjects. They thus permitted the Executive to exercise the right of arrest or detention of individuals even without trial, but they went no further; they did not give in England the right to extradite British citizens – mark you, I always mention the words "British Citizens" – and the law which was passed in I 939, which has been mentioned as the Emergency Powers to the Government or to the Executive the power to deport, therefore it did not grant to the Secretary of State for the Colonies nor to any Governor under a Secretary of State, or one who receives instructions and orders from the Executive in England, the power to deport. This important right of the citizen not to be extradited has been well commented upon in the judgement of the 7th of this month; that very same judgement has stated clearly that the Defence Regulations as applied to Malta, that is to say the Malta

Defence Regulations, did not give power to the Governor to do what was the intention of the Government of Malta to do; at the same time it made it clearly evident by quoting authorities, *inter alia*, Blackstone ... Hawk, and other authorities that no power on earth except the authority of Parliament can send a subject, even if he be a criminal, out of England, out of the land, against his will ... Except Parliament, and Parliament is the King plus the two Houses ... In England no power exists to deport a British subject out of England who had been condemned by a competent court, and I will quote here Hawk on Common Law, that is the unwritten law of England as applied by the judges there. There is no legal method of exporting or removing a subject from his country, no power on earth except the Authority of Parliament could do this. In fact whenever it was felt expedient to do so, the Parliament of England had to pass laws such as the Penal Servitude Acts of 1855 as regards deportation of convicts and other laws such as those passed during the reign of George III regarding the deportation of Indians, which, however, were afterwards altered. Deportation was always looked upon as an extraordinary measure, contrary to the rights of the citizens, which required a particular authority in order to receive execution ... The Court has shown that the Malta Defence Regulations gave no greater power to the Executive here than the Executive has in England, and in England when the Emergency Power Act was passed and promulgated no authority was granted to the Executive to deport people from the United Kingdom. With us something very particular happened; when the law was published a dispatch or rather a law intended to be prepared in Malta in 1939 and intended to be promulgated whenever and when the emergency would arise, was printed and published and therefore enacted in August of 1939. In that law the power to deport did exist; however, when the Imperial Parliament passed the Emergency Powers Act, when therefore the Emergency Powers Act, which was passed by the Chamberlain Government a few days before the outbreak of war, was promulgated, that particular clause, regarding the deportation of British citizens, was deleted, deliberately deleted, because it did not receive the approval of Parliament. It was against the spirit of the British Constitution itself, it was against the birthright of Britishers, and here in Malta we had to publish again, that is the authorities concerned, had to publish again new Malta Defence Regulations, in which Regulations that particular clause was absolutely non-existent and was purposely deleted in order to fall into line with the spirit of the British Constitution. We stand, therefore, in this particular position. In view of the particular legal state of this question, the Law Officers of the Crown of Malta pretend that, by passing the Bill, which we had simply the time to cursorily read and which perhaps might be open to many other objections, this Council will fill up the gap. My contention, my strong contention on Constitutional grounds, apart from political grounds and questions of expediency, is that it will not, and the reasons are clear. There are, or there is, a sovereign law-making body and that is the Parliament of the United Kingdom and the Parliament of the Dominions, which now have won for themselves an equal position. But the Councils or Legislative Assemblies in the Colonies are not sovereign law-making bodies and it has been recognized in Constitutional Law that they cannot – by legislation or by administrative Acts – go against the general principles which are now in Common Law, not only in England but throughout the whole Empire, regulating the rights of the citizens; and amongst others, as I said, there exists the right of non-deportation; and I use the word deportation because it has been mentioned *expressis verbis* by the spokesman of the Government – that is to say, the right to transfer elsewhere people for any reason whatsoever … What has happened to these internees may happen to anybody and we stand here for the rights of the individual. We have always been clamouring for the return of Self Government. Let us begin by respecting our own Constitutional rights for which our ancestors have always fought in this Chamber. Many of us have devoted their life, their money and their health in order to be free men under the British Crown – not be employees or to make money out of their representation of the people by asking for jobs … Deportation is a penalty; a very grave penalty and it means therefore the consequence of a crime. Now, Sir, in the case of these detained persons, there has not been any formal accusation. There has not been any charge proffered against them, much less has there been a judgement of any Court before which, whether as a Court specially constituted, or else as a Court assisted by ajury, these people might have defended themselves. It is for this reason and this reason alone that I had asked that at least a jury of Honour ought to have been appointed to consider their case. For this reason and also on political grounds I interceded a week ago for these people and asked that no execution should be given to the decision to deport them ... I pray God that recriminations like these which I leave an indelible mark in our history will not happen in Malta. I am feeling ill ...'

(At this point Sir Ugo Mifsud was rushed out of the Chamber suffering from a heart attack. He died two days later (11 February) at his residence in Villa Preziosi, Lija, aged 53).

More raids. Tue 10 Feb

Casualties: *Birkirkara*: Paul Pace (48); *Qormi*: Lisa Aquilina (50), Georgia Borg (43), Ġanni Briffa (33), Salvino Cassar (7), Ninu Ciappara (12), Salvo Gatt (47), George Grech (34), Joseph Giordimaina (8), Mary Giordimaina (5), Emanuel Giordimaina (11), Anna Muscat (15), John Portelli (34), Carmelo Saliba (55), Manwel Sammut (7), Maria Sammut (6), Spiru Vella (20); *Gozo* (*Xagħra*): M'Anna Attard (70), Carmelo Attard (72).

Some internees challenge the Government's right to deport them. The case is heard in His Majesty's Civil Court, First Hall, the Hon. Mr Justice AJ. Montanaro Gauci, LL.D presiding. Plaintiffs are seeking to impugn the validity of the emergency Powers (Removal of Detained Persons) Ordinance (No 1 of 1942). The contention advanced is that this law is illegal and *ultra vires* in as much as the enabling Act under which it has been enacted known as the Emergency Powers (Defence)Act of 1939, does not confer legislative powers for the deportation of British subjects from Malta. The hearing takes place under heavy air-raids.

Enemy bombers with fighter escort continue their raids. Intense fire from land defences. Casualties: *Mosta*: Ġamri Chetcuti (12), Emilia Defelice (65). Wed 11 Feb

A number of enemy aircraft attempt to attack a convoy of warships about to enter the Grand Harbour. The ships make port safely under cover of fighter protection.

Thu
12
Feb

Heavy raids.

Casualties: *Għargħur*: Carmelo Micallef (8); *Marsa*: Carmelo Calleja (54); *Paola*: Maria Agius (31), Victor Agius (29), Carmelo Bugeja (76), Antonia Busuttil (4), Emanuel Busuttil (26), Carmela Cachia (52), Carmelo Camilleri(30), John Desira (70), Joseph Fenech (35), Maria Fleri (29), Lilian Fleri (1), Giovanna Gatt (55), Anna Gera (75), Aurelia Grech (19), Carmela Grech (53), Maria Grech (21), Gianna Grima (19), Louis Mallia (9), Rosina Mallia (56), John Mazzello (75), Carmela Morris (68), Regina Pace (64), Carmela Pisani (34), Jane Pisani (50), Joseph Pisani (64), Mary Salsero (17), Lorenzo Scerri (55), Charles Theobold (77), John Vassallo (75), Stanley Warn (13), Andrea Zammit (76), Carmelo Zammit (33), Stephen Zammit (62), Marianna Zarb (50); *Qormi*: Joseph Farrugia (36); *Tarxien*: Alfonzo Camilleri (46), Gio Batta Cutajar (14), Michelina Grech (72); *Żejtun*: Salvina Bonnici (–), Giusa Buttigieg (14).

Order by His Excellency the Governor:

> *'Whereas the Emergency Powers (Removal of Detained Persons) Ordinance, 1942, enables the Governor to make an order directing that any person as therein specified and subject to the conditions therein set forth shall be removed from Malta in pursuance of arrangements made as therein recited;*
>
> *And whereas the persons hereunder mentioned have been lawfully ordered to be detained in Malta;*
>
> *And whereas it appears that, with a view to securing the public safety or defence of Malta, the continued detention in Malta of the persons hereunder mentioned is inexpedient;*
>
> *And whereas arrangements have been made with the Government of Uganda, which is a country to which the Emergency Powers (Defence) Act, 1939, of the United Kingdom has been extended by Order in Council made under Section 4 of that Act, for the removal of the persons hereunder mentioned to that country;*
>
> *Now, therefore, I, Sir William Sheddon Dobbie, Governor and Commander-in-Chief of Malta and its Dependencies, enabled as aforesaid, do hereby Order that the following persons, namely*[3] …

3 The number of persons actually ordered for deportation was 47, namely the 44 shown with the sign (+) against their names in the list; plus

During yesterday's meeting of the Council of Government, the Nationalist member, Dr Giorgio Borg Olivier, paid tribute to the memory of Sir Ugo Mifsud whose funeral service was held at 8 a.m. this morning. He was later interred at the Lija Cemetery.

In his speech Dr Borg Olivier said: 'The loss of Sir Ugo means to me the loss of a leader, a father, and a friend. At the age of 21, Sir Ugo graduated at the University of Malta, that University which remained in his love for all his life, and he then immediately joined the Bar. Sir Ugo Mifsud's forensic career was indeed a brilliant and remarkable one, and all those who are in any way connected with our Courts will bear me out in stating that his loyalty and esteem towards His Majesty's Judges, his clients, and his colleagues should stand as an example to the rising generation. As one of the leading lawyers, he was elected a member of the Chamber of Advocates, in which he maintained keen interest even before he was elected President, which position he held for the last three years. He was extremely proud of his profession, and he strove to keep the dignified position which it deserved. A lover of Constitutional Law, a writer on International Law, he attended many conferences both in England and on the continent, organized by the International Law Association of which he was a member. His country had the honour to have Sir Ugo Mifsud elected as Chairman of the Conference held i'n Berlin in 1928, as well as of that held in Budapest in 1934 on the occasion of the Budapest Law Congress. Sir Ugo Mifsud's career as a public man is well known to all his fellow-countrymen, because it constitutes the actual history of our Island. From the day on which he was elected Secretary to the Assemblea Nazionale in 1919, that is to say at the age of 30, his interest in local politics was incessantly great and he had at heart the welfare of Malta, which he so dearly wished could enjoy a welldeserved Dominion Status, in the British Commonwealth of Nations ... In his private life he had a real charm of manner and courtesy, as well as consideration for the failings and shortcomings of whoever came in contact with him. He had a profound sense of religion, an unfailing sense of honour, and a great sense of humour. He loved good company and a good joke. One

Enrico Emmanuele Galere and Lady Mercieca and her daughter Miss Lilian Mercieca, both of whom volunteered to accompany Sir Arturo to Uganda.

can hardly forget Sir Ugo's smile. Using tact throughout, he never wavered from speaking the truth when and where necessary. He was conscientious and scrupulous in the management of his affairs, professional or otherwise, always generous with sympathizers and political adversaries alike, always ready to see the good points in others and equally ready to condemn the bad. He had a good word for everybody.'

The tempo of war heightens and Malta had a hectic 24 hours. Guns, smoke, fire, bombs, and more bombs. A Royal Navy destroyer suffers a direct hit. Losses inflicted on the enemy include a Junker 88 and a Dornier 24 Flying-Boat.

Casualties: *Floriana*: Michael Debattista (30); *Ħamrun*: Francis Pace (22).

7 p.m. Parlatorio Wharf. The internees[4] left Malta on board the 10,000-ton AA armed merchantman *Breconshire* for Uganda. An air-raid was on when the detainees had boarded the ship and were preparing for departure.

Sat 14 Feb

Intense enemy air activity.

Sun 15 Feb

A day-long alert. Our fighter pilots and AA gunners share in the spoils of the day: two ME 109 fighters were shot down into the sea by Hurricanes; a JU 88 was shot down in flames on land by HAA guns and a second JU 88 destroyed by LAA guns.

In the evening, under cover of clouds, the enemy cross the coast and drop some bombs, causing damage to civilian property, including the Regent Cinema, which was at the time crowded with people, and the Casino Maltese, besides scoring a direct hit on and damaging part of the Grand Master's Palace.

Casualties: *Birkirkara*: Pio Carabott (34); Floriana: Gerald Ciantar (19), Giulio Mifsud (19); *Ħamrun*: Joseph Cassar (30), Mary Cassar (19); Renzo Flores (65), Albert Zammit (26); *Paola*: John Attard (20), Toni Farrugia (14), Michael Wickan (19); *Pietà*: Frances Patsy Cutter (19); *Sliema*: Melita Abela (26), Joseph Amodeo (24); Valletta: Dr R.

4 See footnote 23.ġ

Queuing for meals outside a Victory Kitchen.

Bonello, MD (52), Dr A. Caruana Galizia, LL.D. (46), Joseph Cassar (17), Francis Cremona (16), Joseph Falzon (17), Frank Farrugia (13), Raffaele Mallia (54), Franġiska (Kitty) Mamo (17), Fr Gerald Pace, OC (40), Manasser Reginiano (18).

After a dangerous crossing, during which the *Breconshire* was attacked several times from the air, the deported Maltese reach Alexandria and were thence transported by train to Cairo. Mon 16 Feb

Casualties: *Kirkop*: Michael Farrugia (31); *Qormi*: Carmela Briffa (60); *St Paul's Bay*: Manwel Borg (60); *Valletta*: Joseph Cremona (21).

In a Circular-Letter to Government Departments, Mr G.N. Nunn, Assistant to the Lieutenant Governor, informs all civil officers who are not called upon to report for special duty in the event of invasion or prolonged attack on the islands that they will be required to assist in the distribution of emergency iron rations to the public. Wed 18 Feb

Fri 20 Feb

The bombing continues.

Casualties: *Mosta*: Jimmy Gauci (3), Jessie Borg (40); *Żabbar*: William Miller (55).

Sat 21 Feb

A series of determined attacks on airfields, by large formations of enemy aircraft, throughout the day.

Casualty: *Mqabba*: Anthony Ghigo (24).

To date, we have had 1,690 air-raid alerts.

Mon 23 Feb

Communal Kitchens are established. The heavy blitz on Malta continues incessantly.

Tue 24 Feb

Raids on airfields. Bombs dropped on Valletta.

Casualties: *Għaxaq*: Ubaldesca Vella (32); *Sliema*: Ġanni Brincat (32).

Wed 25 Feb

Casualty: *Gżira*: Anthony Borg (60).

Thu 26 Feb

Casualty: *Valletta*: Reginald Smith (53).

Fri 27 Feb

RAF fighters seriously damage a JU 88 bomber and three ME 109 fighters during determined attacks on the Grand Harbour by the *Luftwaffe*.

Casualty: *Cospicua*: Ġanni Borg (51).

Saturday, 28 February

Casualty: *Valletta*: Capt. W.C. Parnis, OBE, MC (48).

Sun 1 Mar

Heavy *Luftwaffe* attacks continue on shipping in the Grand Harbour, airfields, and other military objectives. Stella Maris Church in Sliema has been hit and reduced to an empty shell.

Casualties: *Floriana*: Robert Attard (60), Joseph Borg (8), Patricia Cameron (18), Giovanna Caruana (43), Joseph Darmanin (60), Stella Debattista (19), Annunziata Demanuele (13), Benjamin Maggi (15),

Grezzju Magro (16), Emmanuel Pace (20), Giovanna Pace (15), Carmelina Portelli (4), Sarah Portelli (39), Antonio Pulo (27), Dolores Zammit (24); *Msida*: Carrie Portelli (23); *Sliema*: Dolores Borg (60), Joseph Muscat (35); StJulian's: Surg. Cdr A.E. Cheeseman, RN (40), Doris Cheeseman (40).

Casualties: *Cospicua*: Anthony Zammit (70); *Kalkara*: Lorenzo Mejlak (55); *Żabbar*: Grezzju Abdilla (45), Maria Abdilla (15). Mon 2 Mar

During last night RAF Wellington bombers carried out a devastating attack on Palermo. This important Sicilian port is used mainly for loading war supplies intended for Rommel's Afrika Korps. Relays of British bombers continued to shower explosive bombs on the harbour. Despite the Italians trying to cover the docks area with a smokescreen, two cargo ships (9,000 tons and 5,000 tons respectively) were sunk. A third ship (5,000 tons) loaded with motor transport was set on fire. During this attack several other merchant ships, an oil dump, a ship-building, and engineering yard, and a seaplane base were also set on fire and were still burning six hours after the attack. Tue 3 Mar

During February, Malta experienced 153 bombing raids – 97 by night and 56 in daylight.

London. The Air Minister, Sir Archibald Sinclair, introducing the Air Estimates in the House of Commons announced that the bombing of Germany is to be resumed on the largest possible scale at the earliest possible moment. Declaring that the RAF's main task since June has been to help Russia and that large numbers of British aircraft are now being operated there by the Russians, he added: 'We have given Russia help in other ways, RAF squadrons in Malta and Africa have engaged large numbers of German fighters and by fighter and bomber sweeps over Northern France, attacks on German shipping and industries, we have forced them to keep a large number of fighters in the West.' Wed 4 Mar

The Air Minister stated that 175,000 tons of Axis shipping has been sunk in the Mediterranean during the six months prior to the last offensive.

After an all-night alert, day raiding was resumed soon after dawn. The enemy followed their usual tactics of first sending reconnaissance aircraft and then small fighter sweeps. The first bombing raid started shortly after noon and this was followed by another determined attack on airfields during the early part of the afternoon. More raids and bombs dropped on widely scattered localities.

Casualties: *Attard*: Joseph Dingli (15), Tessie Dingli (4), Valentino Dingli (1); *Birkirkara*: Michael Gauci (40); *Gozo* (Żebbuġ): Wiġi Vella (22).

The Information Office notified that the following Maltese who are prisoners-of-war in Germany have not received any letters from their relatives living in Malta, and that they also ask for some thick underwear and warm clothing: P. Agius 88539; A. Bugeja 87401; P. Felice 86516; D. Pace 89955; G. Portelli 88801; C. Barbara 87016; N. Bartolo 807650; V. Scerri 90585; C. Tonna 89392; G. Muscat 90288; F. Camilleri 90615; Micallef 86847.

Fri 6 Mar

Casualties: *Rabat*: Domenica Borg (19); *Sliema*: Carmel Balzan (71), Laura Castagna (22), Kenneth Scicluna (6 months).

Sun 8 Mar

Casualties: *Balzan*: Melita Brincat (50); *Luqa*: Peter Farrugia (58), Peter Paul Saydon (45).

Mon 9 Mar

Enemy air-raids continue incessantly and relentlessly, their tactics being to neutralize the island's airfields. Today was to be the last time that our Hurricane fighters fought alone, before the arrival of the Spitfires. A German radio broadcast states that the Island Fortress of Malta is under a hail of bombs by day and night. The ground defences of Malta are in a continuous state of alarm.

Casualties: *Qormi*: Dolores Agius (6), Concetta Briffa (53), George Ellul (17).

MALTA
FOR
EVER

Tue 10 Mar

During the last night Naval aircraft made two torpedo attacks and hit a 10,000-ton merchant ship in the Central Mediterranean. Escorted by three Italian destroyers, this heavily laden ship was on its way to Tripoli with supplies for Rommel's army. Flares were dropped and the destroyers tried to cover the cargo ship by a smokescreen. Despite this device and AA fire, the British pilot came down to only thirty feet above the sea to launch his torpedo. The newly arrived Spitfires go into action for the first time over Malta.

During today's bombing raid, the chapel of St Paul situated near the Gillieru Hotel, St Paul's Bay, suffers a direct hit. This historic and artistic gem is traditionally associated with the site of the landing of St Paul on Malta in AD 60.

London. The new Under-Secretary of State for the Colonies, Mr Harold Macmillan, said in the House of Commons: 'This offers us an opportunity to express our gratitude and pride in the magnificent defence which the people of Malta have put up under the leadership of Gen. Sir Wiliam Dobbie – one of the most gallant officers ever holding the position he now occupies. There has been an inspired defence.'

The deported Maltese start their train journey from Cairo to Uganda.

Casualties: *St Julian's*: Calcedonio Parnis (50).

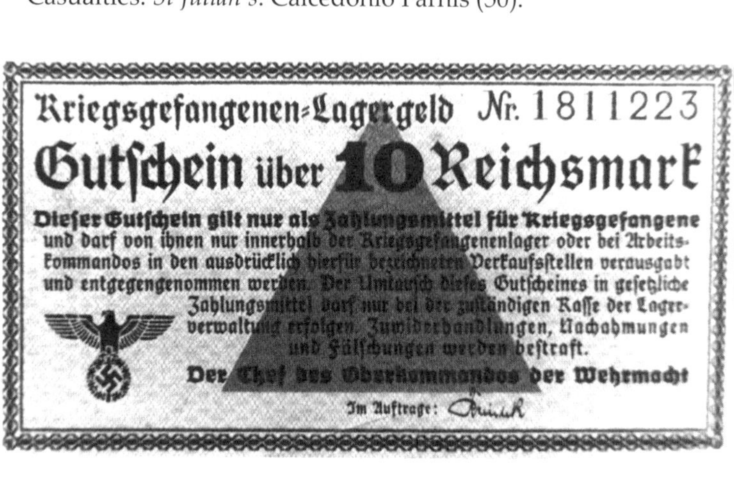

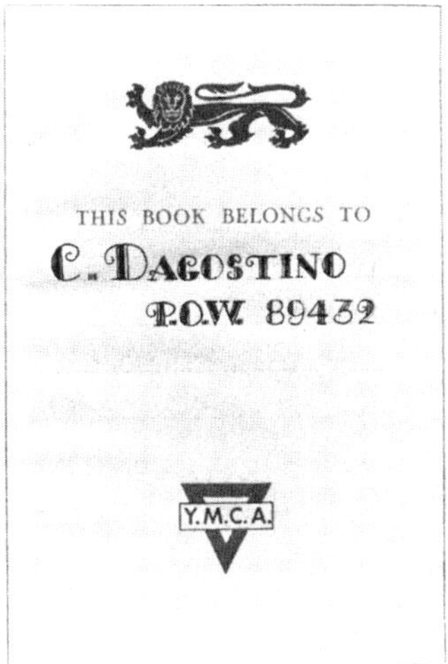

From the wartime log of a Maltese prisoner.

More air-raids. Wed 11 Mar

Casualty: *Sliema*: Georgia Borg (22).

Casualties: *Żurrieq*: Paula Ellul (64), Salvu Sammut (62), Salvu Sammut (64), Mary Zahra (54). Thu 12 Mar

Spectacular air combats in Maltese skies. Fri 13 Mar

This evening an appeal in Maltese is broadcast calling for manpower to work on Ta' Qali airfield which is intended mainly for the newly arrived Spitfires. Sat 14 Mar

Casualties: *Floriana*: Francis Pulo (62); *Żurrieq*: Kalanġ Zerafa (47).

More raids and more gallant dogfights. Sun 15 Mar

Casualties: *Birkirkara*: Salvu Borg (20); *Sliema*: Polly Cannataci (26); *St Julian's*: Chris James Butler (8 months); *Valletta*: Giovanna

A group of Maltese deportees in Uganda.

Attard (56), Domenica Borg Bellizzi (39), Joseph Bellizzi (66), Michelina Busuttil (60), Vincent Busuttil (30), Anthony Formosa (37), Girolamo Fsadni (77), Marianna Mayman (34), Harold Miles (38), Mary Mifsud (57), Melita Vella (35), Michael Vella (74); *Żabbar*: Emmanuele Bongailas (28), Giuseppe Lia (12).

Mon 16 Mar

Great enthusiasm in Valletta, when some Spitfires swooped low over the City and showed off their speed and manoeuvring qualities in a series of stunts. At one time they appeared to be diving recklessly into the cheering crowds. The spectators seemed to have enjoyed this Spitfire 'raid'!

Tue 17 Mar

Heavy raids.

Casualties: *Birkirkara*: Alfred Calleja (35); *Ħamrun*: George Debono (43); *Lija*: Charles Lanzon (PS 89) (36); *Paola*: Giuseppe Delia (60); Joseph Delia (4), George Gauci (80); *Qormi*: Carmelo Aquilina (77); *Rabat*: Francis Mallia (–), Ena Mallia Pulvirenti (12), Salvu Portelli

(37), Andrea Spiteri (11), Samuel Vassallo (25); *Siġġiewi*: Carmelo Baldacchino (44); *Sliema*: Eddie Bartolo (38); Joseph Bartolo (38), Alfred Calapai (54), Antonio Fava (20), Paul Formosa (50), Giuseppa Micallef (54), Joseph Micallef (11), Albert Mifsud (14),Joseph Mifsud (66), Anthony Pisani (38), Carmela Sghendo (15), Francis Spiteri (14), Alfred Vella (PC 547) (45); *Valletta*: Muriel Brocklebank (47); *Żebbuġ*: Giuseppe Petroni (29); *Żejtun*: Joseph Mercieca (45); *Żurrieq*: Ursola Schembri (58).

Wed 18 Mar

Last night, naval aircraft struck another severe blow at Axis shipping. Attacks on two convoys in the Central Mediterranean resulted in torpedo hits on a 7,000-ton merchant ship, as well as a fully loaded 2,000-ton vessel which was set on fire. Two E-boats formed the escort of the first convoy; the second convoy was being escorted by two destroyers. Incessant enemy action; dogfights and losses on both sides.

Casualties: *St Paul's Bay*: Carmela Muscat (72), Francis Muscat (14).

This morning, on her arrival at Marfa, the Gozo-Malta passenger boat *Royal Lady* was machine-gunned by an enemy aircraft. Most of

A censored letter addressed to a Maltese deportee in Uganda.

the passengers had alighted, but three men still on the boat were injured.

Thu 19 Mar

Arrangements are made in respect of departments housed in the Palace, Valletta, for a bell controlled by the party on the Palace signal tower to be rung in each departmental office as the red flag is hoisted on the tower. Bells have also been installed in the shelters under the Palace, which will be rung to indicate that the red flag had been lowered. One long peal on the bells in the offices will indicate the hoisting of the flag, and two long peals on those in the shelters will indicate its lowering. These arrangements are made to avoid unnecessary interruption of work during air-raids.

Casualties: *Gżira*: Paul Vassallo (50); *Lija*: Paul Azzopardi (39); *Sliema*: Mikiel Borg (64).

Fri 20 Mar

Heavy raids continue.

Casualties: *Attard*: Alessandro Camilleri (50), Salvo Gatt (49), Ġanni Portelli (55), Emmanuele Vassallo (47); *Birkirkara*: Anthony Gatt (12); *Ħamrun*: Carmelo Camilleri (11), Giusa Cuschieri (3), Francis Farrugia (13); *Lija*: Salvu Mallia (45); *Marsaxlokk*: Nardu Caruana (56); *Mosta*: Salvu Dimech (70); Giovanna Frendo (75), Duminka Micallef (18), Pietro Micallef (45), Rita Micallef (24); *Naxxar*: Zaru Grech (30), Joseph Sciberras (18); Pietà: Lewis Camilleri (44); *St Julian's*: Joseph Debono (45); *Valletta*: Margherita Buttigieg (44); *Żejtun*: Salvu Spiteri (30).

Sat 21 Mar

Frequent raids, heavy bombing, heavy damage, heavy casualty roll. Attacks on airfields continue throughout the day. Wave after wave of JU 88s came over in close formation. The heavy AA artillery and guns of HMS ships immediately engaged. *Luftwaffe* formations consisted of 50 to 75 aircraft each time. This was the largest single attack, since the Luftwaffe returned to Sicily last December.

Casualties: *Attard*: Anthony Pace (24); *Balzan*: Suor Paola Agius (73), Joseph Muscat (32); *Floriana*: Francis Azzopardi (16), Publio Mercieca (16); Mdina: Vincent Mizzi (13); *Mosta*: Doris Borg (6), Gio Maria Cuschieri (37), Teresa Cuschieri (70), Anthony Degiorgio (79),

Gozo – The broken hull of *Royal Lady* at Mġarr Harbour.

Carmela Degiorgio (77), Maria Degiorgio (34), Giorgina Dougall (42), John Fabri (9), Pacik Falzon, RE (41), Carmelo Fenech (11), Joseph Fenech (11), Giovanni Galea (66), Victor Galea (39), Kalanġ Gatt (42), Francis Gatt (13), Giuseppe Gatt (9), Ċensu Gauci (5), Maria Gauci (8), Mary Grech (54), Alfred Montanaro (63), John Montanaro (18), Mary Montanaro (60), Olga Stjohn (26), Zareno St John (3 months), Pina Tabone (22), Santu Tanna (32), Bartholomew Vella (41), Carmelo Vella (12), Giuseppe Vella (9), Vincenzo Zammit (39), Ġanna Zarb (48); Remains of an unidentified female, unidentified male; *Msida*: Salvu Vella (45); *Rabat*: Carmela Abela (63), Mary Adami (6), Albert Adami (2), Louis Adami (29), Catherine Azzopardi (80), Rev. Robert Calleja (58), Lewis Caruana (2 months), Domenico Ceci (84), Angiolina Ellul (73), Spiru Galea (63), Teresa Galea (42), Peter Giordimaina (65), Alb. Laferla, ACE (Internment Camp) (45), Dolor Mangani (20), Albert Mifsud (19), Felicia Mifsud (26), Gisuarda Mifsud (10 months), Harriet O'Neil (56), Gisuardo Portelli (71), Dr A. Stilon, LL.D. (Internment Camp) (64), Margherita Vassallo (28), one unidentified female; *St Paul's Bay*: Rita Vella (6); *Żejtun*: Carmelo Zahra (15).

Sun 22 Mar

Casualties: *Mosta*: Joseph Bartolo (40), Saverin Galea (45), Grezzju Schembri (9); *Valletta*: John Cachia (48).

Mon 23 Mar

During the last 24 hours, the tempo of the air attacks on Malta has risen. Three times the *Luftwaffe* has launched mass bombing raids on Ta' Qali airfield. Seventeen enemy planes brought down; 10 damaged.

RAF fighters gave continuous protection to a convoy approaching the island and entering the Grand Harbour. It is estimated that the enemy used at least 70 bombers, attacking in relays throughout the day.

A heavy-calibre bomb makes a direct hit on the Greek Church of Our Lady of Damascus in Valletta. Luckily the historic painting of Our Lady of Damascus, which had been brought to Mata by the Knights from Rhodes in 1530, had been removed to a safe place in good time by Revd. Papas Giorgio Schirò, the Parish Priest of the church.

Casualty: *Kalkara*: Agostino Mintoff (16).

Tue 24 Mar

The *Luftwaffe* carries out large-scale determined attacks on the Grand Harbour and airfields.

Casualties: *Birkirkara*: Paul Borg (17), Louis Sacco (60); *Birżebbuġa*: John Callus (49); *Ħamrun*: Joseph Grixti (51); *Kalkara*: Joseph Bartolo (18), Anthony Busuttil (16), Joseph Camilleri (45), Filomena Coster (54), Ġustu Coster (30), Joseph Coster (26), Mary Coster (48), Manwel Gauci (9), Rokku Gauci (2), Stella Gauci (12), Concetta Hili (20), Grezzju Hili (44), John Hili (4), Pawla Hili (12), Mary Micallef (31), Samuel Micallef (10), Toni Micallef (9), Carmela Mintoff (80), Pina Mintoff (48), Marino Stivala (62), Spira Vella (70), Angelica Ventura (66), Kelinu Ventura (75); *Luqa*: Xandru Bonnici (36); *Mosta*: Wiġi Calleja (75); *Paola*: Toussaints Aquilina (17); *Rabat*: Mary Adami (6); *Valletta*: Joseph Mifsud (47), Carmelo Vella (17); *Żabbar*: Katie Cardona (50).

Wed 25 Mar

In one of the biggest air battles ever fought over Malta. Spitfires and Hurricanes swooped on a formation of 30 JU 87 dive bombers that were about to attack a ship lying off the coast and shot them out of the sky.

Casualties: *Floriana*: Publio Mercieca (16); *Gżira*: Alfred Bellizzi (50); *Marsa*: Felice Gatt (80); *Sliema*: Mary Alvarese (88).

Thu 26 Mar

Casualties: *Balzan*: Valent Sammut (33); *Mosta*: Alfred Stjohn (2); *Sliema*: Carmelo Coppola (50), Doris Coppola (17), Herman Mifsud (42); *St Paul's Bay*: Rita Vella (6).

Fri 27 Mar

More air-raids.

Casualties: *Żejtun*: Carmel Zahra (15).

Sat 28 Mar

Today's issue of the *Times of Malta* publishes a sonnet by Maurice Caruana Curran, entitled 'Valletta':

Not for the princely monuments that form
Our ancient heritage we weep today:
Their very stones cry out above the storm,
That they shall rise again in proud array.
Nor for the blood of slaughtered innocents
Seek we revenge. They need it not who go
To rest in halls of bannered firmaments
With those who fought at Birgu and Lepanto.
Valletta! We learn from you the ways
Of dignity. Each token of your power
Steels our breasts for more embattled days.
We take out fate grim-lipped and cannot cower
Who matin and vesper see the sun's warm rays
Catch in their net of rose bastion and tower.

Mon 30 Mar

Dobbie states in a broadcast: 'Malta has suffered much and has been called upon to endure much, and this ordeal has been going on for a long time.'

Casualty: *Birkirkara*: Lewis Fenech (64).

Tue 31 Mar

A restricted bus service is introduced.

Milk distribution from a mobile canteen.

Casualties: *Ħamrun*: Anna Casha (17), Manwela Casha (18), M'Anna Micallef (45), Manwela Micallef (3); *Żabbar*. Antonia Muscat (33).

Wed
1
Apr

At 3.00 p.m. a wave of German bombers destroy the Convent of the Franciscan Minors at Sliema. The adjoining Parish Church (Sacro Cuor) is also hit and the chapels of St Lawrence and of the Holy Rosary are badly damaged. Close to the altar of the Holy Rosary were the Parish Priest, Fr George Xerri, who was hearing confessions, three women and a ten-year-old girl all of whom were buried under the falling masonry. They were rescued after two hours, but two of the women and the child were found dead. During this raid, the German bombs also hit and destroyed a number of houses in the vicinity of the church, killing 22 persons who had had no time to take cover in the shelters.

Shortly before midnight enemy bombs wreck the historic Tagores Palace commonly known as *Il-Palazz tan-Nigret* in the limits of Żurrieq.

The *Luftwaffe* suffers heavy losses in its four daylight mass raids on the Grand Harbour and airfields: 5 JU 87s, 2 JU 88s, and 1 ME 109 destroyed by AA artillery; 2 JU 87s, 2 JU 88s, and 2 ME 109s destroyed by RAF fighters who also damaged a further l JU 87, 5 JU 88s, and 2 ME 109s.

Casualties: *Birkirkara*: Edgar Zahra (43); *Balzan*: Walter Farrugia (43); *Gżira*: John Azzopardi (15), Ophelia Colombo (25), Concetta Mifsud Ellul (43), Mary Anne Miller (10); *Paola*: Anthony Vassallo (22); Sliema: Carmen Bates (6), George Bates (9 months), Imelda Bates (5), George Cassar (27), Vinċenza Cassar (20), Ċensa Cauchi (80), Hilda Clarke (32), Ivy Clarke (5), Joseph Clarke (2), Albert Fava (1), Fr Diego Galdes (52), Alfred Gatt (50), Giulia Gatt (46), Rose Marie Gatt (4), Thomas Lewis (54), Lonza Micallef (50), Michael Riviera (PS 184) (40), Antonia Tabone (7), Giusa Tabone (22), Alfred Zammit (50), Carmelo Zammit (15), Marianna Zammit (45); *Żebbuġ*: Carmel Attard (50), Frances Attard (16); *Żejtun*: Carmelo Camilleri (18), Cristoforo Caruana (77), Annunziato Desira (21), Wiġi Grech (31).

Casualties: *Paola*: Rose Midlane (41); *Sliema*: Joseph Grech (17). Thu 2 Apr

During a raid the schooner *Anna Dacoutros* received a direct hit while on her way to Gozo, and foundered. Fri 3 Apr

HM King George VI assumes the Colonelcy-in-Chief of the Royal Malta Artillery as from today, 3 April 1942.

Casualty: *Żebbuġ*: Joseph Agius (60).

From Secretary of State for the Colonies on behalf of HM the King, to HE the Governor of Malta: 'I have been watching with admiration the stouthearted resistance of all in Malta – service personnel and civilian alike – to the fierce and constant air attacks of the enemy in recent weeks. In the active defence of the island the RAF have been ably supported by the Royal Malta Artillery, and it therefore gives me special pleasure, in recognition of their skill and resolution, to assume the Colonelcy-in-Chief of the Regiment. Please convey my Sat 4 Apr best wishes to all ranks of my new Regiment, and assure them of the added pride with which I shall follow their future activities.'

From HE the Governor of Malta to the Secretary of State for the Colonies, for onward transmission to HM the King: 'The RMA desire to thank Your Majesty for the most gracious message conveyed to them and for the signal Honour Your Majesty has been pleased to accord to them in becoming Colonel-in-Chief of the Regiment. They desire to express their loyalty and devotion to Your Majesty's Person and they will endeavour to prove themselves worthy of the High Honour conferred on them.'

Mass raids continue. Heavy losses inflicted on the enemy. Intensive attacks on Luqa, Hal Far, and Ta' Qali airfields and on Valletta, where the church of St Augustine is hit.

Casualties: *Cospicua*: Paul Bartolo (24); *Ħamrun*: George Degiorgio (22), Carmel Felice (17), Tommy Harmsworth (54), Vincent Miggiani (38), Michelina Psaila (16), Joseph Sultana (2), Pupull Sultana (31), Teresa Sultana (26); an unidentified female corpse; *Marsa*: Joseph Bugeja (19), Carmela Saliba (20); *Paola*: Joseph Caruana (43), Francis Frendo (15), Carmelo Livori (–); Qormi: Joseph Ciantar (49); *Rabat*: William O'Neil (22); *Senglea*: Joseph Galea (77); *StJulian's*: Carmel Sciberras (29); *Valletta*: Ali Abdul Ben (61); *Vittoriosa*: Joseph Gatt (31); *Żebbuġ*: Teodora Coleiro (68); *Żejtun*: Carmel Cioffi (55).

Sun 5 Apr

More heavy raids.

Casualties: *Cospicua*: Carmela Montague (33), Daniel Montague (13), Joseph Montague (11), Mary Montague (8): *Floriana*: Antonia Attard (50), Joseph Borg (70); *Ħamrun*: Agostino Balzan (16), Franġiska Borg (40), Marianna Borda (77), Fr Clement Cauchi, OC (67), Josephine Farrugia (48), Emanuel Grima (15), Concetta Sultana (6); *Marsa*: Paul D'Amato (77); *Msida*: Joseph Abela (–); Rabat: Anthony Camilleri (42); *Tarxien*: Mary Bonello (11), Amodeo Micallef (44); *Valletta*: Philip Camilleri (64); *Żebbuġ*: Alfred Barbara (27); *Żejtun*: Anġlu Agius (29), Dolores Busuttil (2).

Mon 6 Apr

The *Luftwaffe* carried out one of the largest and most determined attacks on the Dockyard and airfields. *The Times* of London in today's leader pays tribute to 'the stout-hearted courage and endurance of the British and Maltese garrison and of the civil population of the island, who have been subjected to an ever sterner, because longer, ordeal than the population of London and our other great manufacturing cities and ports ... The splendour of the defence will be realized when it is remembered that though the number of hostile aircraft engaged in these onslaughts has not approached the strength employed in the major bombings of London, the area of three islands, Malta, Gozo, and the inhabited rock of Comino, is less than one sixth of that of Greater London, and that the inhabitants could not retire like many Londoners to safer areas.'

All valuables, monies and other articles of movable property recovered from buildings damaged by enemy action and held by the Police are on view to the public as from today at Police War Headquarters, Bugeja's Institute, Ħamrun.

Casualties: *Birkirkara*: Gianninu Psaila (12); *Ħamrun*: Joseph Borda (82), Paul Cassar (43), Jane Farrugia (50); *Marsa*: Anthony Pizzuto (38); *Paola*: Joseph Curmi (38); *Qormi*: Salvo Agius (68); *St Paul's Bay*: John Grech (28); *Tarxien*: Antonia Borg (56), Ċetta Borg (25), George Borg (63), Mary Borg (18), Anthony Busuttil (16), Francis Busuttil (44), John Busuttil (13), Joseph Busuttil (7) Mary Busuttil (38), Rose Busuttil (18), Michael Cilia (31), Concetta Falzon (9), Mary Falzon (11), Paola Falzon (38), Carmela Formosa (31), Giorgina Formosa (56), Lewis Muscat (3), Maria Annunziata Muscat (26), Rose Muscat (–); *Valletta*: Paula Abela (55); *Żejtun*: Anthony Spiteri (54); *Żurrieq*: Anna Schembri (75).

The 2000th alert is sounded today. The longest had lasted 11 hours 40 mins. Malta has had 17 alerts within the last 24 hours. 6.30 p.m.: The Royal Opera House suffers a direct hit by high explosive German bombs and is badly damaged. Tue 7 Apr

Casualties: *Birżebbuġa*: Carmela Briffa (6), Caterina Briffa (4), Manwela Briffa (8); *Gżira*: Joseph Caruana (33); *Luqa*: Lawrence Cassar (19); *Naxxar*. Mariano Sammut (24); *Valletta*: Helen Cachia Zammit Slythe (58), Luigia Cachia Zammit Slythe (60), Revd Robert Cachia Zammit Slythe (55), Rosina Cachia Zammit Slythe (50);

Ruins of the Opera House.

Vittoriosa: Giovanna Catania (60); *Żabbar*. Ludgarda Debono (60); *Gozo* (*Qala*): Joseph Buttigieg (60).

Wed 8 Apr

Today's *Times of Malta* publishes the following sonnet by V.E. Borg of Birkirkara to mark the first anniversary of the sinking of the mooring lighter Moor:

They are no more! Those gallant, sturdy men
Who form'd the crew of the ill-fated Moor.
The sea hath swallow'd them into his den,
And there they lie hard by their native shore.
Their lot was such, that all but one, had died
For that same cause, which, others bravely fought.
The hideous monsters all of them defied,
Until with deadly grip their ship was caught.
There's nothing left – no sign – nor sculptured urns,
Their watery graves, in silence to locate.
Their hearts are chill'd, and Love no longer burns
Within those frames now bleak and desolate.

A greater sacrifice no man can make
Than that to give his life for Duty's sake.

Bombing continues.

Casualties: *Gudja*: Fred Scicluna (45); *Marsa*: Salvu Grima (57); *Qormi*: Francis Barbara (56); *Tarxien*: Joseph Bartolo (52); *Valletta*: Joseph Cachia (49).

Thu 9 Apr

The village of Luqa is made the target by enemy aircraft. A bomb hits a shelter killing 25 people who had taken refuge there. Governor Dobbie rushes to the site. Another bomb hits Mosta Dome, piercing through the cupola without exploding. Of the 300 persons then inside the church none is killed.

Casualties: *Cospicua*: Charles Byers (–); *Għaxaq*: Josephine Bugeja (68), David Busuttil (7), Francesco Enriquez (60), Carmela Fenech (6), Esther Fenech (10 months), Mary Fenech (31), Żarenu Fenech (8), Joseph Schembri (13), Pawlu Zammit (7); *Gudja*: Carmela Calleja (33), Carmelo Calleja (54), Grezzju Calleja (51), Joseph Calleja (51), Peter Calleja (30), Teresa Calleja (65), Peter Zammit (62); Remains of an unidentified child; *Luqa*: Giuseppa Abdilla (9), Gnr Giuseppe Attard, RMA (21), Indrì Attard (13), Kola Attard (6), Lucrezja Attard (40), Mikiel Attard (11), Paskalina Attard (3), Salvina Attard (19), Toninu Attard (8), Carmela Azzopardi (62), Francesca Barbara (31), Ġanni Barbara (10), Indrì Barbara (5), Karmena Barbara (10 months), Ġanmarì Ellul (51), Felicissima Farrugia (38), Giuseppe Farrugia (5), Indrì Farrugia (11), Indrì Farrugia (16 months), Karmnu Farrugia (4 months), Rożarju Farrugia (6), Salvu Farrugia (8), Francesco Schembri (11), Grezzju Schembri (53), Ċensa Vella (70); *Mosta*: Gio. Maria Cauchi (56); Unidentified male; *Mqabba*: Gaona Busuttil (39), Mary Busuttil (15), Salvina Busuttil (15); *Qormi*: Emmanuel Agius (16); *Qrendi*: Rose Ellul (65), Gaona Mifsud (60), Joseph Psaila (70), Caterina Sciberras (86); *Valletta*: Anthony Farrugia (43); *Żabbar*: Martha Cordina (45), Toni Portelli (14); *Żejtun*: Emmanuel Rizzo (4); *Żurrieq*: Joseph Barbara (16).

Fri 10 Apr

Enemy action hits the baking and distribution of bread. Many bakeries have been put out of action or destroyed, and others have

The Mosta Dome bomb.

had their power cut off; roads have been blocked and the central area from which flour is distributed has been heavily damaged. Some bread distributors have lost their horses through enemy action.

Following yesterday's heavy air-raid, Archbishop Dom Maurus Caruana visits the village of Luqa.

Casualties: *Ħamrun*: Anthony Bellizzi (65); *Mqabba*: Pawlina Borg (31), Lawrence Mangion (61); *Żabbar*: Żarena Defelice (44), Salvu Grech (35).

Sat 11 Apr

From today's editorial comment in the *Times of Malta* – 'Everything which the German Air Force can spare in aircraft and men is concentrated in the Mediterranean for the attacks upon Malta.'

More air-raids.

Casualties: *Mġarr*: Mary Vella (36).

Sun 12 Apr

About 80 bombers take part in the first raid of today. One of our fighters chased and shot down an Italian BR 20 bomber. It fell in flames at Nadur (Gozo). Four members of the crew: Ettore Pizzi, Capt. Alberto Zampini, WIT De Santis, and L.A.C. De Vito are found dead. A fifth member, Sgt Pilot Gianfranco Viola, is rescued alive in the vicinity of Cominotto.

Casualties: *Msida*: Emmanuel Agius (7); *Qormi*: Joseph Scicluna (52); *Żejtun*: Vincent Ellul (67); *Gozo* (*Xagħra*): Carmelo Azzopardi (17).

Mon 13 Apr

Heavy blitz over Malta continues.

Casualties: *Birkirkara*: Marion Borg (14), Mary Borg (46), Helen Debono (70), Paolina Magro (18), Irene Perini (8 months), Marianna Perini (26), Joseph Sacco (23), Mary Sapiano (17), Paolo Schembri (15), Emilia Tonna Barthet (73), Valentin Tonna Barthet (75); Three unidentified females; Remains of an unidentified corpse; *Msida*: Emmanuel Agius (7).

Wed 15 Apr

From the Secretary of State for the Colonies – Message bearing today's date to HE Sir William Dobbie, Governor of Malta: 'I have it

Valletta – queuing for bread.

THE KING HONOURS MALTA

GEORGE CROSS AWARDED TO FORTRESS OF MALTA

DAILY TELEGRAPH REPORTER 17/4/42

The King, it was announced early to-day, has awarded the George Cross, the civilian V.C., to the scarred but defiant island fortress of Malta, most bombed part of the whole British Empire.

I learn that the King himself suggested making the award, which is the first time a decoration has been conferred by a sovereign on a part of the British Commonwealth.

The award was announced in the following cable sent by the King to the Governor of Malta, Lt.-Gen. Sir William Dobbie:

"To honour her brave people I award the George Cross to the island fortress of Malta to bear witness to a heroism and devotion that will long be famous in history."

Sir William sent the following reply to the King:

"The peoples and garrison of Malta are deeply touched by your Majesty's kind thought for them in conferring on the fortress this signal honour. It has greatly encouraged everyone, and all are determined that, by God's help, Malta will not weaken but will

SECOND FRONT IN EUROPE

"VERY IMPORTANT" ANGLO-U.S. TALKS

By Our Diplomatic Correspondent

Reports from the United States show that the American staffs are convinced that Germany should be forced to fight on two fronts.

George Cross Award. *(Daily Telegraph)*

in command from the King to convey to you the following message: 'To honour her brave people I award the George Cross to the Island Fortress of Malta to bear witness to a heroism and devotion that will long be famous in history'.'

Casualty: *Qormi*: Giuseppa Felice (2).

Thu 16 Apr

Bad weather gives Malta a quiet day.

Casualty: *Żejtun*: Joseph Caruana (12).

Fri 17 Apr

The *Times of Malta* editorial comment is entitled 'Malta GC' – 'His Majesty the King has conferred on the island of Malta the George Cross, the highest award for gallantry which can be won by sailors, soldiers, airmen or civilian alike. The award was founded and established by His Majesty in the early days of the present war, during the heavy air attacks on Britain ... The island has been an inspiration to many ... His Majesty's act brings immense consolation to all in Malta and floods the humblest amongst us with joyous pride in having lived and strived through Malta's greatest hour.'

Broadcast by HE the Governor on the occasion of HM the King having conferred the George Cross upon the Fortress of Malta: 'This kindly gesture of the King in conferring this signal honour to Malta is both heartening and encouraging and very welcome as we face the days which still lie ahead of us.'

Sat 18 Apr

For the first time the heading of the *Times of Malta* carried the emblem of the George Cross.

Casualties: *Birżebbuġa*: Carmelo Cutajar (31); *Cospicua*: (PC 49) Carmel Borg (–), (PS 850) V. Walton (40); *Marsa*: Joseph Formosa (78); *Żejtun*: Joseph Bonavia (9).

Sun 19 Apr

More German air-raids. Soon after midday JU 87 dive bombers, escorted by ME 109s, raid the Grand Harbour and gun positions. A ship is set on fire.

Casualties: *Gżira*: Joseph Borg (15), Giuseppa Gingell (40); *Gudja*: Toni Borg (46); *Ħamrun*: Marianna Attard (70), Filomena Azzopardi

Reading the King's message announcing the award of the George Cross to the Maltese Nation. (*Daily Sketch*)

(70), Rosaria Azzopardi (70), Francesca Bonello (75), Silvia Bono (71), Carmela Borg (91), Giovanna Borg (72), Lucrezja Borg (55), Mary Calascione (40), Rosa Calascione (70), Maria Camilleri (70), Mary Camilleri (70), Joseph Caruana (77), Teresa Casabene (58), Marianna Cassar (65), Joseph Cuschieri (75), Caterina Cauchi (66), Concetta Darmanin (70), Carmela Debono (80), Pawlina Ferro (80), Giuseppa Galea (70), Sister Teresa Garabaldi (53), Antonia Hyzler (75), Mary Kelly (90), Emanuela Laferla (70), Teresa Meilak (90), Teresa Micallef (60), Virginia Micallef (60), Clara Pace (70), Grace Pace (80), Giovanna Potenza (70), Sister Therese Sciberras (85), Mary Vella (69), Rosa Zahra (70); *Msida*: Francesca Bianco (70), Vincenza Caruana Mamo (74), Joseph Grech (76), John Zammit (78); *Sliema*: Emanuel Borg (16); *Valletta*: Violet Bone (16), Joseph Borg (14), Herman Scerri (14); *Żabbar*: Anġla Degabriele (75), Giuseppa Gatt (34), Mary Lia (38), Joseph Mallia (30), Salvu Mallia (33), Grezzja Tedesco (23); *Żejtun*: Paul Despott (16); *Żurrieq*: Carmela Callus (43), Anthony Inguanez (13).

Fierce air-raids over Malta. Mon 20 Apr

Casualties: *Floriana*: Henry Moakes (42); *Ħamrun*: Dr A. Montanaro, LL.D. (79); Mosta: Concetta Mifsud (80); Revd Giuseppe Mifsud (50); *Rabat*: Louis Agius (20), Gio. Maria Bezzina (20); *Sliema*: Carmela Rogers (71).

Raids from dawn till dusk. Tue 21 Apr

Casualty: *Mosta*: Vincent Zammit (39).

Casualties: *Birkirkara*: Emmanuela Gatt (60); *Valletta*: Vincent Schembri (60); *Żejtun*: Joseph Scicluna (18); *Żurrieq*: Emanuel Mangion (18). Wed 22 Apr

At a huge 'Battle of Freedom' pageant staged at the Albert Hall in London, where representatives of the British Commonwealth and Allied Nations took part in a march past, the call 'Malta!' brought forth terrific cheering and handclapping. Thu 23 Apr

Casualties: *Paola*: Vincent Scerri (64), Joseph Vella (43); *Gozo* (*Xagħra*): Francesco Azzopardi (58).

Fri 24 Apr

6 p.m. The heaviest raid of the day! A large force of bombers with fighter escort attacks the Grand Harbour area. Bombs fell in Valletta. Three farmers are machine-gunned by two MEs while crossing over to Ħondoq irRummien, Gozo, from Comino.

Up to Wednesday last, Malta has had 2148 alerts.

Casualties: *Birkirkara*: Joseph Delia (20); *Floriana*: Dolores Abela (60); *Għaxaq*: Gio. Maria Camilleri (67), Anthony Galea (51); *Gżira*: Joseph Borg (15); *Ħamrun*: Charles Demajo (13), Aida Kelly (26), Michael Pace (15), Joseph Spiteri (12); *Marsa*: Michele Cilia (18); *Mosta*: Luigi Calleja (75); Paola: Leone Bartolo (20); Giuseppa Bondin (6 months), Teresa Bondin (2), Gaetano Pisani (31); *Pietà*: Salvu Caruana (21), Petra Christine Dungstaad (30); *Siġġiewi*: Carmel Cachia (53); *Sliema*: James Naudi (45); *Tarxien*: Michele D'Alfonso (18); *Valletta*: Giovanna Muliett (3), Carolina Salnitro (14); Two unidentified corpses; *Gozo* (*Comino*): Rose Zammit (15).

Sat 25 Apr

Daylight heavy bombing attacks by enemy aircraft on hospitals. Telegram from the well-known Dominican writer and preacher, Fr Vincent MacNabb, OP, to the Prior of the Dominicans of Valletta: '*Prior Dominicans Valletta – Ave Melita Intrepida non Mole sed Fortitudine Magna – MacNabb*' (Hail, O fearless Malta, thou art great not because of Thy size, but because of Thy strength).

Casualties: *Floriana*: Onorato Amaira(45); *Għargħur*: Ġanna Camilleri (65); Mary Camilleri (60); *Marsa*: Unidentified male; *Sliema*: Alfred Montefort (75), Perina Montefort (88); *StJulian's*: Albert John Montgomery (41); *St Paul's Bay*: Joseph Grech (52).

Sun 26 Apr

Casualties: *Ħamrun*: Anthony Coleiro (22); *Sliema*: Salvatore Gauci (a–).

Mon 27 Apr

Aircraft of the Fleet Air Arm last night attacked an enemy merchant vessel escorted by two/three destroyers, following bombing and torpedo attacks on convoys the previous night.

The Admiralty has announced that Malta submarines have recently been successful against convoys carrying supplies to North Africa.

Casualties: *Paola*: Concetta Campbell (59); *Rabat*: Andrew Scicluna (40).

Tue 28 Apr

8 a.m. The drone of approaching planes. Soon three enemy bombers detach themselves from the last of four separate formations and diving low over the Church of St Publius in Floriana, they drop their loads which directly hit the church and seriously damage it.

The *New York Herald Tribune* in today's leader says that Malta has shown the astounding durability of a properly prepared and defended fortress position. 'Malta has made an immense contribution to the cause of freedom.'

Casualties: *Balzan*: Annunziato Callus (65); *Floriana*: Annetta Barbara (41), Calcedonio Cardona (79), Joseph Enriquez (65), Joseph Grima (64), Mary Mangion (74), Salvatore Morana (68), Revd Paul Portelli (52), Calcedonio Scerri (63), Assunta Tabone (48); *Ħamrun*: Vincent Vella (50); *Paola*: Saviour Salsero (66); *Qormi*: Carmelo Calleja (58); *Senglea*: Carmel Borg (3), Carmela Borg (27), Adelaide Gau (60), Lawrence Gatt (62), Carrie Gellel (20), Carrie Green (20), William Iles (24), Mary Micallef (39), Josephine Saguna (50), Antonia Sizeland (46), Charles Sizeland (8); *Valletta*: Joseph Dalli (62), Joseph Grech (62), Carlo Rapinett (60); *Żabbar*: Vincent Pulis (37).

Wed 29 Apr

Casualties: *Floriana*: Joseph Buttigieg (64); *Rabat*: Michael Bonello (21); *Żebbuġ*: Philip Grech (24).

Thu 30 Apr

Two Axis aircraft are shot down by the island's AA artillery. The last day of the month brings the AA gunners' score for April to 102 aircraft definitely destroyed.

Casualties: *Mellieħa*: Joseph Debono (40); *Mosta*: Concetta Mifsud (80); *Senglea*: Mary Zarb (10).

Poem by R.A. Willis dedicated to Spitfire Pilots:
Malta, Mediterranean gem

Set in an azure sea;
Guarded by an Empire's sons
Who fight to keep you free.
By day, by night, when you're beset
These sons obey your call,
They gladly give their life for you,
They sacrifice their all.
High in the firmament above
On speedy wings they soar;
Seeking to protect the Island,
Keep it safe for evermore.

AD 1942

May – August

Salvaging household effects from bombed houses in Valletta. *(Bristol Post)*

This morning a fishing boat with four occupants was machine-gunned off the south east coast of the island. Fri 1 May

Casualties: *Ħamrun*: Giovanna Borg (76); *Kirkop*: Leonardo Cassar (76); *Mdina*: Sister Rosaria Abela (Sister of the Order of St Scolastica) (82); *Żejtun*: Carmela Abela (14), Salvu Baldacchino (55), Salvu Bellotti (52), Tarcisio Bonnici (12), Rosario Bugeja (65) Mary Camilleri (68), Gracie Felice (14), Mary Rose Felice (5), Giuseppa Fenech (11), Spira Fenech (46), Victoria Fenech (10), Cikku Frendo (30), Salvu Galea (17), Joe Harris (11), Emanuel Hyzler, MD (56), Giuseppe Mamo (68), Calcedonio Palmier (40), Giuseppe Piscopo (75), Gaetana Portelli (60), Francesca Schembri (30), Emanuel Zammit (24). Sat 2 May

RAF and FAA aircraft strike off Malta at Axis convoy consisting of a merchant vessel and escort of two destroyers. The merchant vessel received a direct hit.

Sun 3 May

Casualties: *Naxxar*. Alfred Azzopardi (56), John Mallia (72); *Żejtun*: Tonina Camilleri (32), Bonvincino Dalli (14), Joseph Grech (64).

Mon 4 May

This evening a small number of Italian bombers, with German and Italian fighter escort, bomb the Harbour area. The MV *Royal Lady* is machinegunned while in harbour at Gozo.

Casualty: *Naxxar*. Carmelo Schembri (14).

Tue 5 May

It is stated in London that during April the RAF based on Malta destroyed 53 Axis aircraft for certain, while 31 were probably destroyed and 118 damaged. With the known total of 102 Axis aircraft destroyed by AA fire during the same period this means that the Axis lost more than 150 aircraft in their attacks on Malta last month – an average of more than five a day. Over the same period we suffered the following civilian casualties – Killed 247; Died of wounds 50; Seriously injured 320; Minor injuries 305.

Life in blitzed Malta. *(Nottingham Guardian)*

This evening, an air-raid took place by a formation of bombers with a large fighter escort and a few fighter bombers. An airfield and the Dockyard area were attacked and some bombs fell on land. AA artillery was in action and badly damaged one bomber. Later a single bomber with fighter escort made a tip and run raid on Valletta.

Casualties: *Sliema*: Louis Sammut Bardon (45); *Valletta*: Giuseppe Portelli (44).

Wed 6 May

This evening, MV *Royal Lady* was sunk and SS *Franco* sustained damage during a raid on Gozo.

Casualties: *Qormi*: Salvu Cutajar (50); *Sliema*: Edwin Azzopardi (21); *Żejtun*: Toni Gatt (71); *Gozo* (*Victoria*): Toni Saliba.

Thu 7 May

It is officially announced that Major-Gen. (temporary Lieut.-Gen.) Sir William Sheddon Dobbie has tendered his resignation of his appointment as Governor of Malta and C-in-C of the Island of Malta to HM the King. General the Rt. Hon. Viscount Gort is to succeed him. Lord Gort arrived in Malta tonight and assumed office.

Casualties: *Mdina*: Anthony Sapiano (53), Giovanna Sapiano (58).

Fri 8 May

Broadcast message from ex-Governor Dobbie to the people of Malta: 'I had very naturally desired to speak to you myself before leaving Malta, but for reasons of high security this was not possible – it was essential that the change of Governor should be known to as few as possible until it was an accomplished fact. So I very reluctantly had to forego my desire and I am now speaking to you by proxy, who is reading to you what I wrote before my departure. I leave Malta with the greatest regret. I have been here for two eventful years, and I had hoped I would be able to see Malta through her present difficulties at any rate. But that was not to be. During my two years we have been through stirring times together, times which I will never forget. I am glad I have had this experience because it has enabled me to get to know and appreciate the people of Malta. I have seen them facing experiences which were unfamiliar to them, and facing them with the determination and courage of veteran soldiers. I have seen them facing experiences which had become painfully familiar by the same courage and determination. I have marvelled at the way they have accepted hardships and disasters with cheerfulness, and I consider that the people of Malta have rightly earned the admiration of the whole world, an admiration crystallized by the award of the George Cross to the island. And now Malta is still facing unprecedented difficulties with the same cheerful courage. I am sure that in God's good providence she will in due course emerge out of her difficulties into smoother water. Until then she will endure, and so ensure the final victory.'

The new Governor, Viscount Gort, today takes the oath of office.

Casualties: *Birżebbuġa*: Randa Zammit (30); *Floriana*: Ċikku Agius (30), Teresa Carbone (36), George Farrugia (51), Francis Sammut (70); *Gżira*: Anthony Pike (4); *Msida*: Manoel Goura (49); Sliema: Alfred Bonello (45); *Żabbar*: John Vella (41); *Żebbuġ*: Fredu Zammit (24); *Żejtun*: Rosaria Azzopardi (25), Wenzu Azzopardi (1), Grazia Ciantar (40), Żarenu Ciantar (40), Antonia Dimech (–).

Sat 9 May

Raids continue. Italian aircraft drop bombs in Grand Harbour area. Farmers are advised that as soon as crops are ripe for collection, they should gather them at once and not leave them uncovered or in the middle of fields, not even for a short time. Incendiary bombs can cause much damage in fields during the hot season.

Warning: The public has been reminded that it constitutes an offence to be found loitering in the confines or the immediate vicinity of airfields. Thefts of RAF property have been increasing for some time. In future, therefore, all RAF Police on duty at or in the vicinity of airfields will be armed and anyone who trespasses or is found loitering in such localities will do so at his own risk.

Casualties: *Attard*: Carmela Muscat (23); *Balzan*: Sister Alexandra Borda (Sister of the Convent of the Good Shepherd) (31); *Floriana*: Mary Polidano (17); *Gżira*: Joseph Mifsud (36); *Qormi*: Teresa Sammut (20); *Żejtun*: Gejtu Mifsud (54).

Sun 10 May

The Spitfires, newly arrived two days previously, went into action with devastating results to the enemy who, on this day alone, lost no less than 63 aircraft.

A typical war scene in Malta: a Maltese trader with Spitfire in the background.

Since much storage space has been destroyed by the enemy and it is imperative to store perishable foodstuffs which cannot be left in the open, Government has decided to requisition at once all available garages.

Casualty: *Mosta*: Joseph Schembri (1 l). Tue 12 May

So far this month 54 enemy aircraft have been destroyed over Malta. Since the beginning of the war the island's defences have accounted for 507 enemy aircraft definitely destroyed. Wed 13 May

In a broadcast to the people, Andrew Cohen, Assistant to the Lieutenant Governor, gives a survey of the siege – Malta's watchwords: endurance and fortitude: 'Therefore steel yourselves to endure until better times come. Remember that here in Malta we are not carrying on the struggle unnoticed by the world. The eyes of the world are constantly on these islands. Here in the centre of the Mediterranean we are in the heart of the struggle and the newspapers of Great Britain, the United States, and Russia are filled with the name of Malta. The people of these countries have learnt to expect much of Malta; they have grieved with us in our sufferings and exulted in our successes. It is a great responsibility which we have to bear, the admiration of the whole civilized world. The world knows what we have suffered in bombing and what our gunners and our pilots have achieved against the enemy. The hardships and restrictions imposed on the public are less well-known. We cannot talk of these outside Malta without telling the enemy of things he should not know. But when the history of the defence of Malta comes to be written the endurance of the public in putting up with all the inconveniences of food shortages will not be forgotten. Let us make sure that we earn the praise which will be showered upon us after victory has been won, as assuredly it will be.'

Gozo, an eyewitness account: Four Messerschmitts flew very low over the Citadel, so low that I could quite clearly see the pilots. The leading pilot, after circling three or four times, pushed back the cover of his cockpit and waves his hand, as if giving signal to the others; the pilot of the second machine did likewise. Then each plane came down in twin and machinegunned the town, at the same time throwing out hand-grenades and dropping anti-personnel bombs.

Thu 14 May **Broadcast by Viscount** Gort to the people of Malta: 'People of Malta, I salute you – I admire you for your courage and endurance

Indelible. *(A Strube cartoon published in the* Daily Express*: 14/5/1942)*

– I admire you for your cheerfulness – I admire you for your trust in Almighty God and I admire the greatness of your Faith. I am proud to come to live amongst you, to share your trials, to share your dangers, to share your privations, and I am proud to have the great honour of being sent here by His Majesty the King to do what I can to assist Malta forward to that great and glorious day when each and everyone of us had fulfilled his or her duty and peace comes once more to this sorely tried but beautiful Island.'

More raids. Residential areas bombed.

Casualties: *Naxxar*: Joseph Deguara (20); *Sliema*: Rosina Busuttil (32), Angelo Falzon (73), Sarah Falzon (67), Alfred Micallef (l 6), Beatrix Scicluna (14), Winnie Smith (56), Dr Hector Vassallo, LL.D. (41).

Nine Axis raiders destroyed. Italian E-boats off Malta are similarly dealt with. Coastal artillery defences engaged. Sun 17 May

Casualties: *Floriana*: Joseph Camilleri (16); *Għaxaq*: Michael Abela (26); *Mdina*: Stella Sant Manduca (76); *Żabbar*: Mary Fava (8); *Gozo* (*Sannat*): Anton Hili (16).

London. High Mass *coram cardinale* for Malta at Westminster Cathedral. The congregation consisting of over 3,000 people included Viscount Cranborne, the Secretary of State for the Colonies, representing His Majesty, Vice-Admiral Sir John Cunningham representing the Admiralty, Lieut. Gen. Floyer-Ackland representing the Secretary of State for War and the Army Council, Air Marshal F.S. Lionel representing the Air Ministry, Viscount Fitzalan and Earl Iddlesliegh, both Knights of Malta, Lord Clarendon, Sir Joseph Lyme and Col. Sleeman representing the Order of St John of Jerusalem. Many members of the Allied forces, French, Belgian, Polish, Norwegian, and others were present. Cardinal Hinsley, the head of the Catholic Church in the land known in history as the 'Dowry of Mary', delivered a stirring address: 'On Malta the gaze of the whole world is riveted in wonder.'

Lieut. Gen. Sir William Dobbie was unable to attend the High Mass as he was operated upon for appendicitis on Friday last.

Moth and the Flame. *(Evening Standard)*

Tue 19 May **Today's score: 1** Italian bomber, 3 Italian fighters, and 6 German fighters, all destroyed.

Casualties: *Birżebbuġa*: Carmel Pace (30); *Paola*: Consolat Bondin (6).

Wed 20 May **London. Harold Macmillan,** Parliamentary Under-Secretary for the Colonies, in the House of Commons: 'All possible measures, which ingenuity can devise and valour execute, have been taken to assist the garrison and the people of Malta in their splendid heroic resistance.'

Sat 23 May **Casualties:** *Kirkop*: Spiro Bartolo (73); *Luqa*: Andrew Farrugia (8); *Sliema*: Antonia Pace (77); *Żejtun*: Vincent Axisa (68); *Żurrieq*: Carmel Axiaq (40).

Rome. Radio Roma comments: 'Theirs [the Italian bomber pilots sent to raid Malta by night] is indeed a hard lot. We are blinded by searchlights, hammered by the AA guns, pursued and ambushed by night fighters. There is no seeing the enemy till the British guns start spitting death at your bomber.' Sun 24 May

Raids over Malta continue incessantly. The people of Valletta are again showing that resident spirit which they have time and again displayed during this war. The streets of the city have now nearly all been opened for traffic, and where this has not as yet been possible, a footpath has been cleared, sometimes rising in steps to the top of a mound of debris. The people of Valletta have settled down to their new way of living – getting water from taps in the streets, getting their meals from the Victory Kitchens, and queuing up for their other necessities. Mon 25 May

Last night RAF aircraft attacked an Axis convoy which included destroyer escort. Bombs were dropped from a low level. Tue 26 May

Casualties: *Ħamrun*: Carmel Borg (3), Carmel Borg (35), Stella Borg (34), Carmela Brimmer (62), William Brimmer (38), Joseph Darmanin (68), Concetta Decelis (64), Adelaide Fabri (32), Antonia Falzon (60), Carmela Felice (66), Carmela Pace (5), Doris Rizzo (18), Paul Rizzo (70).

Last night RAF aircraft stationed in Malta attacked targets at Messina, Sicily. High explosive and incendiary bombs were dropped. Wed 27 May

Casualties: *Luqa*: Rosa Bonnici (60), *St Julian's*: Saviour Magri (58).

It is reported that the Germans are using a new tank fitted with a refrigerating system in the Libyan battle. Thu 28 May

RAF aircraft based in Malta continue for the fourth successive night to bomb Sicily. Sat 30 May

An Information Office Notice hits at the Black Market and advises the general public to boycott known profiteers and to report to the

Police anyone who tries to charge more than the lawful price for a controlled article.

Casualties: *Mosta*: Albino Bezzina (11), Francis Bezzina (12), Edwin Gatt (11).

Tue 2 Jun

Last night RAF aircraft based in Malta were again over Sicily. An Axis convoy was also bombed from a low level by aircraft f the Fleet Air Arm.

Casualties: Ħamrun: Charles Muscat (–), Louis Farrugia (41), Alfred Scicluna (33), Joseph Ward (19); *Żebbuġ*: Nicholas Cutajar (75).

Review of the blitz in Malta: Up to the first week of April this year, 15,500 houses including blocks of flats and *kerrejjiet* have been destroyed or damaged. These figures include: 70 churches, 18 convents and nunneries, 22 schools, 8 hospitals, 10 theatres, 8 hotels, 8 clubs, 5 banks, and 48 other public buildings.

In Valletta itself, amongst the churches destroyed or damaged, there are St John's Co-Cathedral, St Francis Church and the adjacent convent, the Carmelite Church and convent, St Ursola Monastery, St Paul's Anglican Cathedral, All Souls' Church, the Catholic Greek Church, the church and convent of Perpetual Adoration, the church and convent of Mary of Jesus, the Notre Dame de Liesse Church, the Magdalene Garrison Church, St Dominic's Church, St Augustine Church and convent, and the smaller church of Our Lady of Pilar.

At Cospicua and Senglea – the parish church of the Immaculate Conception, St Theresa's, St Paul's, St Margherita's, and the Anglican Church, the parish church of Our Lady of Victory, St Philip Church and convent, St Julian Church, and the Franciscan Nunnery and Crucifix Oratory.

In the villages – the churches of Our Saviour and the Annunciation (Attard); the Good Shepherd Convent (Balzan); Birżebbuġa Parish Church; St Publius Church, St Calcedon Church, the Seminary, the Capuchins' Church and convent, the Chapel of Our Lady of Lourdes (Floriana); Gżira parish church; the convent of the Little Sisters of the Poor (Ħamrun); the parish church, the Capuchins' Church and convent, the chapel of Our Saviour (Kalkara); the Maria Assunta

Rotunda of Mosta; the parish church, the chapels of Taċ-Ċeppuna and Ta' Ċejlu (Marsa); the monastery of St Benedict (Mdina); the parish church and the Carmelite Church (Luqa); the Franciscan Friary, Our Lady of Jesus, and St Agatha churches (Rabat/Malta); the church and convent of the Sisters of Charity (St George's Bay); St Paul's Chapel (St Paul's Bay); the Ursoline Convent (St Julian's); the parish church of Santa Venera; the parish churches of Stella Maris and of the Sacred Heart of Mary, the Nazareth Church, St Mark's Garrison Church, St Elizabeth Church and annexed convent (Sliema); Castelletti Church (Wardija); the Oratory (Siġġiewi); Tad-Dawl Church (Żebbuġ/Malta); the parish church of Żabbar; the Mqabba parish church; and the Immaculate Conception Church of Żurrieq.

Hospital hit include: the Blue Sisters, St Luke's Central Civil Hospital, King George V Hospital, the Hospital for Mental Diseases at Attard, Cini's Hospital, the Poor House, the Connaught Hospital, and St Andrew's Hospital.

Schools destroyed or damaged by enemy action include: St Joseph's Secondary School, the Lyceum, St Elmo Elementary School, the Montessori School, the High School, the Girls' Secondary School, the Orphan Asylum, Flores College, St Edward's College, ten village Elementary Schools, and two boys' Reformatories.

Hotels hit by enemy bombs include: the Savoy, the Royal Hotel, the Great Britain Hotel, the Phoenicia Hotel, the Hotel de France, the St James Hotel, the Melita Hotel, and the Point de Vue Hotel.

Clubs: Sliema Union Club, Casino Maltese, La Valette Band club, King's Own Band Club, and the *Circolo Giovine Malta* (formerly the headquarters of the *Società Dante Alighieri di Malta*).

Theatres include: Gaiety, Royal Opera House, Regent, Plaza, Rialto, Capitol and Trops Hall.

Banks include: Barclays branch, Exchange Buildings, Credit Fonder, Scicluna's Bank.

Auberges: Besides the Magisterial Palace, six of the eight Auberges of the Knights have been destroyed or damaged, namely the Auberges d'ltalie, de Baviere, d'Aragon, de France, de Castille, and d'Auvergne.

Amongst the public buildings destroyed or damaged: the Post Office, the Public Health Office; the University, the Customs House, the Valletta Market Place, the Police Headquarters (formerly the Sacra Jnfermeria).

An unofficial but reliable estimate of the devastated areas in the principal blitzed localities, including buildings which, even if tenable, have to be rebuilt, shows that: 75% of the houses in Valletta have been destroyed or damaged; 65% at Vittoriosa; 70% at Cospicua; 80% at Senglea; 85% in Floriana; 60% at Gżira; 70% at Kalkara; 75% at Kirkop; 70% at Luqa; 30% at Paola. It is estimated that about 55% of the most thickly populated districts have been devastated and require rebuilding.

Up to 8 April of this year, figures relating to civilian casualties are as follows:

Killed	*1,104*
Seriously injured	*1,318*
Slightly injured	*1,299.*

Reckoning the civilian population at 260,000 since the war started, one in every seventy of the population has been a fatal, serious, or slight casualty, and one in every 235 persons a fatal casualty, that is, the highest civilian casualty percentage in the world.

Without the rock shelters, the blitz on Malta would have been a wholesale massacre.

Wed 3 Jun

Our bombers continue their offensive against the enemy when targets in Sardinia and Pantelleria are severely attacked.

Fri 5 Jun

The Blitz: 1,869 tons of bombs dropped on the Grand Harbour between 24 March and 12 April; 162 hours of air alerts; number of bombers engaged amount to 2,159.

All members of the Casino Maltese whose club has been destroyed on February 15 last, are made honorary members of the Union Club, which is housed at the Auberge de Provence.

Valletta – the facade of the Auberge d'Italie partially bombed.

Sat 6 Jun

Civil Defence Awards. His Majesty the King has approved the following awards: British Empire Medal (BEM) to PC 509 Manuel Fenech, Malta Police; Reserve PC 44 Carmel Cassar, Malta Police.

Constables Fenech and Cassar are both members of the Malta Police Fire Brigade. On 26 March 1942 the Brigade was trying to extinguish a fire on a merchant vessel when a heavy air-raid developed on the harbour. Some members of the crew of a Dockyard Fire Float lying alongside the vessel jumped overboard and swam for the shore. As soon as the AA barrage had stopped, the Brigade emerged from cover and these two constables observed a man clinging to a pole in the water. They swam to him and brought him safely to land. At the same time shell splinters from the barrage were still falling in quantity and small arms ammunition which formed part of the cargo of the vessel was exploding continuously. They knew that there was a risk of a large explosion of ammunition and of the petrol catching fire at any moment.

Casualties: *Balzan*: Antoinette Zammit (18); *Żebbuġ*: Anthony Rodo (26).

It is reported that Lord Gort, accompanied by his staff, inspected the whole of the Harbour area a few days ago; he walked from the Customs House to the Cisk Flour Mill and entered the premises to speak to people in the shops and offices.

3.30 p.m. A Grand Charity Boxing tournament was held at the Command Fair, Old Police Depot, Merchants Street, Valletta.

Sun 7 Jun

More enemy activity than of late. Two German bombers, five Italian fighters, and one float-plane destroyed.

RAF bombers continue to raid military targets in Italy.

Tue 9 Jun

RAF Bombers attack military objectives in Sardinia.

Casualties: *Bengħajsa*: Joseph Zammit (72); *Marsa*: Gaetano Attard (28); *Sliema*: John Miceli (21).

Wed 10 Jun

Heavy AA artillery against enemy raiders.

Bombs dropped in scattered localities and more particularly in the north west of the island.

It is now two years since Italy entered the war. During this period Malta has experienced: 2,537 alerts, 492 day bombing raids, and 574 night bombing raids.

During the night lights are placed at intervals along certain roads in connection with a military exercise considered essential to the defence of the island. Sat 13 Jun

Casualties: *Rabat*: Frank Galea (31), Bro. Norbert Vella (20); *Siġġiewi*: Joseph Spiteri (36).

Enemy raiders continue to attack our airfields. Heavy raids take place. Mon 15 Jun

Casualties: *Naxxar*: Paul Vella (11) *Siġġiewi*: Nicholas Farrugia (43); *Tarxien*: Louis Pulis (14).

Meanwhile aircraft of the FAA and the RAF have attacked units of the Italian Navy. Torpedo carrying aircraft score direct hits on three battleships, two cruisers, and two destroyers. One battleship is hit amid ships and flames are seen in its superstructure and hull.

Goods from the convoy now in port are being unloaded and placed in stores and dumps in various parts of the island. The public is forbidden to loiter near or enter any storage dump, except on legitimate business. Armed guards and sentries have been placed at the dumps. During the unloading of the convoy the public is requested not to enter the Grand Harbour area, since every effort is being made to unload the convoy with the greatest possible speed. Roads and quays must be kept clear of all unnecessary persons and traffic. According to a Police Notice, animal-drawn vehicles shall not make use of certain roads in various areas of the island until further notice because of the unloading of the convoy.

It is reported that a powerful squadron of the United States Navy is cooperating with the Mediterranean Fleet. This squadron consists of two battleships, five cruisers, and one aircraft carrier.

Tue 16 Jun

As apprehensions over supplies increase, Governor Gort broadcasts to the people: 'Some days ago, two convoys set out, one from the West and one from the East, to bring us the supplies which we need to restore our situation. The Western convoy had to endure severe and prolonged attacks, and only two merchantships survived the ordeal … The Eastern convoy, after suffering from prolonged and intense attacks by the Luftwaffe was ordered to turn back … I must break to you what the arrival of only two ships means to us. For some time past, we have been short of supplies and further privations lie ahead of us… Every effort will be made to replenish our stocks when a favourable opportunity presents itself. Meanwhile we must stand on our own resources and everyone of us must do everything in his or her power to conserve our stocks and to ensure the best use is made of all the available resources that remain to us … Here on this island there stands on Mount Sceberras the image of Christ the King[1] surrounded on all sides by bomb craters and demolished buildings. It remains, untouched and unscathed after the most intense and prolonged air bombardment in the history of the world. Trusting in Him, guided by Him, we shall surely pass out of the darkness into the light.'

A committee has been set up to make proposals as to the form of the ceremony of the presentation of the George Cross to Malta.

Heavy fighting reported at Kharkov and Sebastopol. Powerful Soviet Black Sea Fleet units and the Red Army are pounding the Germans.

Thu 18 Jun

Yesterday Beaufighters of the RAF met the Malta convoy off Bizerta. Continuous cover provided. During the following 24 hours several hundred fighter sorties were flown from Malta, the majority by Spitfires. Enemy aircraft destroyed: these include 3 Messerschmitt 109s, 5 Junkers 88s, 2 B.R.20s, 2 float planes, 1 Cant 506[2] and 1 R.O. 43. The merchantmen and their escorts had to pass through large

1 This monument of Christ the King was inaugurated in December 1917; it was erected to mark the XXIV International Eucharistic Congress held in Malta in 1913. The bronze monument is the work of the Maltese sculptor Antonio Sciortino.

2 The Cant Z-5068 was one of the most important of the Cant seaplane designs; bomb load: 3,300 lbs; max speed: 217 mph.

areas in the Central Mediterranean which are dominated by enemy shore-based air forces from Sardinia, Sicily, Pantelleria, Crete, and North Africa.

More raids over Malta accompanied by heavy AA barrage.

Lieutenant Governor Sir Edward Jackson broadcasts on the food situation: 'If the enemy failed in his main purpose, he succeeded in part of it. He has delayed part of our much needed supplies. Greater privations than we have known hitherto lie ahead of us here. Fresh supplies will come to us. You need have no fear of that. But we do not know when they will come. We got about 15,000 tons of stores in the two ships that arrived. It is a very small part of what we had hoped for. I have come here this evening to tell you plainly what our arrangements are. And I shall tell you the worst. Small quantities of vitally necessary supplies can reach us from time to time without all the difficulties and dangers that running of a convoy involves. But though small additions to our stocks help us they cannot really change the situation. Our security depends more than on anything else on the time for which our bread will last. In examining our position, we calculated first the time for which our bread could be made to last. That calculation gave us a certain date, I shall call it the Target Date. I cannot tell you what that date is but it is far enough off to give ample opportunity for fresh supplies to reach us before our present stocks run out. England will not forget us and her Navy and Air Forces will see us through. The bread ration will remain as it is. Sugar will remain as it is, except that there can be no issue for the first period in July and the second period in August. Our stocks of edible oil are low. An issue can only be made once in every three periods. Soap and kerosene are two other necessities of which our stocks will not last at their present rate of issue as long as our stock of bread. We can only make one issue of soap in the second period of every month, beginning in July. Kerosene, in our present situation, is the most difficult problem we have to face. We can only issue the present ration once in every two weeks instead of once a week. One issue of rice and coffee will be made in the first period of July. Tea will be issued during the second period of each month. Sat 20 Jun

I come now to the fodder problem. Our stock position is such that no fodder can in future be made available except for horses used for transport and in much smaller quantities for very young pigs and rabbits. It will thus become impossible to maintain a larger part of the population of goats and sheep and cows or grown pigs. The rest will gradually have to be killed off. The very great reduction of the goat population will bring about a great reduction of raw milk. The use of tinned milk is already restricted to young children and to women with child. Our intention is that pasteurized milk shall be limited to hospitals and school children. As raw goat's milk disappears from the market, there will be no milk for the adult population. A drastic reduction of our present consumption of petrol will also be necessary.'

Sun 21 Jun

An attack is made on a convoy by torpedo-carrying aircraft. The convoy consisted of two medium-sized motor vessels with a smaller vessel as escort. Since the outbreak of hostilities to date there have been 2,537 air alerts, 492 of them developed into day-bombing raids, 274 night-bombing raids.

Mon 22 Jun

Night raids continue on larger scale than usual. The main weight of the attack developed when a number of enemy bombers dropped incendiary and high explosive bombs by the light of flares near airfields. The AA defences engage with great intensity. Enemy losses.

During the same night our aircraft attack a convoy, and bombs were dropped on a large merchant vessel. Bursts were seen and a large amount of smoke was also seen issuing from the stern of the ship.

Afternoon. Our torpedo-carrying aircraft made another attack on a convoy consisting of two large merchantmen and four destroyers as escort.

Casualties: *Mosta*: Matthew Bonanno (4), Paul Bonanno (45), James Mangion (67), Catherine Micallef (57); *Mqabba*: Catherine Saliba (72); *Żejtun*: Joseph Spiteri (55), Laurence Spiteri (62).

London. The Deputy Prime Minister, Clement Attlee, speaking in Churchill's absence (who is in Washington, USA for talks with President Roosevelt) in a statement in the House of Commons disclosed that the convoy coming from the West last week, under the command of Vice Admiral Curtiss, got through to Malta, after suffering serious losses, but that from the East, under the command of Rear-Admiral Vian, after passing supply ships into Tobruk, was forced to turn back owing to a fuel shortage caused through delay in dealing with a strong Italian naval force.

Today's *London Gazette* announces that Gen Viscount Gort, Malta's new Governor and Command-in-chief, and Lieutenant General Sir William Dobbie, his predecessor, are among the nine Knights of the Order of St John of Jerusalem – the Order of chivalry for centuries linked with Malta.

Thu 25 Jun

An Information Office Notice invites the public not to touch bombs, shells, mines, bits of aircraft, or any unusual object if they find them but to bring them immediately to the attention of the Police.

Fri 26 Jun

The bus service is being suspended on Saturdays and Sundays and replaced by horse transport.

Casualties: *Gżira*: Anthony Caruana (13), Henry Cassar (2), Concetta Tanti (13), Mary Tanti (17); *Mosta*: Gerald Camilleri (33); *Msida*: Carmelina Dimech (12), Josephine Dimech (7), Lilian Dimech (17), Mary Dimech (6), Rita Dimech (3); *Qormi*: Anthony Borg (59), George Borg (35); *Sliema*: John Attard (25); *Ta' Xbiex*: Agnes Smith (47); *Żurrieq*: Catherine Darmanin (13).

Sat 27 Jun

This morning four Spitfires intercept an enemy patrol.

Casualties: *Sliema*: Ivo Falzon (37); *Żejtun*: Louis Zammit (46).

Sun 28 Jun

This morning a simple but impressive ceremony performed by Archbishop Caruana took place within the historic Fort St Elmo: the consecration of the 1st Coast Regiment, Royal Malta Artillery, to the Sacred Heart of Jesus. On the parade ground an altar, simply decorated with candles and pink gladioli in shining brass vases –

Transport in wartime conditions.

slender shell cases – was erected on a raid dais underneath a canopy of crimson velvet; palms and white flowers in large brass shell cases were placed at the side of the carpeted platform. A painting of the Sacred Heart of Jesus by George Preca surmounted the altar. Mass was celebrated by Mgr Canon L. Catania, Ph.D., B.Litt., B.L., Can D.D. who was assisted by Fr J.W. Orr, C.F., chaplain of the Regiment; hymns were sung and the Royal Artillery (Malta) Band under its conductor Bandmaster Busuttil played appropriate music. Holy pictures commemorating the event were distributed. After Mass, a sermon was delivered in Maltese by Mgr Catania. At the close of the sermon, the Blessed Sacrament was carried to the altar – Lieut. Col. T. Dunkerley, RMA, Officer Commanding 1st Coast Regt holding the *ombrellino* and Capt. Cremona, RMA, Capt. Fiteni, RMA, Lieut. Cuschieri, RMA, and Lieut. Diacono holding four lighted candles; Mgr Catania read in Maltese the Act of Consecration. The *Te Deum Pro Gratiarum Actione* was sung to the accompaniment of the organ played by Sgt Zammit. The men's voices resounded in the large courtyard. The proceedings ended with the playing of the Maltese Hymn followed by the singing of God Save the King. Brigadier C.T. Beckett, MC, Commanding Royal Artillery, who, together with

Fort St Elmo – the solemn Consecration of the 1st Coast Regiment Royal Malta Artillery to the Sacred Heart of Jesus.

Brigadier CJ. White, MC, attended the ceremony, then took the Salute at the March Past of detachments from each company of the regiment, headed by the Royal Artillery (Malta) Band.

Casualties: *Attard*: Veneranda Scicluna (45); *Safi*: Concetta Cachia (34), Carmela Cachia (2), John Farrugia (5).

Wed 1 Jul

Government introduces very severe penalties as part of its campaign against the Black Market; the new measures include imprisonment up to a maximum of five years.

Two formations of enemy bombers over Malta. Heavy AA defences engaged. Our Spitfires were airborne, and air combats ensued.

Casualty: *Qrendi*: Carmela Spiteri (70).

Enemy shipping bombed and torpedoed. A merchant ship received two torpedo hits.

Washington. A Navy communiqué announces that aeroplane reinforcements for Malta were carried out from the United States aircraft carrier *Wasp*; during one of these ferry trips, the enemy were surprised by the increased number of defending fighters and suffered considerable losses. The planes which took off from the *Wasp* engaged the enemy over Malta before landing on the island.

Fri 3 Jul

More heavy raids.

Casualties: *Attard*: Grace Borg (30), Mary Gauci (53); *Floriana*: Laurence Cauchi (26); *Ħamrun*: Eleonora Apap (66); *Rabat*: Consiglio Portelli (53); *Siġġiewi*: Laurence Cutajar (62), Emanuel Muscat (22), Josephine Muscat (51), Mary Concetta Muscat (16), Rosanna Muscat (20), Saviour Muscat (7), Joseph Schembri (50); *Sliema*: Peter Cordina (57).

The public is informed that any person cutting a military telephone or telegraph cable will be treated as a wilful saboteur and will be liable to very severe penalties.

Sat 4 Jul

Casualties: *Luqa*: Andrew Coleiro (53); *Siġġiewi*: Concetta Frendo (16).

The Admiralty announce loss of HM ships in the Mediterranean during recent convoy operations. No details are disclosed.

Sun 5 Jul

Shortly after dawn a steady stream of people made its way on foot, in flat carts or in *karozzini* (cabs) to the Cathedral Church at Mdina in order to be present at the consecration of His Lordship Bishop Emanuel Galea. The ceremony was private and no invitations had been issued on account of the exigencies of war. The consecration took place in a wartime setting with the Cathedral stripped of many of its treasures and with the severe background of bomb-blasted windows, and empty frames on the walls above the altars. Archbishop Dom Maurus Caruana, the consecrator, was assisted by H.L. Mgr Michele Gonzi, Bishop of Gozo, and by Mgr Giuseppe Apap Bologna, Archdeacon of the Cathedral. The Revd Canons of the Cathedral Chapter were present in their stalls. The Archbishop with great fortitude, and clearly suffering from a considerable strain, celebrated Mass, and solemnly performed the impressive consecration ceremony. HG was visibly deeply moved. As the newly consecrated Bishop walked down the aisle and blessed the faithful, his gentle bearing impressed itself upon those present. Bishop Galea then took his place next to the consecrator near the High Altar. The notes of the organ pealed out for the first time and accompanied the singing of the Te Deum. The Cathedral was packed with a representative gathering – side aisles being reserved for the clergy and religious communities, alt of whom were well represented. The Chief Justice, Sir George Borg, Mr Justice Edgar Ganado, and Mr Justice Robert Ganado occupied the seats reserved for His Majesty's Judges, and on the other side of the aisle were members of Bishop Galea's family, including Mgr Canon F. Galea, His Lordship's brother, and his sister. The drone of fighter planes was at times clearly audible overhead, while the loud explosion of a delayed action bomb, dropped in a previous air-raid, shook the church. When the three Bishops had withdrawn, the congregation poured out of the cathedral onto the square, and shortly afterwards Bishop Galea appeared on the balcony of the Archbishop's Palace;[3] he was

3 This magnificent building is annexed to the Cathedral and dates back to 1733. It is the residence of the Archbishop of Malta.

greeted with rousing cheers. The crowd knelt as he raised his hand to give his blessing.

London. The total RAF losses in all operations during the month of June were 422 aircraft against the Axis losses of 318. The RAF lost 271 over Germany and German-occupied territory, and 151 in air combats in the Middle East. The Germans lost 35 over Britain, 65 over Europe, and 218 in the Middle East, including 53 over Malta.

Tue 7 Jul

Heavy raids. Six German bombers, 1 Italian bomber, 4 German fighters, and 1 Italian fighter destroyed.

Four German bombers, 3 Italian bombers, 9 German fighters, and 3 Italian fighters damaged.

Casualties: *Mosta*: Rose Mary Grech (3), Joseph Vella (14); *Siġġiewi*: Nicolina Borg (62); *Valletta*: Francis Ciarlò (14), Anthony Vella (74).

Thu 9 Jul

The Director of Transport issues requisition orders to owners of horsedrawn vehicles, excepting cabs. Heavy raids continue.

London. The Financial Secretary to the War Office, Duncan Sandys, was told in the House of Commons that the power to relieve soldiers stationed in Malta continuously since December 1938 was severely restricted by operational needs and shipping limitations. The problem is particularly difficult with regard to Malta.

Fri 10 Jul

Casualties: *Birkirkara*: Rosario Borg (21), Doris Galea (30), Francis Galea (3 months), Laurence Galea (39), Mary Mamo (4), Stella Mamo (32), Carmel Pisani (10), Mary Pisani (8), Paul Pisani (3), Victoria Pisani (45); *Paola*: Frances Mifsud Speranza (17); *Siġġiewi*: Rita Cachia (13).

Sat 11 Jul

Eighty-two Axis aircraft have been destroyed over the last ten days – an average of over eight a day.

Casualties: *Balzan*: Giorgina Borg (52); *Birkirkara*: John Galea (18); *Rabat*: Carmel Bugeja (47), Pauline Deguara (9), Rita Sammut (18), Joseph Scerri (70); *Żebbuġ*: Carmel Bonnici (12).

Mon 13 Jul

As from today, any person registering with the Communal Feeding Department will be provided once a day with one hot dish consisting of meat or vegetable stew, and no reductions in ration will be made.

Casualties: *Imtarfa*: Florence Mary Hamilton (–); Qormi: Saviour Mifsud (34); *Rabat*: Emanuel Darmanin (11), Joseph Gauci (60), George Zammit (65); *Żejtun*: Saviour Desira (50).

Wed 15 Jul

Heavy raids. Enemy losses.

Casualties: *Ħamrun*: Joseph Grech (8); *Naxxar*. Carmel Grech (15); *Rabat*: Felice Gauci (30).

Il Popolo di Roma says that the destruction of Malta is essential in order to render impossible the intermediate landing of British planes coming to Egypt.

Wed 22 Jul

Casualties: *Attard*: Edward Mifsud (12), Walter Mifsud (14); *Ħamrun*: Concetta Borg (66), Alfred Sacco (3); *Rabat*: Paul Zammit (13).

Figures for June: Killed or died of wounds – 54; Seriously wounded – 97; Slightly injured – 50.

Fri 24 Jul

Casualties: *Luqa*: Carmel Mallia (75); *Rabat*: Carmela Borg (10); *Żurrieq*: Josephine Bondin (10 months), Catherine Bugeja (13), Jane Bugeja (11), Revd Joseph Cuschieri (63), Carmel Ellul (70), Anthony Gauci (60), Joseph Saydon (48), Carmel Schembri (16), Joseph Spiteri (3 months), Saviour Zammit (54), Revd Joseph Zammit Psaila (68).

An Axis convoy proceeding southwards is attacked by torpedo-carrying aircraft. The convoy consisted of a medium-sized merchantman, escorted by two destroyers and E-boats. The merchant ship is torpedoed and hit forward.

Sat 25 Jul

IMPORTANT NOTICE: If there is no air-raid in progress at 12 o'clock noon today, there will be a test of the new signal for the 'General Alarm'. The sirens will be sounded as though for an air-raid five times with intervals of half-a-minute between each sounding. Half-a-minute after the last time the 'All Clear' will be

The statue of Our Lady of Mount Carmel carried in procession through blitzed streets in Valletta.

sounded. At the same time the church bells will be rung. The public should not be alarmed; it will be nothing but a TEST. If there is an air-raid in progress at noon, the test will be held immediately the raid is over.

Today marked the 2,800th alert with heavy barrage engagements. Sun 26 Jul

Today's edition of the *Sunday Times of Malta* reproduces a poem entitled 'Isle of the Triple Cross' by Dom Ambrose Agius, OSB; the poem was first published in the *Daily Telegraph* of 2 July 1942:

Malta! Resolute thrice-crowned citadel: fortress wreathed in undying glory:
Still thy flag of unbought allegiance, Freedom's symbol, on high unfurled
Greets dawn: is caressed by moonlight, Splendid as thy immortal story.
Stirs hearts to a faster rhythm, million-folded across the world.
La Valette of the stainless scutcheon, Lady St Mary's knight unyielding,
Kept intact the Shield of Christendom, Turk-infested by land and sea:
Stood intrepid on crumbling bastion, still his tireless weapon wielding.
Till the eve of Our Lady's birthday saw the baffled armada flee.
Now the ruins of church, and palace cumber, shapeless, the lovely city:
All her skies are ablaze with lighting, death thunders by night, by day:
Limbs are sundered and hearts broken by winged furies estranged to pity:
Yet Malta, still Help of Christians, sees her knights unafraid at bay!
Knights surely: for toil, vigil and courage never surpassed in splendour
Prove thy men to be Knights of Malta, noblest Order of ancient days.
What should a grateful Sov'reign give thee?
What return for they merit render?
Lo! the Cross of King George acclaims thee, blazoned over thy strucken ways!
Yet Malta, thy King is older: Who first came with apostle's preaching:
Christ crowned with the thorns of sorrow: Christ gave thee His Cross to bear.
Loyal Island, for twenty centuries steeled to patience by Christian teaching,
Ah, 'Sliema!' Hail Malta! Thrice chosen a Cross to wear!

Parachutes dropped into the sea as enemy pilots baled out of planes shot down by local defences in air action. Total losses inflicted on the enemy: 13 aircraft destroyed; 8 damaged. Mon 27 Jul

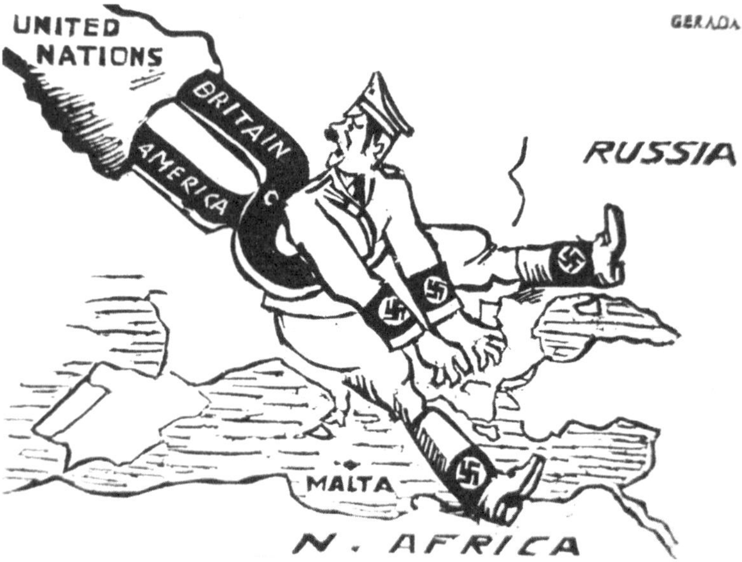

The 'Pincers' Pincered. *(Sunday Times of Malta)*

Tue 28 Jul

An enemy float-plane landed in the sea not far from the coast and the crew were rescued.

Casualties: *Għaxaq*: Joseph Abela (13); Mosta: John Fenech (11); *Żurrieq*: Carmel Buhagiar (10), Joseph Buhagiar (–), Salvina D'Amato (18).

Fri 31 Jul

Casualties: *Birkirkara*: Anthony Agius (29), Carmel Borg (27), John Busuttil (16), Pauline Busuttil (5), Joseph Calleja (75), Giorgina Dimech (28), Michael Fenech (47), Orazia Grech (4), Mary Melita Medati (50), Mary Scerri (9), Amabile Sammut (21), Carmela Sammut (23); *Mġarr*: Joseph Deguara (45).

Sat 1 Aug

Casualty: *Birkirkara*: Joseph Galea (13).

HM the King approves the award of the British Empire Medal (Civil Division) to Joseph Panzavecchia, Boy Scout Special Coast Watcher. 'This Boy Scout has displayed unusual courage and devotion to duty in the face of many air-raids, during which he has with coolness and accuracy passed reports and information of the greatest importance to the defence.'

During July 153 Axis planes were definitely destroyed by the Malta defence.

Casualties: *Birkirkara*: Gaetana Abela (20), Samuel Zammit (63); *Gozo* (*Għarb*): Kalanġ Mizzi (60); *Gozo* (*San Lawrenz*): Carmela Farrugia (35), Josephine Farrugia (66), Mary Farrugia (35), Nazzarena Attard (28). Wed 5 Aug

Air combats in Maltese skies continue. Thu 6 Aug

The Pope has given Malta ten thousand dollars (£2,445) for the relief of those who have suffered because of the war. The transaction was carried out through the Apostolic Delegation in London which sent the money to the Archbishop of Malta to distribute among the people. Sat 8 Aug

Rome. The newspaper *Voce d'Italia* is quoted as saying: 'So long as the Island of Malta remains in British hands with the possibility of adequate supplies, it can again become an instrument for a British offensive.' Tue 11 Aug

New York. Comparing the Battle of Malta to the Battle of Britain, Air Vice-Marshal Sir Hugh Lloyd, former Air Officer Commanding Mediterranean, when interviewed by Reuter, called the island the 'greatest factor' in preventing the complete loss of the Mediterranean area to the Axis. Malta was more important than Gibraltar. The Convoys to the island were large but few and far between. He doubted very much if there would be an invasion of Malta, which was proving a 'very great nuisance' to the Axis. Considering the scale of the attacks, – three or four daily – the casualties were very light. The future is in the air beyond doubt – in war or peace.'

News is received of 13 Maltese now held as prisoners-of-war at Tobruk.

Wed 12 Aug

Malta-based RAF attack enemy airfields in Sardinia.

Thu 13 Aug

Five enemy bombers approached the island. Heavy AA artillery in action.

Ships of the mercantile marine in harbour. They have run through the worst gauntlet the Axis air forces and underground craft could bring against them in narrow waters. Men, women, and children cheered the ships as they come into harbour. Viscount Gort was among the people, in the midst of the craters and ruins of the Upper Barracca Gardens, welcoming the ships of the convoy as they entered the Grand Harbour. In between the clapping and cheering, the waving of flags and of handkerchiefs, there were moments of deep silence. The rattle of the anchor chains was a sound which gave one a choking feeling of deep emotion. The ships were arriving in Malta's war-scarred harbours, and the Spitfires had met them out at sea. There was none of the bombing seen on other occasions at the entrance of the harbour; but all in Malta knew that the ships had come through living hell.

Yesterday in the early evening, people living in the harbour areas raised their cries: '*Wasal il-Konvoj! – Dieħel il-Konvoj*! – 'The convoy is here, the convoy is entering the harbour.' Then all roads that lead to the gardens and bastions that surround the Grand Harbour were packed with hurrying people. The atmosphere was electrifying. There were smiles on all faces and excited whispers. People climbed on rubble heaps that were once happy homes. They manned the blitzed bastions. Flags were perched on the top of the slender archways of the Lower Barracca Gardens. A band was playing on battle-scarred St Elmo. The roar of the Spitfires overhead was continuous. They were seen in flights landing and taking off non-stop, giving umbrella cover to the ships out at sea. Some units of the Royal Navy that had run the gauntlet with the mercantile marine were outside the harbours. Suddenly from St Elmo and Fort Ricasoli and the breakwater, cheer after cheer was heard. A merchant ship had the honour of leading the heroic ships of the convoy into port. An old woman was heard saying: '*Imbierka s-Sapjenza t'Alla – Waslu!*' – 'They have arrived – Blessed be God's Wisdom!' These were the simple words with which she greeted the men who had fought a gallant three-day action to keep the flag flying over this vital outpost. Hardly had the ships dropped anchor, when the waiting gangs of stevedores and port labourers, and the military, were in contact with the incoming crews for the unloading of the ships. An air alert sounded and the fighting merchant ships that had just arrived pointed their guns again at the sky; they themselves now form part of Malta's great barrage. The alert was of a short duration.

People going home were all conscious that a great battle had been fought at sea and that they had set eyes on some of the ships that had fought and won therein. The ships came in – with guns pointing up, and gun crews standing by, stripped to the waist. They came in towards the close of a raidless day, the first for many weeks. It was an unforgettable sight, reminiscent of the arrival of the first convoy in Malta on 3 September 1940, but under different conditions. A young man said as he watched the ships and their deck cargo: 'Flour for us, and nuts [bombs] for the Germans. That is what they've brought us, I hope.'

The Santa Marija Convoy brings deliverance. The crippled American tanker *Ohio* between her escorts limps into Grand Harbour.

Watching the arrival of the convoy.

Viscount Gort called on the captains on board their ships and learnt from them first-hand accounts of their ordeals and escapes on the voyage to Malta.

The King as Sovereign Head has approved to the promotion of Gen. Sir William Dobbie to the grade of Bailiff Grand Cross of the Venerable Order of St John.

Fri 14 Aug

Today's leader of the *Times of Malta* is dedicated to the 'Convoy Heroes'. – 'Through the mercy of Providence and the courage of our seafarers, Malta has been given succour in an hour of need borne by people and garrison alike with fortitude and an abiding faith in the justice of our cause ... Daring all, braving all, and succeeding against all attacks delivered by the Axis, ships of the merchant navy escorted by units of the Royal Navy, and of the FAA [Fleet Air Arm] and assisted by the shore-based aircraft of the RAF have smashed through the barrier which the enemy had directed across the Gibraltar–Malta route ... Ships of convoy, bearing a precious argosy of supplies and war cargoes, have reached the island. They are now in harbour. The strain of what is known today as the Second Siege of Malta is a hard one, of which the hours which precede the arrival of the ships, is the hardest part of all...The full story of convoy work has yet to be written. The world has yet to learn fully of the matchless gallantry which our Navy and mercantile marine have displayed in maintaining sea communications in the face of a ruthless foe. Occasionally the veil is lifted and we are permitted a brief glimpse of what is faced and overcome by the men who go down to the sea in ships in wartime.'

This morning Lord Gort visited the Dockyard and all other areas where unloading was taking place.

This afternoon cheers and applause again echoed from one end to the other of the Grand Harbour as yet another ship entered port. From St Elmo Point, along the bastions of Valletta, down the Marina Road to the Marsa, and on the other side at St Angelo and Senglea Point, thousands of people gave a rousing welcome. Lord Gort was again amongst the people welcoming the merchant navy.

The tanker *Ohio,* deck almost awash, steering gear smashed, hit six times and once set on fire, limps into Grand Harbour. One of the few survivors of the August convoy (1942), she brought fuel at a time of desperate shortage.

Welcoming the arrival of the convoy.

IMPORTANT NOTICE: During the unloading of the convoy which is now in port, all members of the public are requested NOT to enter the Grand Harbour area. Goods from the convoy in port are being unloaded and placed in stores and dumps in various parts of the island. The public is warned that it is forbidden to loiter near any storage dump.

Health authorities notify that there is no need for alarm as to possible ill effects to the health of any person from the smokescreen, provided those who are obliged to remain in the area of the concentration take the precaution already advised by covering their nose and mouth with a wet cloth or handkerchief. People going to air-raid shelters in the locality affected should take with them handkerchiefs or cloths and a bottle of water. The Military Authorities would not use poisonous smoke. Only persons with weak lungs or of an asthmatic condition are likely to be affected by the smoke if they do not cover up their noses and mouths with a wet handkerchief. The smoke has a drying effect on the bronchial tubes which is harmless, though irritating, to normal healthy persons. If possible, it is advisable to move away from the area of the concentration. It is also advisable to keep doors and windows shut. The smoke can be cleared from enclosed spaces by waving blankets.

London. This afternoon the Admiralty has announced the safe arrival at Malta of supplies and reinforcements despite heavy enemy concentrations designed to prevent their passage. It is learned in London that British battleships and several aircraft carriers accompanied the Malta convoy. An Admiralty communiqué confirms that the British aircraft carrier *Eagle* was sunk, also the 9,600-ton British cruiser *Manchester*. Measures taken by the enemy consisted of packs of E-boats, barges, a number of torpedo-carrying and dive-bombing aircraft, and strong forces of U-boats operating in the central narrows.

Feast of Santa Marija – the Assumption of Our Lady into Heaven. Today's editorial comment of the *Times of Malta* is entitled: 'Santa Marija'. – 'Today is the Feast of St Mary, the celebration of the Assumption of Our Lady into heaven. It will be celebrated without any of the traditional manifestations of rejoicing, which accompanied '*Santa Marija*', Patroness of Malta, in pre-war days ... '*Santa Marija*' is a day of thanksgiving to God through Our Lady, for the mercies received and of prayer for added strength to resist the material powers of evil, and also a day of rededication to the cause which we are convinced is sacred and just.' Sat 15 Aug

Heavy raids during which many aircrafts were hit.

Casualty: *Żurrieq*: Pauline Grech (46).

Message by Lord Gort to Admiral Sir Dudley Pound, GCH, GCVO, Chief of Naval Staff, Admiralty:

> *Malta is filled with admiration for the gallant efforts made to pass the convoy to the island. We thank you and are most grateful.*

Aircraft based in Malta attack and hit an enemy merchant vessel which formed part of a hostile convoy. Mon 17 Aug

Two RAF torpedo-carrying aircraft, with fighter escort attack an Axis convoy. A line, about a mile-and-one-half in length, of oil Tue 18 Aug barrels, spars, and general wreckage give conclusive evidence of the sinking of one of the enemy ships.

The New York Times comments: 'Malta is the war's key fortress. In convoying supplies to Malta, the risk was deliberately taken – a proof not only of audacity, but of the desperate importance of holding this speck of an island. That Malta stands isolated, and, interminably bombarded as it is, is one of the miracles of the war.'

Wed 19 Aug

Heavy raids. Heavy barrage.

Casualty: *Birkirkara*: Gaetan Mansueto (40).

Thu 20 Aug

Further details are released by the Admiralty regarding the Malta Convoy. The communiqué says that at least 66 Axis aircraft were destroyed and two U-boats and two E-boats lost. The Royal Navy lost four warships in the action: the aircraft carrier *Eagle*, the 9,600-ton modern cruiser *Manchester*, the 23-year old 4,200-ton anti-aircraft cruiser *Cairo*, and the 1,350-ton destroyer *Foresight*. The convoy operation was under the command of Acting Vice-Admiral Syfret, flying his flag in the battleship *Nelson*.

Notice: A certain amount of pilfering and looting from the ships now being unloaded in the harbour is going on. The Government has emphasized, in the strongest possible terms, that this practice has to cease at once. The heaviest penalties are contemplated for persons convicted of the crime of looting from the convoy.

Tue 25 Aug

It is reported that Lord Gort has returned to Malta from a visit to Cairo in the course of which he attended consultations presided over by Prime Minister Churchill. HE was accompanied by Major the Earl of Minster.

Wed 26 Aug

A large fighter sweep was sent over Malta, and dispersed by Spitfires. Heavy artillery fired pointer rounds.

This afternoon an airfield in Sicily is bombed.

An Historical Branch attached to the Information Office has been set up for the purpose of examining, collating, copying, and

Clearing the debris. The priest waits amid the ruins to pray for those who are dying.

preserving documents bearing on the history of the civilian war effort in Malta.

London. The Duke of Kent, the youngest brother of His Majesty, is killed in a flying accident while en route to Iceland.

The Master of King's Music, Sir Arnold Bax, is writing the music for a film on the defence of Malta. This is revealed in a message of greeting and encouragement from British composers to Russian composers, which was handed to Madam Miasky, wife of the Soviet Ambassador in London.

At dusk RAF strike on Axis shipping. A fair sized enemy merchantman, escorted by a destroyer, is attacked with torpedoes and bombs and sunk. She is hit amidships by a torpedo and also suffer a direct hit in her stern. The merchant vessel blew up, blazing from bow to stern. Fri 28 Aug

Lord Gort in a broadcast message: 'Recently we have seen four merchant ships and an oiler reach Malta; this represents the largest number of ships which has arrived in the Grand Harbour since

WHEN GOD SAVED MALTA

CATHOLIC TIMES 29.5.42.

By Gordon Albion

THE Grand Turk had sworn to fulfil his grandfather's oath that he would feed his horses at the High Altar of St. Peter's. It was no idle boast. Italy would be easy prey if he took Sicily and Sicily was less than sixty miles from Malta. This then was the first nut to crack. And why should not Islam over-run the little honeyed isle of Melita, as it had done in the 9th century, exacting tribute from the Popes? Why should not the Knights of St. John be driven from the Island given them in 1530 by Charles V, as they had already been driven from Rhodes? Once master of Malta, the Sultan would have the whole of the Mediterranean and Southern Europe within his grasp.

✦ ✦ ✦ ✦

And so on 18th May, 1565, the very day on which Pope Pius IV ordered prayers for the passing of the Turkish peril, the black ships of Solyman the Magnificent hove within sight of Malta. There were a hundred and fifty of them, bearing heavy artillery and 30,000 men. They were not unexpected. The Pope, Venice and their own spies had warned the Knights of the impending attack and old Jehan Parisot de la Valette had received *carte blanche* from Philip II of Spain to lay in stores, set up defences of every kind and increase his garrison to eight thousand men, six hundred of them sent by the Pope.

As the Crescent fleet appeared, the Blessed Sacrament was carried in solemn procession and exposed for forty hours, while the white-haired Grand Master prayed with his troops for God's [illegible] and set out to batter down the covering fortresses, St. Michael, St. Angelo and St. Elmo with heavy artillery. Day after day they pounded at St. Elmo, the weakest of the three, pouring men into the broken walls, merely to be driven off time and again, leaving hundreds of dead behind them. Only under cover of darkness could the Knights and their gallant Maltese repair the breaches and replace their dead and wounded. For a whole month it went on till on 22nd June at dusk the Moslems launched their heaviest assault. The C[illegible] fought like men possessed and when night fell the enemy had lost two thousand killed and had withdrawn, but only a handful of wounded Knights were left in grim glory for five hundred of their own lay slain around them.

✦ ✦ ✦ ✦

They passed the night in earnest prayer, salving one another's wounds, making ready for their last fight to the death that they knew would come with the dawn. It was quickly over, for fresh Infidel hoards fell on them with fiendish fanaticism and soon their heads were piked above the walls they had for twenty-nine days so heroically defended. It was the Vigil of St. John the Baptist.

Heart-broken at the cruel slaughter of his brethren, old Jehan sent word to Don Garcia de Toledo, Captain of the Spanish fleet being feverishly assembled at Messina, for immediate help in God's name, lest the whole Island meet the fate of St. Elmo. It was typical, both of the dauntlessness of the Maltese and of the straits in which they had been left by the overcautious Philip II, that the message was rowed by night across sixty miles of sea in a leaky skiff.

✦ ✦ ✦ ✦

Five days later four Spanish galleys landed a thousand men, welcomed by the beseiged as saviours from God. With fresh heart Valette and his men steeled themselves too defend the two remaining harbour-fortresses. Wherever a break was made by Moslem mines and artillery, there stood the gallant Grand Master, sword in hand "with white and flowing beard, fighting like an angel of wrath." Even the Maltese women fought on the walls, while their children brought up food and supplies and tended the wounded. Towards the end of August, the enemy nearly broke through, but a saintly Capuchin Friar, who had escaped badly wounded from St. Elmo, cried out to the exhausted defenders that he had seen a vision of Saints, and heard a voice saying "God will save Malta." With renewed courage the Christians flung back the attacking Turks.

✦ ✦ ✦ ✦

In unbearable heat, the struggle went on into September till 16,000 Moslems lay dead. The brave Maltese had lost seven thousand and the Knights and their men two thousand five hundred. Only six hundred Christians remained, wounded and weary, but full of faith in God, as they crouched beneath the dusty rubble of their shattered walls.

As 6th September dawned, the Turk, sick with dysentery, prepared to finish his few remaining foes when news came that the Spanish fleet had put in unse[en] and was fast landing troop[s]. Hastily taking off his guns an[d] men, the Infidel sailed away to th[e] East.

The seige was raised with th[e] eight-pointed cross, white o[n] black, tattered, but still flutterin[g] over the ruins which the battle stained old Valette had defende[d] with undying glory. Refusing a Cardinal's Hat, he has left an immortal name in his new "City built by gentlemen for gentlemen," Valetta, giving it, through the bounty of Pope and Princes, fortifications unrivalled in the world, an enduring bulwark of Christianity against the enemies of the Cross.

✦ ✦ ✦ ✦

"*Nothing could happen to give me greater satisfaction and pleasure; and everything you have done and arranged has been what your prudence and experience has led us to expect. This service has been so foremost and distinguished, of such quality and importance for the good of Christianity and of our possessions and estates, that you have placed me under a new obligation: and so you can be sure that I intend to honour, favour and reward you, as is right I should, and as you deserve.*" These noble words were Philip of Spain's grandiloquent way of voicing a pride and gratitude that Malta's present Sovereign has expressed in the two letters, G.C.

Malta report by Gordon Albion. *(Catholic Times)*

September of last year. No sight could have been more welcome to all of us than the arrival of the convoy after so many weeks of anxious waiting. 15 August was the last day of the Novena and also the Feast of St Mary the celebration of the Assumption of Our Lady into Heaven. When the last ship of the convoy, the US tanker *Ohio*, entered Grand Harbour as the sun rose on 15 August, everyone in Malta was mindful of how the nine days of united prayer had been answered and was thankful. We are also conscious that, when so many have risked so much and when so many lives have been lost to bring supplies to us from Britain, we also have a duty to perform ourselves. These convoys are very hazardous operations, and, were we to be improvident about the supplies which have reached us, we would do a real disservice not only to those who dared all to succour us, but also to ourselves. It is our bounded duty to eke out our available stores to carry us forward as far as possible on the road to victory ... Convoys, such as this last convoy, are magnificent achievements, but they cannot be constantly repeated, and we must now steel ourselves to last out until a new target date. We will play our part, as Malta has consistently played it in the past. Our aim must be to keep our consumption of all foodstuffs and other commodities at the lowest possible level and so put off, for as long as we can, the date when another convoy has to reach our shores.'

Two Sicilian airfields are bombed and hangars severely damaged.

Raids continue with less intensity. Mon 31 Aug

Casualties: *Birżebbuġa*: Carmela Ellul (30); *Mqabba*: Emanuel Zammit (7), Joseph Zammit (6); *Paola*: Emanuel Paris (–); *Qormi*: Spiro Saliba (40).

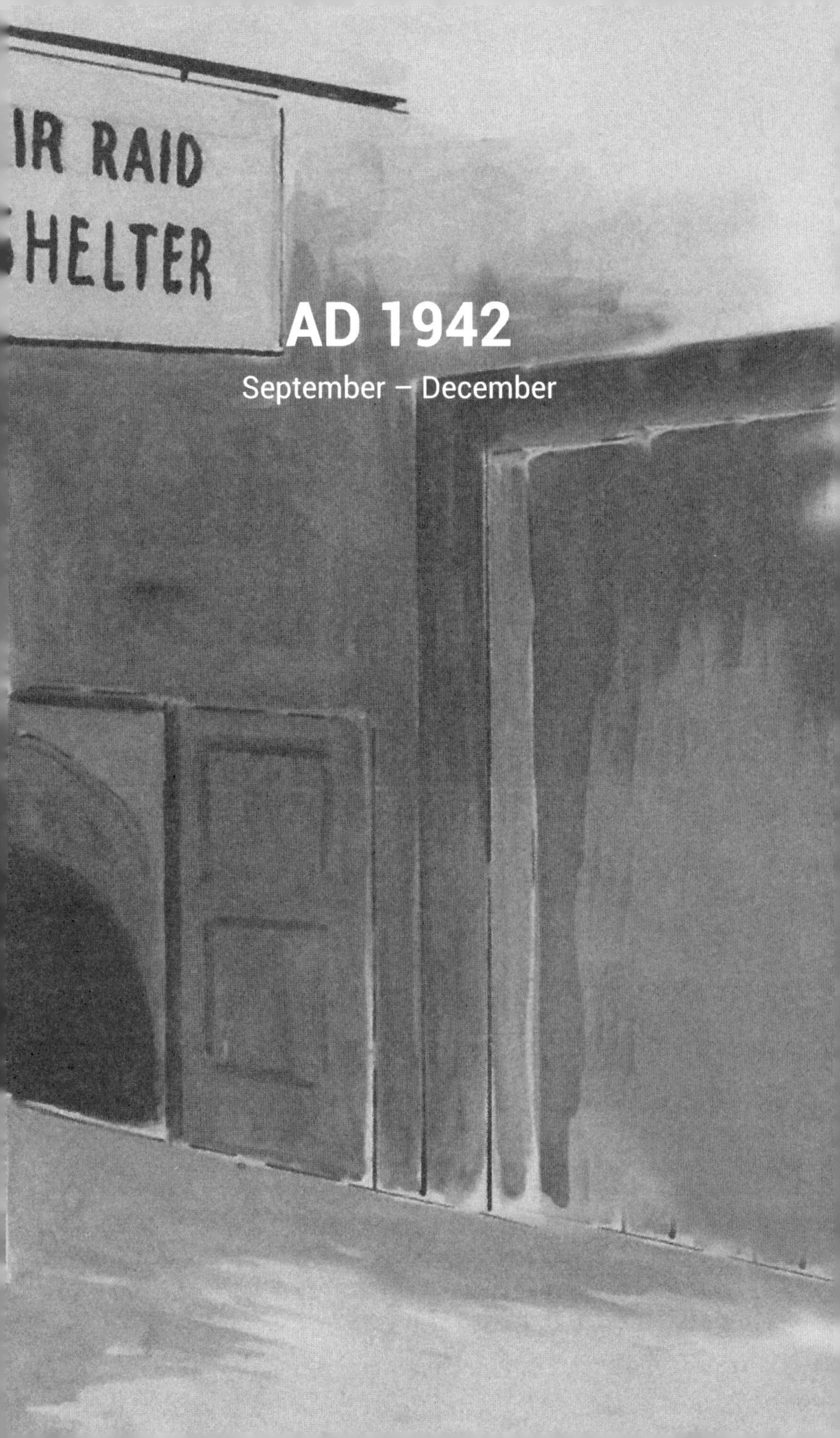

AD 1942

September – December

Casualties: *Rabat*: **Francis** Sammut (16), Carmel Tanti (14). Tue 1 Sep

During August aircraft based on Malta accounted for 50 raiders destroyed. July ended with a bag of 153 Axis planes definitely destroyed, a figure which fell short by one of the record set up in April this year. The total of enemy aircraft destroyed over Malta or by aircraft operating from this base since Italy entered the war is now 936.

The Ack Ack have a great war record behind them. By 1 August our gunners had accounted for 227 enemy aircraft definitely shot down, of which 172 this year. Their peak month was April, when they destroyed 102 raiders. Wed 2 Sep

The Santa Marija Convoy – More information is available on the Malta Convoy. Destroyers and minesweepers were attempting to tow the unwieldy tanker, the *Ohio* (Capt. D.W. Mason). The next day they were joined by another minesweeper, and two destroyers (HMS *Penn* and HMS *Bramham*) were placed on each side of the *Ohio*. A further dive-bombing attack developed, which was driven off without any further damage being done. By nightfall the ships were nearing Malta and, throughout the last night, despite the danger of mines and numerous E-boats alarm, the minesweepers and destroyers struggled on to get the valuable ship home. Early the next morning she was skilfully manoeuvred into harbour.

Rationing. Schedule showing rations entitlement for September 1942: Fri 4 Sep

1st Ration Period (6 to 15 September)

Bread: 3/8 ratal per head per day up to 7 Sept. From 8 Sept. ½ ratal for men between the ages of 16 and 60 years; 3/8 ratal for women, children under 16, and men over 60.

Kerosene: 1 quart for families of one graded down to 1½ gals for families of 12 and over. Every other week only. Will be distributed in weeks 31 Aug. – 4 Sept. and 14 and 18 Sept.

Sugar:	*1½ ratal*
Fats/Lard:	*No. in family* *1–1/8 ratal* *2–½ "* *3–1 "* *4 & 5–½ "* *6 & 7–5/8 "* *8 & 9–¾ "* *10, 11, & 12– 7/8 "* *13, 14, & 15– 7/8 "*
Matches:	*1 to 5–2 boxes* *6 & over–3 boxes*
Corned beef:	*1 & 2–l tin of l4 ozs* *3 to 5–2 tins* *6 to 9–3 "* *10 and over–4 "*
Laundry soap:	*Nil*
Edible oil:	*1–1 terz* *2–2 triezi* *3 & 4–3 "* *5 & 6–4 "* *7 & 8–5 "* *9 & 10–6 "* *11 & 12–7 "* *13, 14, and 15–8 "*
Coffee:	*1 to 3–1/8 ratal* *4 to 5–½ "* *6 to 7–¾ "* *8 to 10–1 "* *11 to 13–1¼ ratal* *14 and over–1½ "*
Tea:	*1–1/16 ratal* *2 to 3–1/8 "* *4 to 5–¼ "* *6 to 8–3/8 "*

	9 to 11–½ "
	12 to 14–5/8 "
	15 and over–¾ "
Tinned fish:	*1, 2, or 3–1 large tin*
	4, 5, 6, or 7–2 large tins
	8 and over–3 " "

The president and members of the Casino Maltese entertain to luncheon at Valletta the captains and officers of the merchantships that arrived in the last convoy. The luncheon was held in the partly-destroyed Ball Room of the club.

London. Roll of Honour: killed – Psaila John, cook, died of wounds; Borg Salvu, petty officer; Falzon C., canteen manager, prisoner-of-war.

Casualties totalling 160 were published by the Admiralty as a result of the sinking of the aircraft carrier *Eagle* during the Malta convoy.

Casualty: *Tarxien*: **Joseph** Bonnici (56). Sat 5 Sep

Last night aircraft of the Royal Navy air squadron made torpedo and bomb attacks on a merchant vessel. A torpedo hit was seen to cause a large explosion and a column of smoke 60 ft high. A bomb-hit on the stem of an escorting destroyer was also scored.

Aware that the service of goats' meat at Victory Kitchens on five days of the week is not popular, a new menu is introduced as from today, viz: Sun 6 Sep

Sunday	*stewed meat with tomatoes and baked beans;*
Monday	*Macaroni with cheese and tomatoes;*
Tuesday	*Balbuljata;*
Wednesday	*Minestra;*
Thursday	*Stewed meat with tomatoes and peas;*
Friday	*Minestra;*
Saturday	*Macaroni with cheese and tomatoes.*

Tue 8 Sep

Today's leader in the *Times of Malta* is entitled 'Our Lady of Victory'. – 'This day is the birthday of Our Lady and it is to Our Lady of Victories that prayers for intercession arise ... Today, Malta commemorates the Victory of the First Siege, a victory which marked the beginning of the end of Turkish Power. The triumph was all the more notable because up till then the Turks had carried all before them ... The parallel between 1565 and 1942 is distinct. Malta is undergoing its Second Siege. Its strategic position is every whit as important today as it was in the days of La Valette.'

7a.m. Today, the anniversary of Malta's victory in the Great Siege of 1565, the miraculous Icon of *Sidtna Marija Damaxena,* in front of which Grandmaster La Valette knelt in prayer during that epic struggle, is carried in solemn procession from the church of St Nicholas (*Tal-Erwieh*) to St John's Co-Cathedral, where the *Papas* of the Greek Catholic Church celebrated High Mass. Immediately after Mass at St John's, the Icon was taken back in procession to the church of St Nicholas where High Mass was sung. Until the Greek Catholic Church of Our Lady of Damascus, destroyed through enemy action, is rebuilt, the *Papas* of the Greek Church will officiate at the former Greek Church of St Nicholas.

Wed 9 Sep

RAF bombers from Malta continue their attacks on enemy convoys.

Sat 12 Sep

Casualty: *Qrendi*: Grezzju Dalli (52).

Sun 13 Sep

Presentation of the George Cross: (from an eyewitness report) – 'Everyone felt the greatness of the occasion as they hastened into the ruined city of Valletta from towns and villages all over the island, everyone of which bore the cruel and honourable scars of the heaviest aerial bombardment in history. The four sides of the Palace Square were crowded. It was a typical holiday crowd, everyone in their Sunday best, glossy black faldettas,[1] side by side with cool

1 The *faldetta* – originally a skirt or petticoat thrown up over the head – is Malta's traditional costume. In earlier times the *faldetta* used to be of different colours in silk or satin. But tradition says that the *faldetta* commenced to be worn only in black as a sign of mourning for Count Roger the Norman who died in 1101.

Palace Square, Valletta – The presentation ceremony of the George Cross and Citation. *(Times of Malta)*

summer dresses, the sombre cassocks of the priesthood, mingling with the spick-and-span parade dress of the services and the white duck suits of the civilians. Lining the Square were representatives of the Royal Navy, the Army, the Royal Air Force, the Police, the Special Constabulary, and the ARP. Here and there in the crowd, white-capped hospital nurses. The captains and officers of the Malta Convoy had special reserved seats. Two mounted policemen heralded the martial music as the Royal Malta Artillery marched down Kingsway accompanied by the band of the King's Own Malta Regiment and took up its position in front of the Main Guard. The scene was set: the ruined Palace of the Grandmasters cast its shadow forward across the Square. From the flagstaff fluttered the Union Jack, with Malta's Red and White superimposed, for the first time since the bombing of the Palace. In the sunlight, was the rose-coloured façade of the Casino Maltese, its cornice blown away, some of its interior showing plainly where the roof had collapsed; on its balcony were draped the Union Jack and the Maltese flag. To the right of the Square, a Maltese flag floated above the rococo façade of the Palais de Verdelin. In the centre of the Square, on a carpeted dais, were gathered Vice-Admiral R. Leatham, KCB, ViceAdmiral,

Malta; Major Gen Mack Scobie, General Officer Commanding Troops, Malta; Air Vice-Marshal Park, Air Officer Commanding, RAF, Mediterranean; the members of the Executive Council; Mr Bell, Legal Secretary; Dr Louis Galea, Attorney General; and other personalities. Before them stood the centre of the day's ceremonial – an empty plinth, on either side of which stood a sentry of the 1st Bn King's Own Malta Regiment. To the left of the dais, a pile of debris, and a shattered door-panel from the Magisterial Palace. The black-clad figure of His Grace, Mgr Maurus Caruana, OSB, Archbishop of Malta, and his suite, made their way to the dais, accompanied by Mgr Michele Gonzi, Bishop of Gozo, and Mgr Emanuel Galea, Bishop of Tralles and Auxiliary Bishop of Malta, their magenta robes and green-tasselled hats making a brilliant patch of colour in the group of khaki and white-clad figures on the dais. HE Viscount Gort, the Governor and C-in-C, accompanied by HH Sir George Borg, Chief Justice and President of the Court of Appeal, preceded by Mr J. Axisa, OBE, Commissioner of Police, walked quickly up to the dais. The Guard of Honour gave the Royal Salute and the Band of the Royal Malta Artillery played the opening bars of the National Anthem. HE, addressing the people, said: 'On my appointment as Governor of Malta, I was entrusted to carry the George Cross to this Island Fortress. By the command of the King I now present to the people of Malta and her Dependencies the Decoration which His Majesty has awarded to them in recognition of the gallant service which they have already rendered in the fight for freedom ... Now it is my proud duty to hand over the George Cross to the people of Malta for safe keeping. I repeat the words of His Majesty written with his own hand: "To honour her brave people I award the George Cross to the Island Fortress of Malta to bear witness to a heroism and devotion that will long be famous in history".' On concluding his address, HE received the case containing the George Cross from Mr Axisa and presented it to Sir George Borg who received it on behalf of the People of Malta and its Dependencies. Sir George Borg, in his black and gold magisterial cap and robes stepped down from the dais and placed the case containing the George Cross and His Majesty the King's personal message on the plinth and stood at attention as the Band played the first eight bars of the Maltese National Hymn. Returning to the dais,

Sir George Borg spoke in reply to HE: 'For, my Lord, nothing is dearer to the hearts of the inhabitants of these islands than liberty, for which they fought and fell since time immemorial.'

Throughout the day the George Cross was in the custody of the 1st Bn The King's Own Malta Regiment who mounted guard at the Main Guard. In the evening, during a short ceremony, the George Cross was carried on its way to a safe place of custody.'

Mon 14 Sep

Today's editorial comment of the *Times of Malta* is entitled 'Malta G.C.' – 'Yesterday's ceremony of the presentation of the George Cross to the people of Malta by Viscount Gort on behalf of H.M. the King was one of austere and fitting simplicity, admirably carried out. Those who were privileged to be present were conscious of the stern chapter in the island's history through which we are all living, and His Majesty's award of the George Cross marked his kingly appreciation of the importance of Malta's resistance in the cause of free men.'

Sword of the Spirit. *(Sunday Times of Malta)*

Thu 17 Sep

Heavy raid. One German fighter shot down.

Casualties: *Mġarr*: Saviour Bugeja (8); *Mosta*: Carmel Bezzina (73).

Sat 19 Sep

In the course of reconnaissance sweep this evening our Spitfires destroyed two enemy seaplanes.

Mon 21 Sep

Aircraft from Malta attack enemy shipping.

Tue 22 Sep

p.m. The George Cross is brought to the village of Dingli by Josephine Bonnici, accompanied by a small police force. Buglers of the Durham Light Infantry precede the cortege. The Malta Cross is carried by the delegate of the Commissioner of Police and was followed by delegations and flags. Then came the Dingli Boy Scouts and members of the Dingli Club. Schoolchildren carried in their hands branches of leaves. The George Cross was carried to Church Square, where it was received by the people, the District Committee, the Regional Protection Officer (Brigadier Gatt), and the local Protection Officer (Mr Ebejer). The buglers sounded a fanfare. The

Blitzed houses.

Cross was then handed over to Prof. J. Ellul, Hon. President of the District Committee, who placed it on the plinth, which was guarded by two policemen. The *God Save the King* was played and, immediately after, the schoolchildren sung the Maltese Hymn. Prof. Ellul delivered an address in which he explained the meaning of the award of the George Cross to Malta. During the ceremony the Malta Police Band played a short musical programme. When that ceremony was concluded the Parish Priest of Dingli entertained to tea the guests and bandsmen at the *domus curialis*.

Washington. Two United States merchantmen were lost in the Mediterranean early last month during a three-day attack by Axis sea- and aircraft on the Malta-bound convoy. One of the American vessels was torpedoed and sunk by a motor torpedo boat at night after the third day. The other merchantman was scuttled by the crew, after being torpedoed.

Wed 23 Sep

London. The *London Gazette* announces further awards for gallantry in the recent Malta Convoy Battle. The awards are for bravery and resolution in HM ships *Antelope, Argus, Cairo, Charybdis, Hebe, Hythe, Itsuriel, Kenya, Liverpool, Marne, Middleton, Onslow, Partridge, Rye, Speedy, Vidette, Westcott, Wishart, Wrestler,* and the Polish ship *Kujawiak,* while escorting the convoy to Malta. In addition, 30 officers and 91 men are mentioned in Dispatches. Capt. Mason was awarded the George Cross for gallantry on board the *Ohio* which formed part of the Malta Convoy.

Cardiff. The Parliamentary Secretary to the Minister of Agriculture, the Duke of Norfolk, said: 'We have been extremely well fed in this war. When you hear people grumbling about food, I suggest that you talk to them of the incredible patience and sacrifices of the people of Malta and Stalingrad.'

Washington. More than 200 survivors from two US merchantmen which were sunk in the Malta Convoy are taken to England in British warships. They have now arrived back in the United States.

Thu 24 Sep

Last night heavy AA artillery was in action.

At dusk this morning a torpedo attack was made on an enemy merchant vessel. Two hits were claimed.

The Director of Manpower, Lieut. Col. A.L. Bartolo, notifies that the Governor has decided that the minimum height for service in the Armed Forces of the Crown, under the National Service Regulations 1941, shall now be 5 feet. The Director of Manpower therefore requires all persons between the ages of 18 and 31 years, who have already reported and who have been exempted for being under 5 feet 2 inches, but who are 5 feet and over, to report again at the National Service Headquarters, Ħamrun. Free bus tickets to and from the National Service Headquarters will be provided. Moreover, the Director of Manpower directs that all male persons in Malta and Gozo, born in 1919–1920, shall register on 26 and 27 September 1942, at the Registration Depot of their village. When registering, persons in possession of a certificate of exemption from Military Service or Discharge papers must show them to the Registering Officer. All those liable are reminded that the penalty for not registering is a fine of £ 1.

Fri 25 Sep

More raids and heavy AA artillery. Spitfires shoot down two German fighters into the sea.

The George Cross is being taken round the towns and villages of Malta and Gozo. Today it is displayed at Cottonera.

Starting today and on all subsequent Fridays, the Band and Drum of the 2nd Bn the Queen's Own Royal West Kent Regiment will beat the retreat on Castille Square.

Sat 26 Sep

Last night hostile shipping was attacked by torpedo-carrying aircraft based on Malta.

The George Cross is brought to Luqa – the bomb-battered village situated close to the military airfields. The George Cross was first brought to the *domus curialis* of the Parish Priest Fr Debono, where the chief guests were assembled. The guests included Group Captain Le May and officers of the 11th Bn the Lancashire Fusiliers; Major Allfrey, representing Col. Pulverman of the 2nd Bn the Queen's Own Royal West Kent Regiment; Lieut. Matthewman, Instructor

Luqa Home Guard; Major Mifsud, Liaison Officer; Dr Muscat, District Medical Officer Luqa; the Regional Protection Officer; and the President and members of the District Committee. The George Cross was then carried by Supt. Kissaun, who represented the Commissioner of Police, to Church Square, where it was placed on a plinth. In the midst of the ruins of this village, with the battered church in the background, the Parish Priest delivered a stirring address. This was followed by the playing of the Maltese Hymn and the *God Save the King*.

The villagers of Luqa filed past the George Cross. At the end of the ceremony guests were entertained by the President and District Committee at the Luqa Home Guard Headquarters.

The George Cross is today displayed at Marsa. Sun 27 Sep

The George Cross is today displayed at Mellieħa. Mon 28 Sep

This morning enemy plane approach in several small formations but evade combat. Heavy AA artillery fired pointer rounds to assist our fighters. Tue 29 Sep

Casualty: *Mġarr*. Santo Abela (14).

The George Cross is today exhibited at Mġarr for the Mġarr and Żebbiegħ areas.

London. The need for secrecy regarding shipping movements is raised in the House of Lords. The Earl of Cork said that before the last convoy to Malta, a part of ore cargo at a great port in the north-west of England, within easy reach of the German Legation at Dublin, had been clearly marked 'Malta' according to his information.

The Valletta District Emergency Committee notifies that the mobile gas chamber will be in Valletta to enable the public to test and, if need be, to replace their respirators.

Last night our bombers attacked Axis shipping and a near miss on a merchant vessel was observed. Torpedo-carrying aircraft scored a direct hit amidships on a destroyer. Wed 30 Sep

The George Cross is displayed at Mosta. A modified menu served by the Victory Kitchens is announced as follows:

Monday	*Balbuljata with peas;*
Tuesday	*Macaroni with tomatoes;*
Wednesday	*Tinned fish, beans, and tomatoes;*
Thursday	*Minestra;*
Friday	*Macaroni with tomatoes;*
Saturday	*Minestra;*
Sunday	*Meat with tomatoes and tinned beans.*

The Secretary of State for War has notified that the following Maltese prisoners-of-war have been transferred from Internment Camp Stalag VIII to Hag VIII, Germany: Charles Aquilina, Paul Carabott, Antonio Portelli, Joseph Lia, Spiridione Lia, Spyredon Pace, Eduardo Mefsut, Eleftherios Mefsut, Franziskus Lia, Jean Lia, Antonio Allul, and Victor Ellul.

Thu 1 Oct

The George Cross is displayed at Mqabba.

Rome. 'Malta still constitutes a serious threat to Italian convoy traffic which plies between the Italian mainland and the North African coast. It is only by continuous air bombardment that the offensive potentiality of the island can be neutralized.'

Fri 2 Oct

The George Cross is displayed at the Empire Stadium for Gżira, Msida, Pietà, Guardamangia, and Ta' Xbiex.

Sun 4 Oct

This morning there have been three hostile fighter sweeps. Heavy AA artillery put up.

The George Cross is today exhibited at Paola for the Paola and Tarxien areas.

Mon 5 Oct

Last night an Axis merchant vessel with destroyer escort was attacked. Today the George Cross is displayed at Qrendi.

Tue 6 Oct

A number of carrier pigeons belonging to the Military Authorities have recently been shot. These birds perform a very important

On the High Sea of Stress to the Port of Victory. *(Sunday Times of Malta)*

function in the defence of the island. All persons are warned that a serious view will be taken of the shooting of these birds.

This afternoon the George Cross is displayed at St Paul's Bay. Broadcast by D.C. Campbell, Acting Lieutenant Governor of Malta: 'Victory Kitchens were introduced because it was thought that they are the only satisfactory means of distributing local produce fairly among the public. Meat is too scarce to ration and no country has found a satisfactory means of rationing vegetables. Secondly, they were designed to assure to those who are poorest among us something in addition to their rations. Thirdly, in the Victory Kitchens we have available an organization for distributing food evenly among the whole population, should more arduous siege conditions impose the need to reduce rations still further.'

Wed 7 Oct

This afternoon the George Cross is exhibited at Siġġiewi.

Casualty: *Naxxar*: Teodoro Azzopardi (23).

Thu 8 Oct

The George Cross is displayed at Sliema for the Sliema, St Julian's, and St George's areas.

Fri 9 Oct

Heavy raids.

The George Cross displayed at Rabat for Rabat, Mdina, and Mtarfa.

Sat 10 Oct

Heavy-calibre bombs dropped by JU 88s on Gozo.

Casualties: *Gozo* (*Sannat*): Michael Azzopardi (6 months), Joseph Cini (50), Saviour Curmi (80), Pauline Farrugia (70), Joseph Galea (4), Josephine Galea (30), Margaret Galea (6), Michael Galea (8), Grazia Muscat (50), Mary Muscat (30), Frances Pace (45), Catherine Saliba (35), Mary Tabone (17), Carmela Theuma (64), Lydia Zammit (2). Anthony Bartolo, assistant steward, previously reported missing, is now known to be a prisoner-of-war.

The George Cross displayed at Żabbar.

Sun 11 Oct

Heavy raids continue. Enemy losses: 7 German bombers, 5 German fighters, and 3 Italian fighters destroyed; 7 German bombers, 16 German fighters, and 7 Italian fighters all damaged.

Casualties: *Mtarfa*: Paul Azzopardi (17); *Paola*: Doris Hockey (4), Joseph Hockey (30), Rosy Hockey (25); *Qormi*: Joseph Cardona (76); *Rabat*: Anthony Caruana (10), Angiolina Falzon (14), Joseph Fsadni (28), Maddalena Galea (28), Antonia Grixti (46), Peter Vella (63), Mary Zahra (44); *Tarxien*: Concetta Attard (47), Joseph Baldacchino (36), Anthony Barbara (55), Antonia Camilleri (76), Maggie Cook (56), Joseph Debono (25), Lonza Debono (25), Joseph Degabriele (9), Calcedonio Farrugia (15), Emily Gleaves (28), Joseph Manicolo (44), Laurence Piscopo (24), Charles Porter (71), Edward Redman (64), Charles Salsero (3), Vincent Scerri (60), Mary Tabone (12); *Żebbuġ*: Spiro Borg (25); *Żejtun*: Carmel Grech (30).

The George Cross is displayed at Żebbuġ.

Tue 13 Oct

Today marked Malta's biggest day for air battles since 10 May of this year. Twenty-two enemy aircraft were destroyed and 41 damaged. The Luftwaffe has returned in greater strength than Malta has experienced for months. Malta's defences claim the 1,000th Axis plane since the opening of hostilities in the Central Mediterranean. Increased enemy air activity indicates the enemy's attempt to wrest air supremacy from the Malta fighters.

Casualties: *Birkirkara*: Emanuel Mifsud (20); *Sliema*: John Block (20).

The George Cross is today displayed at Żurrieq.

A number of Victory Kitchens are being attached to Government and Boarding schools for use by schoolchildren.

Slogan. Wartime Reminders – I must remember that imported fuel is used for pumping water; Reduced consumption of water saves fuel; A saving in fuel saves freight; Saving in freight helps to win the War.

The thousandth aircraft to be destroyed by the RAF (Malta) was a Junkers 52. It fell to fighter pilot in command of one of the island's Spitfire squadrons, Squadron Leader J.J. Lynch, who is seen in the cockpit of his Spitfire while an aircraftsman is chalking 'Malta 1000th' on the side of the aircraft.

Wed 14 Oct

Reports say that 82 Axis aircraft were definitely shot down within the last four days; the *Luftwaffe* is attempting a great new bid to smash Malta's landing grounds.

Casualties: *Birkirkara*: Francis Fenech (18); *Msida*: Anthony Zahra (11).

It is announced that *balbuljata* is to cease being served by Victory Kitchens in order that dried egg may be issued in rationed form to the public. The reason for this decision is the wish of the public themselves, who so greatly desire to have the egg powder for use in their own homes, for their children and invalids. Unfortunately, the supply position is so tight that the transfer of dried egg from the Kitchens to the ration makes it necessary for the Kitchens to close down on one day of the week. This is rendered unavoidable by the fact that the Government has no alternative food with which to supply the Kitchens for that day.

London. Message by the Secretary of State for Air, Sir Archibald Sinclair, to the Air Officer Commanding Malta: 'Congratulations to your squadrons on their brilliant exploits in recent battles. Destruction of more than thousand aircraft by airmen and gunners of Malta is glorious, significant achievement.'

Thu 15 Oct

Ground defences continue to put up a heavy barrage against enemy raiders.

Casualties: *Gżira*: Joseph Scicluna (48); *Mellieħa*: Arthur Calleja (6); *Sliema*: Joseph Letard (65).

Fri 16 Oct

The *Luftwaffe* **continues** its attempts to knock Malta's fighting capacity. Owing to the closing of Victory Kitchens on Sundays, the Kitchens' menu for next week will be:

Monday	*Macaroni;*
Tuesday	*Veal, loaf, beans with tomato;*
Wednesday	*Minestra or soup;*
Thursday	*Macaroni;*
Friday	*Fish, beans, and tomato;*
Saturday	*Soup or minestra.*

Vichy. The Berlin Correspondent of the *Neue Zuricher Zeitung* is quoted as saying: 'A direct attack against Malta is not impossible. This belief is based on: firstly, air offensive against the island; secondly, powerful submarine attacks against enemy shipping on the Cape route; thirdly, Rommel's return to North Africa.'

Sat 17 Oct

Large-scale air attacks continue.

Casualties: *Birkirkara*: Anthony Camilleri (40), Carmela Gatt (45), George Zammit (8).

The George Cross is exhibited at Safi.

Sun 18 Oct

Casualties: *Birkirkara***:** Paul Parlar (62), Doris Spiteri (8), Maria Carmela Spiteri (6).

The George Cross is exhibited at Senglea.

Mon 19 Oct

German 2 kg anti-personnel Butterfly bombs are being dropped with delayed action fuses. These bombs are liable to detonate up to 20 minutes after being dropped.

Tue 20 Oct

Today's daylight raids consisted of small numbers of enemy fighters which escorted a few fighter-bombers. Heavy AA artillery in action. Airfields suffer damages.

Wed 21 Oct

On Monday/Tuesday night torpedo-carrying aircraft and bombers had a busy time. The weather was bad, with thick low clouds and rain squalls, but the largest merchant vessel in a heavily-escorted convoy was hit by torpedo. A flash was seen followed by a thick cloud of smoke. Later a large tanker in the same convoy and another merchant vessel was hit by a heavy bomb, causing a dense pall of black smoke.

London. 6,704 buildings in Malta have been destroyed or damaged by Axis air-raids. The Secretary for Air, Sir Archibald Sinclair, further disclosed in the House of Commons that up to 19 October, there have been 1,660 bombing attacks and 1,069 Axis aircraft destroyed. Up to 20 September, 1,386 civilians had been killed.

Cairo. R.F. Roland, Reuters' correspondent: 'Kesselring's 8-day assault on Malta has failed in its main object – to improve the supply position of Gen. Rommel's troops. The Axis is being hit in two ways. Their convoys are sought out and vitally important cargoes are sunk at sea or in harbour.

Fri 23 Oct

This evening there was an escorted fighter-bomber raid in two waves, one German and one Italian.

Casualties: *Birkirkara*: Michael Sultana (73), Carmelina Grech (9); *Ħamrun*: Carmela Calleja (37), Mary Calleja (11), Anthony Debono (54), Carmela Debono (42), Alfred Fenech (73), Alfred Muscat (4), Jennie Scerri (17), Filippa Whiddat (12), Joan Whiddat (10), William Whiddat (8); *St Julian's*: Carmela Sciberras (56).

Wartime Reminder Slogan:

I may contract Typhoid Fever, Dysentery, and other diseases if I eat vegetables, fruit, or seashells which are not properly cleaned or cooked; if I drink water from wells that have not been examined and purified by the Sanitary Authorities. Accumulations of filth and rubbish attract

Fighting Fit. *(Sunday Times of Malta)*

flies and flies disseminate disease germs. Typhoid fever is very prevalent just now and I can protect myself and my family by inoculation.

The George Cross is displayed at Żejtun. Sat 24 Oct

As from noon today, persons requiring tickets for Victory Kitchen meals must, when withdrawing their tickets, present their Ration Book to the Victory Kitchen Supervisor. This procedure is to be observed every week, irrespective of whether registration at the kitchens is made for one month in advance or not. The purpose of this arrangement is to prevent persons withdrawing more meal tickets than they are authorized to obtain. Any person attempting double registration at Victory Kitchens is liable to heavy penalties. Wed 28 Oct

Casualties: *Gżira*: **Rita** Falzon (19), Carmela Micallef (42), Vincenza Rice (40); *Naxxar*. Emanuel Grech (52). Thu 29 Oct

Casualties: *Lija*: **Anthony** Camilleri (56), Saviour Cutajar (48), Peter Fenech (82), Joseph Galea (55), Anthony Zammit (10), Carmela Zammit (24); *Żebbuġ*: Joseph Abdilla (11), Antonia Bonanno (16), Salvina Bonanno (7), Emanuel Buhagiar (29), Anthony Muscat (18), Carmela Muscat (5), Philip Muscat (57); *Gozo* (*Victoria*): Carmela Galea (56). Tue 3 Nov

London. One-hundred-and-thirty-one Axis aircraft were shot down by Malta's pilots during October and many more reported damaged. AA gunners destroyed another seven. So ended perhaps the most momentous month for the island. The Axis have forced a trial of strength, but after ten days they had to call a halt.

Ottawa. Pilot Officer George Frederick (Skew Ball) Beurling, Malta's air ace, escaped unhurt when a passenger plane crashed near Gibraltar. Beurling was on his way home to Canada from Malta. The plane crashed on a hilltop in the eastern part of the Rock. Beurling shot down a total of 22 Axis planes over Malta. He has recently been awarded the Distinguished Service Order (DSO).

Wed 4 Nov

Heavy raids.

Sun 8 Nov

The George Cross is today exhibited at Għargħur.

Tue 10 Nov

This afternoon Lord Gort opened the Qrendi Aerodrome. Performing the inauguration ceremony, HE said: 'The opening comes at a time when we can sense that the initiative in this, the Second World War, is passing into the hands of the United Nations … And now it is my privilege to hand over this aerodrome to the Royal Air Force. May it prove as faithful a friend in service as our three well-tried veterans, Ħal Far, Luqa, and Ta' Qali.'

Wed 11 Nov

During the last 24 hours our bombers carried out more attacks and obtained hits on enemy airfields in Sicily. Bursts were reported on runways, in dispersal areas, and on buildings.

At dusk long-range fighters from Malta attack a Tunisian airfield.

This afternoon, while on patrol, Malta fighters destroyed a German flying-boat and shot up an enemy schooner.

Casualty: *Żejtun*: Joseph Busuttil (58).

Thu 12 Nov

RAF planes based on Malta continue to raid enemy airfields in Sicily.

Notice: Owing to the shortage of meat and in order temporarily to conserve the food supplies of the island, it has become necessary to make a very slight reduction in the quantities of food issued through Victory Kitchens until the winter potato crop is available. Recent successes of the British 8th Army in North Africa will, it is hoped, relieve the supply situation in Malta, but their effect has not yet made itself felt on our supplies. Until a convoy arrives in our harbour, it is only prudent to rapidly conserve all our stocks. From the week commencing on Monday next, 16 November, the quantity of *żibeġ* in the vegetable soup or *minestra* will be reduced by half; the portion of beans and peas served on Tuesday and Fridays will be reduced by half; and the portions of tinned fish will be cut by 1/10, each portion equalling the weight of 4½ pennies; all other ingredients, including paste other than *żibeġ*, will remain at the present quantities.

Fri 13 Nov

p.m. While on patrol, 8 of our aircraft met an aerial armada of some 30 Italian troop-carriers, 15 to 20 German troop-carriers, and some German flying boats with a fighter escort. An engagement ensued.

Sat 14 Nov

a.m. Malta Spitfires on patrol came across an Italian bomber flying low over the sea and destroyed it. From the way it burned, it was suspected that it may have been carrying fuel. Large formations of enemy transport machines, with twin-engined fighter escort, were intercepted.

RAF attacks on enemy airfields continue.

In today's issue of the *Times of Malta,* May Butcher publishes the following poem entitled 'Air-Raid Warning!':

See
how the foe
sows death while hearts grow numb!

We
cannot know
how soon the Call may come:

Grief
meets us now
in shape we dread to see –

Leaf
on the bough
more sure of life than we.

Why
should we fear?
Time counts not in the strife. Die! –
but, while here,
serve others: this is life.

London. *The Times* comments: 'The reduction in German air activity on the Russian front and continued immunity of this country from air attack show clearly that Hitler is collecting as many scattered units of the *Luftwaffe* as he can from all over Europe in order to hamper Allied operations in the Mediterranean area ... The role of Malta, from which our bombers operated in attacks on the Sardinian airfields, has completely changed from defence to offence, since the Allied move into North-West Africa.'

Tue 17 Nov

Aircraft flown by FAA pilots sank a large tanker *en route* for Tripoli. The tanker had destroyer escort. Meanwhile RAF planes operating from Malta continue to bombard enemy airfields at Catania, Augusta, Germini, and Comiso with the object of rendering them unusable to reinforce Tunisia.

London. It is reported that 21-year-old Lieutenant Dennis Arthur Copperwheat, RN who scuttled a blazing ship laden with ammunition in the Grand Harbour at Valletta has been awarded the George Cross.

Thu 19 Nov

Following directives by the Archbishop, in most of the churches a solemn Mass is today being celebrated *Pro Re Gravi* for the repose of the souls in Purgatory as a sign of thanksgiving to God for the Allied victory in Egypt.

The Chief Justice Sir George Borg, Mr Justice Edgar Ganado, and Mr Justice William Harding passed the death sentence on Carmelo BorgPisani, who was found guilty of (l) espionage, (2) taking up arms against the Government, (3) forming part of a conspiracy to overthrow the Government. The proceedings were held in camera but the sentence was read in public.

The Governor authorizes the further issue of paper currency:

Notes of l s. Series A/1 – originally printed as 2 s. notes and now overprinted as l s./–notes, to be legal tender for payments not exceeding £2.

London. The *London Gazette* announces further lists of awards for deeds of gallantry in the recent Malta Convoy operations.

His Majesty awarded the MBE (Civil Division) to Pius Muscat Azzopardi for good service rendered during air-raids on Malta.

Fri 20 Nov`

Late yesterday evening a convoy entered the Grand Harbour.

During last night RAF planes stationed in Malta carried out more raids on enemy airfields in Sicily. Hangars were hit.

a.m. A successful sortie is carried out by RAF twin-engined fighter aircraft against enemy shipping.

Four merchant vessels loaded with essential supplies both for the population and the Services enter harbour. Their arrival marks the beginning of the end of the siege. Crowds flocked to the bastions overlooking the harbour. Gort visited the harbour area when the unloading was proceeding in full swing. Throughout the day our fighters formed a protective umbrella to the convoy.

Casualty: *Birżebbuġa*: Mary Farrugia (44).

The Swiss Minister in Tokyo has reported that the following Maltese Sisters are interned at Tokyo: Carmela Camilleri, Maria Camilleri, Rosina De Gabrieli, Annunziata Grech, Josephine Mifsud, and Teresa Orlando.

Sat 21 Novem

p.m. Our fighters destroyed a German aeroplane and shot up a 'flak' ship with cannon and machine-gun fire.

The Italian Authorities have intimated that, after 31 January 1943, letters received in Italy for prisoners-of-war in their hands which bear place names instead of, or in addition to, the number of the Camp, will be confiscated.

More awards announced in London for gallant service in the August convoy to Malta.

Sun 22 Nov

Last night a big fire blazed, following an explosion at an oil and petrol store. HE sustains severe burns in the arm and leg while helping to extinguish the fire.

Casualty: *Birkirkara*: Vincent Sciberras (44). RAF plane twice attack North Africa airfields.

p.m. Two German transport aircraft destroyed. A second squadron destroys 3 Italian transport aircraft.

African Bridgehead. *(Sunday Times of Malta)*

Mon 23 Nov

RAF planes continue their attacks on vital ports and airfields in Sicily and against Axis shipping.

Tue 24 Nov

Enemy aircraft carry out a fighter sweep. Heavy AA artillery in action.

London. Some 500 officers and men of the cruiser *Manchester* (Capt. Harold Drew), sunk in the Malta convoy battle in August, were among the 1,000 British internees from North Africa who have arrived in Britain.

Cairo. RAF medium bombers operating from Malta raid Bizerta harbour.

Thu 26 Nov

Malta's mounting offensive. Widespread operations by RAF planes operating from Malta.

Casualty: *Birkirkara*: Mary Tonna (60).

Repeated attacks by RAF planes operating from Malta against Sicilian airfields. Fri 27 Nov

7.30 a.m. The death sentence by hanging, passed on Carmelo Borg-Pisani on charges of treason and espionage, is carried out at the execution cell of the Civil Prisons, Kordin. Sat 28 Nov

Casualty: *Żejtun*: **Emanuel** Carabott (53). Sun 29 Nov

Malta continues its offensive and keeps up the blitz against the enemy in Sicily and North Africa. Mon 30 Nov

This morning a small squadron of fighters approached but a heavy barrage was put up. There was a bomb explosion in Gozo. Tue 1 Dec

More attacks by RAF fighter-bombers on Sicilian airfields. Our longrange fighters harass enemy merchant vessels carrying deck cargo of oil drums.

Feast of St Barbara, Patron Saint of Artillery. Fri 4 Dec

This morning gunners from all over the island were assembled to celebrate the feast of St Barbara, Virgin and Martyr, their patron saint. RMA representatives were gathered for Mass in the little chapel of St Anne in Fort St Elmo. Amidst all the destruction the tiny chapel stood in flawless beauty. The baroque carving of the altar arch, embodying the arms of the Order of St John and of Grandmaster Cotoner, contrasts effectively with the simple lines of the new altar, built from the stones of the blitzed churches of Valletta and stones from St Elmo's ancient bastions. Above the altar hangs a painting of the *Sacred Heart of Jesus* from the brush of George Preca, the soft pastel colours blending harmoniously with the background. In a recess is displayed the 16th-century carving of *St Anne with the Virgin and the Child Jesus,* formerly carried on the flagship of the grandmasters, and lately rescued from the ruined harbour church of

Notre Dame de Liesse.[2] Mass, which was attended by the CRA and representative officers and other ranks of the RMA, was celebrated by Revd Ferriggi, CF, RC (II HAA Regt RMA). A hymn was sung by the choir of officers of the 1st Coast Regt RMA. On the conclusion of the service the CRA took the salute as the units marched past to the strains of the RA (Malta) Band. The parade was under the command of Major J. Gatt, RMA.

The following Maltese, previously reported missing, are now reported to be prisoners-of-war: Joseph Camilleri, Officers' Cook; William Debono, Assistant Steward; and Joseph Salafia, Steward.

Sat 5 Dec

More enemy raids. Heavy land defences in action.

Meanwhile Malta maintains its great share in Mediterranean offensive against Axis convoys.

By decree, the *Comitè National de la France Combattante* in London, headed by Gen. De Gaulle, has appointed M. Xavier Gauthier, Consul de France, as his delegate in Malta. The British Government has given its consent to this appointment. The address of M. Xavier Gauthier is Villino Delicata, 91, Old College Street, Sliema, where all communications concerning Fighting France can be sent.

Sun 6 Dec

RAF fighter-bombers attack large north-bound transport enemy aircraft.

Tue 8 Dec

Incessant attacks by RAF planes continue against ports in Sicily.

Wed 9 Dec

Malta-based aircraft intercept and shoot down Axis troop carriers.

Thu 10 Dec

London. *The London Times* reports that four of Malta's Beaufighters have emerged victorious from one of the most one-sided air battles of this war. Fifty of Goering's giant three-engined JU 52 troop

2 The church of Our Lady of Liesse is situated on the foot of the hill which leads to Victoria Gate in Valletta. It was erected in 1620 at the expense of the Bailiff d'Annenia, Fra Giacomo Chenn de Bellay, a member of the Langue of France.

Bombs thunder across the suburb of Floriana.

carriers, en route from Tunisia to Sicily, were escorted by formations of heavily armed Messerschmitt 100s and Junkers 88 long-range fighters. The four Beaufighters led by the Canadian Flight Lieutenant Dallas Schmidt, DFC, spotted the great air force of Lampedusa Island, 100 miles west of Malta. Long-range Allied fighters patrolling off Malta in bad weather also spotted a formation of three six-engined transports, and at once swooped to attack. A single four-engined Focke-Wulf 200 which ventured near Malta was severely knocked. The giant six-engined transports Bloehm-Voss 222s are reported to be capable of carrying 80 armed men; weighing 45 tons, they have a range of 4,500 miles and a speed of about 175 miles per hour.

The Germans continue to suffer heavy losses in their efforts to reinforce Gen. Nehring's troops in Tunisia by air as a result of attacks by Malta-based fighters. Fri 11 Dec

RAF Beaufighters, the most heavily-armed aircraft in the world for its size, had the support of Spitfires against enemy fighters. Sun 12 Dec

Raising the Siege – Duce yields to the Army. *(Sunday Times of Malta)*

Sun 13 Dec

Malta launched the biggest bombing raid yet on North African docks.

Mon 14 Dec

Last night aircraft of the RNAS attacked a convoy on one of the enemy's main supply routes.

Sat 19 Dec

a.m. Beaufighters and Spitfires on offensive reconnaissance encounter a Junker 88 and a Dornier 24 flying-boat and later a formation of three Heinkel torpedo bombers.

Casualties: *Qrendi*: John Attard (17), Catherine Magro (60), Francis Magro (66), Vincent Sciberras (78); *Siġġiewi*: Philip Camilleri (28).

Sun 20 Dec

The Dominican Fathers of Vittoriosa, after a forced absence of nearly two years, inaugurated their new premises in the Inquisitor's Palace[3] put at their disposal by the Government. Masses were

3 The Inquisitor's Palace or Palazzo del Sant'Uffizio dates back to the sixteenth century. The Inquisition or Holy Office was set up in Malta in

celebrated this morning, and the ceremony of the blessing of the chapel was held this afternoon. The ceremony was conducted by the Prior, Fr Alphonsius Spiteri, OP, in the presence of the Vicar-Provincial, Fr Seraphim Zarb, OP, and was attended by Revd Can. Paolino Galea, DD, Archpriest of St Laurence Parish Church, together with a large congregation. The church and priory of the Dominicans at Vittoriosa had been reduced to a mass of ruins as a result of a direct hit in January 1941. The Friars then took refuge in their priory at Rabat. Preparations were under way to enable them to use St Philip Oratory at Vittoriosa, but before anything could be decided that building too was hit and rendered uninhabitable. The Fathers then proposed the Armoury at Vittoriosa as their next abode. But again an enemy bomb destroyed that part of the Armoury which was to have been used by them. In March 1941 they decided to move temporarily to Birkirkara, but continued in their efforts to return to Vittoriosa. Their wish has now been fulfilled because the Government consented to hand over the historic palace to the Dominicans, who set up a public chapel on the first floor which was blessed today. Meanwhile at Vittoriosa Mass and the Holy Sacraments are celebrated in the Police Chapel by the Archpriest of St Laurence – the only priest in the place to whom is entrusted the parish work of the city.

London. The former Governor of Malta, Lieut. Gen. Sir William Dobbie, in a broadcast to the Maltese people: 'Malta, now enjoys a measure of relief for which we thank God, and Malta is, I know, ready to play its part to the full in the hard time which may still lie ahead.' Tue 22 Dec

A small squadron of enemy fighters come over Malta. Heavy AA barrage ensues. Wed 23 Dec

Malta-based Spitfires intercept an enemy supply ship and a destroyer, escorted by six JU 88s.

Lord Gort to the Civil Government and People of Malta: 'I send my greetings and my good wishes for Christmas. During the past

1562 with the purpose of suppressing heresy.

twelve months Malta has faced many trials which she has borne with fortitude and courage.'

Thu 24 Dec

Christmas Eve.

p.m. Message by Archbishop Dom Maurus Caruana, OSB: 'This is the fourth Christmas that find us engaged in war … Much as every one has desired peace and the cessation of strife, the sequence of events has proved to every one of us the necessity of this war.'

Radiant weather after heavy thunderstorms and torrential rains.

The restored bus service made a lively din at Castile Place and outside Porta Reale. The owner of the petrol pump at Castile Place was doing business for the first time since the blitz, when petrol shortage forced the buses to stop at Portes-des-Bombes.

A great storage dump has been formed and a host of labourers and soldiers were busy amongst the piles of crates loading the lorries and trucks on their way to various distribution centres all over the island.

Skeleton-like horses dragged heavily laden *karrozzini* (cabs) or smiling people up to Porta Reale. As the sun sank, the churches began to fill with the scent of incense and the sounds of chanting soon spread along the streets. In the blitzed Carmelite Church in Old Theatre Street the golden glow at the altar contrasted with the gaunt rent in the roof, through which the first evening stars gleamed in the sky. In the little church of Our Lady of Victory,[4] the baroque interior was lit to a golden colour by the light of the altar candles in their tall silver candlesticks as they shone from amongst the silver figures of saints upon the white and gold-embroidered-vestments of the bowing and swaying clergy. The churches were crowded with kneeling people. Heads and hearts were bowed down, full of hope and gratitude.

Sat 26 Dec

RAF Intruders operating from Malta over Sicily.

4 This church stands on the site where the ceremony of the laying of the foundation stone of Valletta is traditionally believed to have taken place on 28 March 1566.

Tue 29 Dec

Last night RNAS aircraft made a spectacular attack on enemy shipping. A supply ship which was squarely struck, disintegrated in a terrific explosion and a mass of flames.

Wed 30 Dec

Roosevelt's message to Malta: 'The mighty blows which you and your ships have struck the enemy during the past week have been an inspiration to the people of the United States of America and their armed forces. The last war had its Verdun. The present conflict brought us Stalingrad and the epic struggle of the Battle of Britain. Now Malta, after endless months of sacrifice and valour, strikes back with devastating power of your sailors and aviators to bring us a complete victory in North Africa.'

Thu 31 Dec

RAF reconnaissance aircraft, long-range fighters, Intruders, bombers, and torpedo-bombers have all been active throughout yesterday. Torpedo-bombers made an attack on a convoy steaming south from Sicily. The convoy was illuminated with flares and attacked in spite of heavy fire from the escorting destroyer. Other

An enemy sweep on Grand Harbour.

RNAS aircraft attack two enemy ships. RAF Intruders were active over enemy aerodromes in North Africa and Sicily and barracks lying in the same vicinity. Our aircraft were also on armed reconnaissance patrols for enemy shipping, anti-submarine patrols. and offensive sweeps.

Today's leader of the *Times of Malta* is entitled: 'The Verdict of 1942' – 'The year 1942 will live in history as the year in which the Axis lost the war.'

HE Field-Marshal Viscount Gort speaks to the people in an end-of-the year message: 'I have come to the microphone tonight, the last night of a year which has brought not only great trials, but also great glory to Malta, to wish you all, fighting Services and citizens alike, good fortune in 1943 ... May the year which begins tomorrow carry us far along the road which leads to the portals of victory! Let us go forward with confidence into 1943.'

Viscount Gort left Malta for Gibraltar for urgent consultation with the British Ambassador in Madrid, Sir Samuel Hoare, American Army Generals, and the Governor of Gibraltar, Gen. Macfarlane.

HH Vice-Admiral Ralph Leatham, KCB administers the Government as the Governor's Deputy during Viscount Gort's absence.

AD 1943

January – April

New Year's Day. Fri 1 Jan

The *Times of Malta*: 'We wish all our readers a Victorious New Year.' Today's leader of the *Times of Malta* entitled "Welcome to 1943".

'Tenacity and endurance have been virtues displayed in abundant manner in Malta since the war began, and especially during the year which has just passed away ... 1943 now breaks with greater promise than ever. A hold has been secured upon the 'bellowing enemy', and, although a stern fight might still be ahead, the quarrel will be dragged down into utter defeat.'

The Pope has set aside the sum of £5,000 to help the rebuilding of the damaged churches of Malta.

In December 1942 fines to a total of £970 were inflicted at a sitting of the Magistrates Courts on one single day. Four persons who made a false declaration in connection with registration under the Rationing Regulations were fined £50 each, and three persons who failed to report that a member of the family had left the house were each fined a similar amount.

London. This year's New Year's Honours include: VC – Field Marshal General Lord Gort, governor of Malta; OBE – Prof. Victor Vassallo, resident doctor at the hospital for mental diseases.

The Christmas and New Year School holidays are extended because of an outbreak of poliomyelitis or infantile paralysis. Sat 2 Jan

The General Officer Commanding the Troops, Major General R. Mack Scobie, CB, CBE, MC, was present at the passing-out parade of the University class at Fort Ricasoli, which was watched by a number of friends and relatives of those taking part. The 80-strong parade, under the command of Capt. T. Page, RA, the Chief Instructor, comprised students of the Royal University of Malta, who had been undergoing an intensive three month course at the RMA Depot at Ricasoli. A number of these students will enter the Faculty of Medicine at the University and the others will continue their military training as officers or in specialist employment in the ranks. The GOC was met on his arrival at the Fort by the CRA Major General C.M. Christie, MC; the Hon. Prof. R.V. Galea, OBE, ACE, Rector of the University; and Brig. W.E. Walter-Symons, MC,

Commander Fixed Defences, and proceeded to the Saluting Base where he received the General Salute. He then inspected the parade which afterwards marched past the Saluting Base to the sound of the RMA Band. In his address, the GOC said: 'Some of you are now to take up your University Courses and others are destined to become officers, but all, I feel sure, have benefited by this course. A period of military training for those who are young and receptive, even if it is only a short one, is always of benefit to the manhood of a country. It tends to promote regular habits, smartness, a sense of discipline, comradeship and self reliance ... I congratulate you very heartily on your bearing and turn-out today.'

Tue 5 Jan

This afternoon our Beaufighters on patrol destroy a Heinkel bomber. Our Intruders continue intercepting enemy JU 52 transport aircraft. More attacks carried against enemy installations in North Africa.

Cairo. Lady Tedder, wife of Air Chief Marshal Sir Arthur Tedder, has been killed in a plane crash while returning from a visit to welfare centres in Cyrenaica. There were no survivors of the crash.

Wed 6 Jan

4.30 p.m. A vocal and instrumental concert is held at the La Valette Band Club under the direction of Mro Giuseppe Camilleri.

Official figures released today show that RAF planes based on Malta and the AA defence destroyed more Axis aircraft over and around Malta in 1942 than Fighter Command operating over Britain and the Channel. During the year Malta-based fighters lost 195 aircraft as compared to 733 Axis aircraft destroyed and 261 probables. In addition AA gunners shot down 182 Axis aircraft. This total compares with the numbers of enemy aircraft destroyed over Britain and France by Fighter Command and by AA gunners, a total of 738. Of these 443 were shot down over the French side of the Channel, 118 over Britain and its seaboards by fighters and AA gunners, and 117 by night fighters and AA gunners. During the same period Fighter Command lost 593 aircraft. During 1942 the RAF in Malta also attacked 46 convoys, six single vessels, and five naval forces. They sank, severely damaged or left ablaze 46 ships and damaged about 40 others. RNAS and FAA aircraft hit 37 ships

Strikes from Malta. *(Sunday Times of Malta)*

by bombs or torpedoes, including four cruisers and two destroyers. The grand total of Malta's shipping strikes is 83 ships hit and more than 40 probables. Considering that a medium-sized supply ship carries an equivalent of six large troop trains of munitions and stores, Malta has, during the year, sent to the bottom something like 500 goods trains. As the Axis attempt to neutralize the island, they have dropped 12,000 tons of bombs on Malta. Now that Malta is striking back, 1,500 tons of bombs have already been dropped on North Africa and Sicily. Malta's aircraft are now flying three times as many operational hours as in the most active week during the summer.

Last night RAF Intruders operating from Malta have carried out raids over Sicily and North Africa. Fri 8 Jan

All places of public entertainment, such as cinemas, theatres, dance-halls, and similar establishments are to be kept closed as a measure against the spread of infantile paralysis.

Sat 9 Jan

Off the North African coast our aircraft sighted a JU 88 which was later destroyed following an air combat.

According to a Notice released by Protection Officer to Birkirkara residents, it is desired to ascertain in respect of the Birkirkara District whether there are any orphans who have lost both parents through enemy action or one parent either by sea, abroad, or in any other way or whether there are any orphans outside an Institution.

Sun 10 Jan

Throughout yesterday RAF bombing of military installations in North Africa continued.

a.m. Firing practice from seaward against Filfla Island.

The Infantry in Malta: The Buffs (East Kents) – The King's Own (Lancaster) – The Devons – The Lancashire Fusiliers – The Cheshires – The Hampshires – The Dorsets – The Queen's Own (Royal West Kent) – The Manchesters – The Durhams – The Royal Irish Fusiliers – The King's Own Malta Regiment.

Mon 11 Jan

7.30 a.m. Archbishop Dom Maurus Caruana celebrate Mass at St Gregory's Church, Sliema, to mark the centenary of the coming to Malta of Blessed Emilie de Vialar, foundress of the Congregation of the Sisters of St Joseph of the Apparition.

The Administrative Branch and the Mail Department of the General Post Office are transferred from Ħamrun to the upper floor of the Museum buildings at the Auberge d'Italie, Merchants Street, Valletta, as from today.

Fri 15 Jan

RAF planes from Malta continue in their intensive offensive against positions in North Africa and Sicily.

Sat 16 Jan

Today marks the Second Anniversary of the day that *Luftwaffe* carried out its first mass dive-bombing attack against Malta.

Malta's all-out air offensive has been resumed, pivoting from Tripolitania through Tunisia to Sicily.

4 p.m. The ancient ceremony of the blessing of animals is held in Valletta at the church of Our Lady of Victory. This ceremony goes back to the time of the Order and is held in honour of St Anthony the Abbot. During today's ceremony a few horses and donkeys in their gay trappings, led by their owners, were lined up outside the church, while many children brought their pets, including dogs, cats, a canary, and a guinea pig. Mgr Bonnici, attended by two acolytes, a cross-bearer, and three servers carrying baskets, appeared at the church door. After a short address in Maltese, in which the priest explained the significance of the ceremony, saying that in former days the ceremony was preceded by a horse race and that rusks were also given with the barley, which this year was not possible, the priest blessed the baskets of barley held by the servers. The first blessing was then given, and the token gift of barley was distributed, each owner of an animal receiving a share. The second and third benedictions followed and pictures of St Anthony the Abbot were then distributed to the assembly. Sun 17 Jan

7 a.m. On the initiative of the Confraternity of St Publius of Floriana, the feast of St Publius is today celebrated at the parish church of Naxxar where the statue of St Publius is being kept. Thu 21 Jan

Last night RAF fighter-bombers from Malta continued their offensive with appreciable successes. Sat 23 Jan

Early this morning Malta receives with unbounded enthusiasm the news of the capture of Tripoli by the British Eighth Army.

RAF Spitfires and fighter-bombers from Malta continue their relentless blitz on Italy's railways. Thu 28 Jan

London. The submarine *Porpoise* has returned to Britain after fourteen months in the Mediterranean; she was the first submarine to embark a cargo of petrol and mines. Her supply trips to Malta are recorded by the white bars on her flag, which bears the letters 'P.C.S.z, – 'Porpoise Carrier Service'. She is also one of the Royal Navy's largest mine-laying submarine and has taken her share of the offensive patrols in the Mediterranean. In one patrol she was attacked by 100 depth charges without suffering any casualty.

London. Supplementary Civil Estimates were issued today for over £11,250,000 for Colonial and Middle Eastern Services, of which £10,000,000 is for reconstruction in Malta.

Mon 1 Feb

Enemy aircraft over Malta. Heavy barrage.

For the week ending 2 January, the number of people registered with the Victory Kitchens was 175,536. For the week ending 31 January, the number declined to 20,000.

Thu 4 Feb

It is officially reported that the enemy in 1942 has dropped 12,300 tons of bombs on Malta, mainly on airfields, Naval Bases, and Harbour installations.

Fri 5 Feb

Sig. Mussolini has dismissed his Foreign Minister, Count Ciano.

Tue 9 Feb

Francis Borg, 5, finds an anti-personnel bomb at Siġġiewi and gives it to his brother Emmanuel, 11. The bomb explodes killing the two brothers and Karmenu Cutajar, 7, and Salvu Saliba, 12, and injuring seven other persons, one of whom, Indrì Xerri, 56, seriously.

Wed 10 Feb

Feast of St Paul Shipwrecked in Malta.

The feast of St Paul's shipwreck is celebrated at the Collegiate church of St Paul in Valletta. The statue[1] and relic[2] of the Apostle are carried in solemn procession through the main streets of the City.

It is officially disclosed that in night attacks during January, Malta-based aircraft sank four enemy supply ships and damaged two others; six more ships were hit by torpedoes. Other aircraft operating by day shot up and damaged three small supply ships, five schooners, and six other craft, all off the North African coast. Our fighters and Intruders destroyed or damaged fourteen trains

1 The statue, carved in wood, dates back to 1659, and is attributed to the Maltese sculptor Melchiorre Gafà.

2 The relic consists of part of the right wristbone of the Apostle Paul.

in Tunisia, Sicily, and Italy, bringing the total of railway engines shot up in these areas to 33 up to the end of January. During the same period, our aircraft destroyed 6 enemy planes, with five others probables. The total of enemy aircraft destroyed by our fighters was thus brought up to 962 destroyed, 336 probables, and 873 damaged. Our Intruder fighters kept up the offensive over Sicily.

Casualties: *Gżira*: Paul Camilleri (–); *StJulian's*: Dominic Darmanin (–); *Żurrieq*: Anthony Sacco (18). Thu 11 Feb

This morning a private graduation ceremony marking the conclusion of the Academic Course of Laws 1939–43 is held at the Jesuits' Church in Merchants Street, Valletta. The scene was reminiscent of pre-war days, though in much reduced form. The old spirit was revived and the large attendance indicated the gradual return to normal times. The students sang the University anthems as they came down in procession from the University building into the church. Mass was celebrated by Mgr Emanuel Galea, Titular Bishop of Tralles, Dean of the Faculty of Theology. Sat 13 Feb

There is an appeal in the Press for games, magazines, and other reading material for distribution to men of an HAA battery stationed in a lonely part of the island.

Casualties: *Sliema*: Aristide Formosa (–); *Vittoriosa*: John Boxall (42); *Żejtun*: Saviour Saliba (50). Sun 14 Feb

London. The Colonial Secretary, Mr Stanley, informed the House of Commons that he is not yet able to make a statement regarding the rebuilding of Malta after the war as, under the conditions of active warfare, there had been little opportunity to prepare detailed plans. He gave an assurance that the preservation of historic monuments and buildings would receive most careful consideration. Wed 17 Feb

London. Lord Gort, after seeing the film *Malta George Cross*, was presented by Sir Arnold Bax, Master of the King's Musick, with the original score of the accompanying music he had specially composed Fri 19 Feb for the film. The manuscript bears the inscription: 'This original MS of the music specially written for the film 'Malta G.C.' is dedicated to the heroism of the Maltese People by the composer, Sir Arnold Bax, Master of the King's Musick.' Sir Arnold added in his own handwriting: 'To heroic Malta G.C. from Arnold Bax.' Lord Gort, accepting it on behalf of the People of Malta said: 'Times have changed. Now, the garrison, the Royal Navy, Army, Royal Air Force, and citizens alike, look forward keenly to the part Malta's destiny will demand of her in the days to come. Eager and resolute George Cross Malta stands prepared.' The presentation was attended by former governors of Malta: Gen. Sir John Du Cane,[3] Gen. Sir Charles Bonham Carter,[4] and Gen. Sir William Dobbie.[5]

Mon 22 Feb

Casualty: *Valletta*: **Francis** Pxinga (56).

RAF torpedo-bombers from Malta strike at a very large enemy tanker off Sicily. 3,000,000 gallons of Axis petrol go up in flames.

Casualty: *Gudja*: **Mary** Ellul (13).

London. A posthumous mention in dispatches, announced in the *London Gazette*, recalls the bravery and devotion to duty of Capt. George Leslie, hero of the epic journey of a Malta-bound convoy last August. His ship was hit by an enemy torpedo and rapidly started sinking. All his crew was rescued, except Capt. Leslie, who preferred to go down with the vessel.

Sun 28 Feb

Casualty: *Żabbar*: **Carmel** Ebejer (24).

Our fighter-bombers attack a factory in Sicily with bombs and cannon fire. AJU 88 and a JU 52 are destroyed during the operation.

The Supreme Naval Command in the Mediterranean, Admiral Sir Andrew Cunningham, and the C-in-C, Levant, Admiral Sir Henry Harwood, have been conferring in Malta with the Flag Officers in

3 Governor of Malta 1927-1931.

4 Governor of Malta 1936-1940.

5 Governor of Malta 1940-1942.

charge of Malta, Vice-Admiral Sir Stuard Bonham Carter and Vice-Admiral Sir Ralph Leatham.

Message from Stalin to Lord Gort: 'There is not the slightest doubt that the gallant defence of Malta has played a great part in the offensive against the common enemy. Please convey to the garrison and population the fighting greetings of the Red Army.'

RAF fighter bombers from Malta attack Comiso aerodrome. One ME 109 damaged. Mon 1 Mar

This morning the alert sounded but AA artillery did not engage. Wed 3 Mar

The War Time Gang are holding a Grand Dance today at the Odeon Theatre, Ħamrun.

The Command Recruiting Office at 8, Don Rua Street, Sliema, will today close and re-open at Fra Diego Institute, Ħamrun, on 6 March (Tels. Fortress l and Central 4062). Thu 4 Mar

RAF fighters operating from Malta destroy a JU 88 over the sea and a reconnaissance aircraft destroy a JU 5 2. Torpedo bombers attack a convoy in the Central Mediterranean. A hit is seen to cause fire on a large supply ship.

The first issue of shoes applied for under the priority scheme will be made in the next few days. The Clothing Board is vetting the applications received since requests are much more than the stocks available, and it is therefore not possible to meet in full all the applications submitted. In the case of shoes for men, it is only possible to supply 20% of the applications, in that of shoes for ladies about 40%, and in the case of children 55%. To ensure a fair and equitable distribution, and in order that each applicant may receive a permit for a pair of shoes, in respect of at least one member of his family, the Board has decided to meet, in the first instance, all requests made for one pair only, irrespective of whether the shoes are required for a man, woman, or child. The balance left will be distributed as fairly as possible amongst all applicants, and in the case of children permits for one half of the quantity applied for will Sat 6 Mar be issued. Prices per pair: Men – £2 5s.; Women – £2 2s.; Ladies' sandal shoes, not with leather, £l 6s.; Youths and Maids – £l 12s.; Children – sizes 2/5 – 10s., 6/10 – 15s., 1 1/l – £1.

Mon 15 Mar

Malta's fighter bombers scored five ship hits over the last two nights. Von Arnim's Tunisian supplies are suffering the same fate as Rommel's.

a.m. Malta's part-time soldiers paraded to be reviewed by Brig. F. Brittorous at Rabat. They included platoon from Rabat, Dingli, Imtarfa, Santa Caterina, and Baħrija.

p.m. Governor Gort has returned to Malta from Britain. He has been absent from the island since 31 December 1942.

Wed 17 Mar

St Patrick's Day. Early this morning spread the news of the death of Cardinal Hinsley, Archbishop of Westminster, who died in his country home at Buntingfor, Hertfordshire.

Malta witnesses its first Naval Parade of the war when Naval personnel took part in a route march. Field-Marshal, Viscount Gort took the salute at the Palace Square. The parade marched off, with the massed bands leading. The route covered the Floriana Granaries – Kingsway – the Palace Square – St Christopher Street – St Paul Street – Bishop Street – Merchants Street – Castile Square – Duke of York Road – and back to Floriana Granaries.

The 2nd Bn the Royal Irish Fusiliers celebrated the feast of St Patrick in the traditional manner by distributing shamrock and attending a church parade. The battalion paraded to Naxxar Parish Church where Mass was celebrated by Revd B. Navin, SCF. After the Gospel Fr Anwyl, CF gave a short homily on the life of St Patrick. With the prayer for the King and the singing of the hymn 'O Glorious St Patrick' the Church service came to an end and the battalion marched back to billet to the skirl of its regimental marches by the drums and pipes.

p.m. The Governor attends the first performance of the film *Malta George Cross* at the Manoel Theatre.

Thu 18 Mar

Today marks the second anniversary of the formation of the Third Light AA Regiment of the Seventh Light AA Brigade. It was formed under the command of Lieut. Col. E.J. Salomone, OBE, who had relinquished his post as ADC to the Governor to take over the command.

Our fighter bombers attack Comiso aerodromes. Our torpedo bombers, escorted by long-range fighters, make a daylight attack on an enemy convoy off the south-eastern coast of Italy. The convoy was heavily escorted by German fighters. One Messerschmitt 110 was destroyed.

Mon 22 Mar

Our Intruders carry out night attacks on enemy rail communications in Southern Italy and Sicily. Trains, railway stations, and shipping suffer damage by cannon fire.

Wed 24 Mar

a.m. The Archbishop of Malta Dom Maurus Caruana assists at a High Mass de Requiem for the repose of the soul of the late Cardinal Hinsley at St John's Co Cathedral. The Bishop of Gozo, Mgr Michele Gonzi, was also present.

Thu 25 Mar

A squadron of enemy fighters flew over Malta. One ME 109 was shot down. A second alert followed. Heavy AA artillery fired pointer rounds.

Malta's Intruders bring the total of trains destroyed in Sicily and Southern Italy to 117 this year.

Fri 26 Mar

a.m. A simple but impressive ceremony at Wardija, when the 2nd Heavy Anti-Aircraft Regiment of the Royal Malta Artillery is consecrated to Our Lady of Victories. The parade of fifty men was under the command of Lieut. Agius, MC, while Lieut. Dunbar-Vella was second in command. In the courtyard, the Guard of Honour, composed of men of the 6th, 7th, and 9th Batteries of the Regiment, was drawn up in line. A small group of officers and their guests were assembled outside the tiny chapel. Major Gen. Christie, CRA and Acting GOC Malta, arrived attended by Lieut. Col. Weldon. Almost immediately afterwards Bishop Galea arrived, wearing his

Hitting Out! *(Sunday Times of Malta)*

magenta robes and biretta and lace chasuble. These distinguished visitors were received by Lieut. Col. Sammut. Gen. Christie inspected the Guard of Honour, while the Band of the RMA played a salute. The ceremony then moved to the small chapel dedicated centuries back to St Simon. Twenty candles gleamed on the altar which was decorated with arum lilies and blue irises. The sermon was delivered by Bishop Galea who referred to the fitting choice of the feast of the Annunciation for this ceremony of Dedication to the Blessed Virgin. The sermon was followed by the Act of Consecration. The Blessed Sacrament was then carried from the chapel to the roof of the headquarters, the canopy being carried by Col. Dunkerley (1st Coast Regt), Col. Salomone (3rd LAA Regt), Col. Ferro (5th Coast Regt), and Col. Terreni (11th HAA Regt RMA[T]) while Col. Sammut carried the *ombrellino*. Fr H. Born gave the benediction of the Blessed Sacrament which was followed by a fanfare of trumpets. The ceremony ended with the playing of the Maltese Anthem, followed by *God Save the King*.

Sat 27 Mar

The original manuscript of the music specially written for the film *Malta George Cross* by Sir Arnold Bax has been handed by HE Viscount Gort to the Librarian of the Royal Malta Library for safe-keeping.

Sun 28 Mar

The Home Guards of Żebbuġ and Siġġiewi held a parade at Siġġiewi; inspection by Brig. F. Brittorous, DSO, MC.

Tue 30 Mar

As from today the ration of cigarettes will be increased from 50 to 70 cigarettes per week. Pipe-smokers will not be entitled to the ration of cigarettes in case they register for pipe tobacco. The weekly ration of pipe tobacco will be 2 oz.–, or a 4 oz.– tin per fortnight.

Wed 31 Mar

One alert was sounded but no engagement reported.

Fri 2 Apr

London. The British Submarine flotilla operating from Malta has during the past two years sunk a total of 82 Axis ships, including 12 warships. The flotilla's record in the dangerous Mediterranean waters is two battleships torpedoed; four cruisers sunk; and several more damaged; eight destroyers sunk; 70 merchantships, including six liners, sunk, and others damaged. The flotilla commander Capt. G.W.W. Simpson gave these figures today. He added: 'In the two years I was at Malta, we sank about half-a-million tons of Axis shipping, the majority carrying supplies to North Africa.'

Sat 3 Apr

Today morning the Royal Malta Artillery held a ceremonial parade to mark the first anniversary of the assumption of the Colonelcy-in-Chief of the Regiment by HM the King. Representative detachments of the various RMA Regiments and Batteries took part. Brig. AJ. Gatt QBE, MC, Colonel Commander, took command of the parade. Then Lord Gort inspected the Corps at the Floriana Parade Ground. The Corps marched through Kingsgate and down Kingsway preceded by the RA (Malta) Band. They marched past the Governor who took the salute on the Palace Square.

Detachments taking part were: 1st Coast Regt. under Lieut. Col. A.J. Dunkerley, 11th HAA Regt. under Lieut. Col. J. Terreni, OBE;

2nd HAA Regt. under Lieut Col. J.A. Sammut; 3rd LAA Regt. under Lieut. Col. E.J. Salomone, OBE; 5th Coast Regt under Lieut. Col. H.A. Ferro; 8th S/L Battery under Major H.R. Micallef; 5th HAA Battery under Major L. Mifsud; and the 14th HAA Battery under Major F. Amato-Gauci. This was the first time the RMA paraded as a Corps since its expansion in 1939. The Corps then proceeded to Upper St Elmo where the officers and men toasted the health of their Colonel-in-Chief, HM the King. Within St Elmo's bastions Brig. Gatt mounted a dais and delivered a short address in Maltese. (Translation): 'This Corps was raised in 1800, soon after the British troops landed in Malta. Its title and its establishment have been changed several times since, but the history of the Corps has been unbroken ... It is the duty of every member of the Regiment to do his utmost to live up to the very high standard which such an honour [Colonelcy-in-Chief by HM the King] demands, an honour which is coveted by all regiments.'

Mon 5 Apr

a.m. A small squadron of enemy aircraft flies over Malta. During a second alert heavy AA artillery fired pointer rounds.

p.m. At the British Institute a lecture was given by the distinguished historian and biographer Philip Guedalla on 'Modern Biography'.

Thu 8 Apr

As from today men over 60 will be allowed a ration of ¾ *ratal* of bread per day.

The New House – Draper and Hosier in Valletta displayed this sign on a board on his premises:

'Blitzed three times
Back I came
Three Times More?
Shall do the same!'

Sat 10 Apr

a.m. Our Spitfires on an offensive sweep destroyed a JU 88 of Pantelleria. Malta Mosquitoes over Catania aerodrome.

Sun 11 Apr

Malta fighter-bombers operating attack Lampedusa. Aircraft of the Royal Navy Air Service (RNAS) score hits on a supply ship off the Tunisian coast.

The Governor, accompanied by his Chief of Staff, Capt. A.W. Clark, DSO, RN, returned to Malta this evening, after a five-day visit to North Africa. Lord Gort stayed for two days with the British Resident Minister, the Rt. Hon. Harold Macmillan, at Algiers, where he called on General Eisenhower, the Allied Force Commander-in-Chief; Admiral Sir Andrew Cunningham, British Naval Commander-in-Chief in Mediterranean, and other senior officers. In Algiers, Gen. Giraud gave a luncheon party in Lord Gort's honour, when they were able to renew a long-standing acquaintance which began before the war. Gen. Giraud commanded the 7th Army which was on Lord Gort's left during the campaign in France. HE subsequently went to the headquarters of Gen. Sir Harold Alexander, Deputy C-in-C; he also made visits to the Front and had the opportunity of acquainting himself with some of the British and American forces now engaged in the advance in Tunisia.

Mon 12 Apr

The Military Authorities, jointly with the Malta Police, take steps to enforce curfew most strictly; any person found during prohibited hours in an area to which the regulations apply will be detained by the Police. According to the curfew rules now in force, no one may be on any road bordering an aerodrome or near a military post between the hours of 9 p.m. and 5 a.m.; and no one may be out of doors between the same hours within half-a-mile of the coastline, except in Marsascala, Marsaxlokk, Birżebbuġa, St Paul's Bay, St Julian's, Sliema, Gżira, Msida, Pietà, Ħamrun, Valletta, Marsa, and the Three Cities.

Tue 13 Apr

Extract from the Report (published today) drawn up by the Chief Government Medical Officer, Prof. A.V. Bernard, on the health conditions in Malta for 1941: 'Schemes were formulated during the year to meet the contingency of an invasion or special attack on the island, during which communications between the several districts might become so difficult as to prevent the conveyance of the sick and wounded to hospitals or the dead to ordinary cemeteries. The basic idea was to have a self-contained medical and sanitary service in each town and village. Maternity cubicles in bombproof shelters were established in many of the villages ... The scheme worked satisfactorily, made many mothers happy, and no cases of sepsis occurred. Many of our hospitals were hit by bombs during the year under review [1941]. Very extensive damages were caused to the Leprosy Hospital, the Mental Hospital, and the Central Hospital, and the latter had to be temporarily evacuated.'

Wed 14 Apr

Mgr Francis Spellman, Archbishop of New York and Bishop of the Catholics in the US Army and Navy, arrives on a brief visit to Malta as the guest of the Governor at San Anton Palace. Mgr Spellman was met on his arrival at the airport by Major Gordon Duff, Asst. Military Secretary to the Governor, the Bishop of Gozo Mgr Gonzi, and other personalities.

Thu 15 Apr

Enthusiastic welcome to Archbishop Spellman. He drove from San Anton Palace to St John's Co-Cathedral where he celebrated 7 o'clock

Mgr Francis Spellman, Archbishop of New York, during his Malta visit. Picture shows Bishop Maurus Caruana, Mgr Gonzi, Bishop of Gozo, and Governor Lord Gort.

Mgr Francis Spellman, Archbishop of New York, receives enthusiastic acclamations from the people.

Mass. He was assisted by Revd Fortunato Cachia, chaplain to the Archbishop of Malta, and Mgr G. Xuereb. It was most fitting that Spellman should celebrate Mass in the old conventual church of the Order of St John for His Grace is the Head of the Knights of Malta in America. The lapis-lazuli of the High Altar were hidden behind a blast wall of stone and sandbags; in front, the temporary wooden altar was lit by six candles in silver candelabra, and before it, on its bare steps, the Archbishop knelt in prayer.

Mgr Francis Spellman, Archbishop of New York, receives enthusiastic acclamations from the people.

Later in the day, Spellman proceeded to Palace Square where the RMA Band saluted as he passed by. One of the bandsmen happening to drop a sheet of music, Mgr Spellman quickly retrieved it and handed it back with a smile. The Archbishop was presented with a bouquet of tulips by one of the spectators and then proceeded to the Customs House, crossed the Grand Harbour, past St Angelo and war-scarred Senglea, to the battered Dockyard. He also visited the ruins of the Senglea church dedicated to Our Lady of Victory where he was welcomed by a few hundreds of citizens who have survived the terrific ordeal of the blitz. Throughout the afternoon Mgr Spellman continued his tour of the island and accompanied by Bishop Caruana, he visited the ancient citadel of Mdina and St Paul's Bay, traditionally associated with the Apostle's shipwreck.

Today marks the first anniversary of the award of the George Cross to Malta by HM the King. The George Cross is ceremonially displayed to the People on Palace Square. A Guard of Honour of the RMA, under the command of Capt. A.H. Debono, 1st Coast Regt RMA, paraded on Castile Square, and, preceded by the band of the Regt. marched down Kingsway to the Palace Square where the band played a programme of martial music. Meanwhile four sentries were posted at the four comers of the plinth on which was placed the George Cross. The crowds broke ranks and queued to view the George Cross together with the autograph Letter of HM the King. Throughout the day the sentries were changed every half-hour; these were drawn from Royal Navy, Army (King's Own Malta Regt.), Royal Air Force, Home Guard, Civil Police, and ARP personnel. A musical programme was provided by the band of the RMA, the KOMR, and the Pipers of the 2nd Royal Irish Fusiliers in turn. Beating the Retreat was performed by the Band and Drums of the 2nd Queen's Own Royal West Kent Regiment – the setting sun added lustre to the white parade uniforms. The Palace balcony was draped with the English and Maltese flags and a rich crimson hanging. The Lieutenant Governor and Mrs Campbell, His Lordship the Bishop of Gozo and other personalities took their place on the balcony. The clapping of hands broke out as Mgr Spellman, accompanied by the Archbishop of Malta, appeared on the balcony. As Lord Gort appeared on the balcony, the Band played the National Anthem. Then followed a splendid performance of Beating the Retreat, when the day's anniversary ceremonial was brought to its conclusion.

Fri 16 Apr

Mgr Spellman ends his visit to Malta this morning.

RAF plans operating from Malta continue their offensive against enemy positions in Sicily and North Africa. Sat 17 Apr

Malta Mosquitoes active over Sicily. Wed 21 Apr

Good Friday. Fri 23 Apr

This year unlike the past two years, the faithful could visit the churches both in private groups and in public processions as in peacetime. Good Friday processions were likewise held in many parts of the island. However, only one statue was carried in the procession.

Casualties: *Gozo* (*Xagħra*): Victor Mifsud (7), Emanuel Sultana (5), Francis Sultana (7).

Our fighters destroy a Caproni 313 aircraft off Sicily. The offensive against Sicily continues. Mon 26 Apr

a.m. An American fighter pilot commanding one of the island's Spitfire Squadron shot down the thousandth enemy aircraft (a JU 52) over Malta. Wed 28 Apr

Our fighter bombers hit on an E-boat base in Syracuse. Thu 29 Apr

Because of frequent occurrences of children being killed or injured by tempering with unexploded bombs, there is an urgent warning to children who on no account should touch any of these dangerous missiles. The public is reminded of the presence of numerous unlocated anti-personnel bombs and cannon shells on the island.

9.15 p.m. The air-raid warning sirens are sounded to warn the public in the Sliema– Gżira– Valletta– Floriana– Ħamrun– Marsa and the Three Cities areas to remain indoors or under cover against the danger of falling splinters from an AA artillery barrage. The 'All Clear' is sounded half-an-hour later at the end of the practice. Fri 30 Apr

VICTORY
KITCHEN
V
G.C

AD 1943

May – August

Detachments of the Żejtun and Żabbar Home Guard are inspected by Brig. F. Marshall, DSO, MBE, MC, in Church Square, Żejtun. Sun 2 May

Casualty: *Gudja*: Joseph Farrugia (10).

A football match between the RN Malta Force and the 1st Coast Regiment RMA played at the Empire Stadium for the Victory Cup attracts 14,000 spectators – the biggest attendance at a soccer match in Malta since before the war. The final score: 4 to 2 for the RN Malta Force.

A small squadron of fighters over Malta. Heavy AA artillery engaged the enemy and fired pointer rounds to assist our airborne fighters. Wed 5 May

Malta's bombers continue their relentless hammering of Italian ports. Fri 7 May

The public is warned against thermos-type bombs with delayed action fuses.

To mark the victory of the Allied Forces in North Africa – the capture of Tunis and Bizerta – hundreds of people stood on the Barrakka and the bastions of Valletta and the Three Cities just before noon, awaiting the first notes of the bell from St Angelo, the signal for all churches on the island to ring out a peal of victory. Silent since the outbreak of the war, the bells seemed to manifest the feelings of the people. Sat 8 May

On this occasion of the Allied victories in North Africa, the Governor, in exercise of his prerogative of pardon, has extended a measure of clemency to 141 prisoners at Kordin Civil Prison.

Our fighters destroy a Fieseler Stroch aircraft off Sicily.

Cairo. It is revealed that Malta is being used as a 'service station' for giant American Liberator bombers based in North Africa for bombing military targets.

The main streets of Valletta are crowded with people who have come to celebrate the Allied victory in North Africa, including Sun 9 May

Aftermath of the air-raids.

representatives from the civic band clubs with their respective banners. As the procession moved slowly down towards Palace Square, a shower of flowers drifted on the bandsmen, most of whom were in the uniform of the gallant RMA.A banner carried the words: 'Tunis is ours/This is free/Thanks to our troops/And to Montgomery/ Victory is coming/Victory is near/Mussolini and Adolph/are shaking with fear'. As the La Valette Band reached the Palace Square, it was applauded by the crowds, and the flags of the United Nations, Britain, and Malta filled the square. Shortly afterwards, the Lieutenant Governor Campbell, accompanied by other Services personalities, appeared on the Palace balcony. He said: 'People of Malta, His Excellency the Governor, Field-Marshal Lord Gort (cheers) has asked me to tell you how very sorry he is that he is not able to be with you today. He has had to leave the island for a few days in order to attend a Conference. Praise be to God that we can stand here today and rejoice together over the glorious victories of the Allied Armies. (applause) Tunis and Bizerta have fallen ... Malta has played a glorious part in these victories. First as a besieged fortress she formed a most vital outpost of defence. Recently she has joined in the glorious offensive. (cheers) Submarine, planes, and the fleet operating from Malta have dealt blow after blow. (prolonged applause)'

Two alerts over Malta; During the second one heavy AA artillery was put up.

Casualty: *Siġġiewi*: Lawrence Vassallo (9).

It is officially disclosed that the Governor has left Malta to attend an important conference of Military representatives in Cairo. Mon 10 May

Two CANT seaplanes, a Junker 52, and three Messerschmitt 210s were destroyed by our Spitfires over Sicily.

A man is sentenced to 18 months' imprisonment with hard labour for theft of oranges from a garden at Mosta.

Malta Spitfires escort American Liberators on a bombing mission over Sicily. Wed 12 May

The Government is actively engaged in the consideration of post-war problems. Town planning, buildings, and reconstruction must necessarily be commenced immediately the war is over and for this purpose all kinds of machinery will be required. In order to be prepared for the commencement of this work, details are required of all available machinery in the island, such as hoisting equipment, drilling machines, stone-breakers, and crushing concrete mixers, elevators, and engine-driven machinery for all kinds of wood work, tool-making, road construction, etc. This Census of Machinery is being carried out up to Monday 24 May.

The Military Authorities give urgent notice that certain areas of Malta are to be rendered dangerous by operations to be carried out immediately. The areas affected are Wied Żnuber (south of Ħal Far) and Wied ilBassasa, in both places from the water-line to a distance 200 yards inland.

Fri 14 May

Lord Gort returns to Malta.

Casualty: *Qormi*: Carmel Mifsud (35).

Sat 15 May

Our fighter bombers attack Comiso. Our long-range fighters destroy a Dornier 24 flying-boat.

A new aerodrome at Safi is inaugurated by Governor Gort. A Guard of Honour formed by the Royal Air Force regiment, under the command of Squadron Leader A.B. Wyndham Thomas, gave the Royal Salute as HE arrived. The parade, which included detachments of Service and civilian units who had helped in constructing the aerodrome, was under the command of Wing Commander L.B. Westmacott, DFC; large crowds of villagers gathered from the neighbourhood to witness the ceremony. HE then inspected the parade. Gort's speech: 'It was on 10 November last year that we assembled at Qrendi for the opening ceremony of an aerodrome which we had built during the months when the siege was pressing hard upon us, when our stomachs were empty, but our spirits were high. On that occasion, I remarked that we could look forward with confidence to the day when Malta, no longer closely besieged, would become an advanced base for the relentless and remorseless prosecution of war against Italy ... This new aerodrome which I now open is a proof of our preparedness as also of our purposefulness. Therefore to those who have so successfully constructed this aerodrome, to yourself, your staff, the Air Ministry Works Directorate, the contractors, and the personnel who have laboured to such good purpose our thanks go out as well as our congratulations. To those who will service the aircraft operating from Safi, as also to all those who will protect it, we extend our good wishes – we know they will never falter no matter how exacting their duty may prove to be.' As the RAF Ensign was broken on the flagstaff, Lord Gort handed over the aerodrome to Sir Keith Park. The Air Officer Commanding, Malta, replying said: 'It was just about six months ago that in taking over Qrendi aerodrome from HE I promoted that the squadrons at Qrendi will be used offensively. They have been used in the last six months on offensive operations over Sicily and in escorting convoys and protecting Malta. I assure you that the fighter wing that will occupy Safi aerodrome will also be used offensively. This aerodrome has been constructed in record time of two-and-a-half months from the word Works squadron to come to Malta – , the Military Labour Companies, the built by the Royal Engineers Unit, the RAF Works squadron – the first Works Squadron to come to Malta – the Military Labour Companies, the ARP workers, who had put in most excellent work, Maltese workers, and contractors.' Sir Keith inaugurated the new aerodrome by taking-off in a Spitfire.

Two JU 52s and a JU 88 were destroyed by our long-range fighters over Sicily. Mon 17 May

RNAS aircraft operating from Malta last night attacked a convoy between Pantelleria and Marettimo. Long-range fighters attacked trains near Catanzaro. The offensive continues. Fri 21 May

For the first time since December bombs were dropped on Malta today in an early morning raid. About 36 Focke-Wulf 190 fighter-bombers[1] with an escort of Messerschmitt 109s took part in this

1 Focke-WulfFW-190: single-seat fighter; one of the outstanding aircraft of the war; speed 404 mph; armament: two 7.92 mm machine-guns, four

attack. Heavy and light AA artillery engaged. The attacks were mainly concentrated on airfields.

Sat 22 May

a.m. Alert sounded. Heavy AA engaged.

Michael Mifsud, a master mason in the Demolition and Clearance Department, has been awarded the British Empire Medal. He has served in the Cottonera District since the commencement of the war and has on a number of occasions saved, at a great risk to himself, persons who had been buried under debris. On one occasion he rescued a boy who was buried besides a bomb which exploded just after he had succeeded in his rescue work.

Mon 24 May

The air-raid warning sounded. Heavy AA artillery engaged.

It is rumoured that the Commander-in-Chief Mediterranean Admiral of the Fleet, Sir Andrew Cunningham, is in Malta and has called on the Governor.

Tue 25 May

Alerts sounded twice. Heavy barrage put up.

Our aircraft lay mines in enemy waters.

Sat 29 May

As from today permission is given for the ringing of church bells throughout the island at 8 a.m., 12 noon, and 7.15 p.m. daily until further notice. The bells will not ring for more than three minutes on each occasion and so will not be confused with the invasion warning.

Lord Gort visits Gozo. On arrival, he inspects a Guard of Honour formed by the 1st Battalion of the King's Own Malta Regiment. He visits several villages and is the guest of Bishop Gonzi at luncheon. The Governor is attended by his personal staff and accompanied by the Commissioner for Gozo, G. Nunn. It is rumoured that the motive of the Governor's visit is the construction of an airfield in preparation for the invasion of Sicily.

---

20 mm cannon.

Six alerts were sounded when formations of JU 88s raided the island. Heavy barrage put up. Sun 30 May

A bomb hit a crowded inhabited area. Heavy barrage put up. Mon 31 May

Casualty: *Valletta*: Gerald Mifsud (27).

The air-raid alert sounded when a small squadron of enemy aircraft flew over. Heavy AA artillery in action. Tue 1 Jun

Today marks the third anniversary of the formation of the Malta Home Guard. Unlike the regular Army, the Home Guard is a national force intended solely for local service.

The Governor has authorized an increased kerosene ration to civilian consumers for the two weeks ending 12 and 19 of June 1943.

A small enemy squadron flew over Malta. Wed 2 Jun

Four alerts were sounded. During one raid a formation of enemy F.W. 190s and M.E. 109s flew over Malta. Heavy AA artillery put up. One of our fighters reported missing. Thu 3 Jun

There is continued shortage of small change in circulation.

It is disclosed today that Marshal of the RAF Viscount Trenchard paid a visit to Malta last week. During the one-day visit he was accompanied by Air Vice-Marshal Sir Keith Park, Air Officer Commanding, Malta AirCommand, and visited Malta's aerodromes. Mon 7 Jun

Enemy formations over Malta. Tue 8 Jun

More raids over Malta. Thu 10 Jun

Today marks the third anniversary when Malta was first attacked by the *Regia Aeronautica*. Fri 11 Jun

Malta's war figures to date:

Killed – 1,185; died of injuries – 394; seriously injured 1,818; slightly injured – 1,889; total killed and died of injuries – 1,579.

Malta planes resume their offensive over Sicily and Italy. Pantelleria surrenders.

Wed 15

Small enemy formations over Malta. Barrage.

Casualties: *Żejtun*: Alfio Testaferrata de Noto (12); *Gozo* (*Kerċem*): Laurence Attard (23).

Meanwhile RAF fighter-bombers continue their offensive over Sicily.

Fri 18 Jun

Governor Gort visits Connaught Hospital (Mdina) and Santo Spirito Hospital (Rabat).

Sat 19 Jun

Enemy planes over Malta.

Mosquitoes operating from Malta continue to harass installations in Sicily.

Message sent by Lord Gort to the Commander, 234 Infantry Brigade, on the Brigade's departure from Malta: 'We have now come to the end of the chapter which records the part that you and the three famous battalions under your command have played in the Siege of Malta.'

Reply to Viscount Gort from the Commander, 234 Infantry Brigade, Brig. F.G.R. Brittorous: 'We will try to maintain not only those traditions but also the very high standard of discipline and courage which you have given us by your example. May we assure Your Excellency that it has been a great privilege to serve Malta under your distinguished command. We are proud of these honours. We leave with regret, tempered only by the knowledge that, in our little way, we are carrying Malta's offensive spirit into other theatres of war.'

Sun 20 Jun

A Royal Visit – HM King George VI in Malta. The cruiser HMS *Aurora* with HM the King on board majestically entered Grand Harbour. When she came into sight past the Lower Barracca, there

Blitz-battered buildings in Valletta.

was an outburst of clapping of hands and waving of handkerchiefs from the crowds that thronged the bastions. The King, clad in white, stood on the bridge of the warship and saluted and acknowledged the cheering. The bugles from Fort St Angelo sounded the Salute. The cruiser then crept forward to her anchorage in the shadow of the blitz-battered walls of St Angelo and Senglea. Meanwhile the steel-helmeted Guard of Honour of the Royal Malta Artillery, under the command of Major H.R. Micallef, drew up at the Customs House and the Band stood with their instruments in readiness. Vice-Admiral Power conducted HE to the waiting launch which made its way slowly out to the anchored cruiser, flying the Royal Standard. There was a tumultuous outburst of clapping and cheering as the pinnance conveying His Majesty approached the Customs House steps, and across the water the newlyrestored bell of St Angelo's historical chapel gave the signal for all the bells of Valletta and the Three Cities to peal forth their welcome. When he came ashore, the King stood saluting, while the Band of the RMA played the National Anthem, and then HE presented Brig. A. Gatt, Colonel Commandant.

King George VI during his visit to blitzed Senglea is accompanied by the Archpriest of Senglea, Can E. Brincat.

The King then inspected the Guard of Honour which was composed of Capt. Micallef-Eynaud and Lieut. J. Agius, as officers, and personnel of the Light and Heavy Anti-Aircraft searchlights and coastal Batteries of the RMA, whose Colonel-in-Chief is His Majesty. Following the inspection, Lord Gort presented the Lieutenant

Governor, Vice Admiral Power, Major General Oxley, Air Chief Marshal Sir Arthur Tedder, and Air Vice-Marshal Sir Keith Park. The open saloon car made its way to Valletta; it passed down Kingsway amidst large crowds. As the King appeared on the balcony of the blitzed Palace, a single uninterrupted roar went up from the crowds. He saluted the crowds to the sound of the Hymn of Malta. In the Red Drawing Room, local personalities were presented to His Majesty. Viscount Gort then conducted His Majesty to the Hall of St Michael and St George, where the George Cross was displayed, with a Guard composed of the Regimental Sergeant Major, RMA, the RSM of the KOMR, and two representatives of the civilian Services. The royal car emerged from the Palace onto Palace Square and through the crowds made its way up Kingsway and then to Senglea. Here His Majesty alighted from his car and proceeded on foot. The Lieutenant Governor presented Revd Emanuel Brincat, Archpriest of Senglea, and Victor Dillon, R.P.O. Senglea. Here was the only city, outside Valletta, where the King stopped. Then the royal car drove through Cospicua, Paola, Marsa, Ħamrun, Birkirkara, Attard, and Rabat. On arrival at Verdala Palace,[2] His Majesty inspected the Guard of Honour formed by personnel of the Buffs Regiment. The tour of the island included the little village of Luqa, whose church steeples have kept watch with the control towers of the nearby aerodrome. The King also visited the aerodrome where he was received by Air Vice-Marshal Sir Keith Park, AOC Malta, and Air Chief Marshal Sir Arthur Tedder, C-in-C Mediterranean, Air Command. He then inspected a Guard of Honour of men of the RAF Regiment. The King's stop at Malta lasted some ten hours.

His Majesty's message:

'It was with great eagerness that I seized the occasion of my visit to North Africa to come to Malta and bring to the Armed Forces and to the Maltese People a message of good cheer on behalf of all other peoples of the British Empire ... I thank the People of Malta from my heart and send them my best wishes for the happier times that surely lie ahead – George R.I."

Poem entitled 'Farewell to the King' by the Gozitan poetess Mary Meylak:

2 This summer residence of Grand Master Loubenx de Verdalle, after whom it is named, was built in 1586.

Say farewell to His Majesty,
A hearty farewell sing!
Now loose your tongue and echo
A farewell to the King!
Your eyes twinkling upon him,
Your beating heart will ring
One lengthy, cheery message,
A farewell to the King!
Each eyelid be a banner
A tiny flappy wing
That bids the biggest welcome
And farewell to the King!
The lips whisper a blessing
While aching heart, like sting,
Is bathing eyes in tears:
Say farewell to the King!
The band is waving farewell,
The mind brings out a string
Of thoughts, of luck and wishes
And farewell to the King!

Mon 21 Jun

Today's leader of the *Times of Malta* is dedicated to 'The King' – 'The personal inspiration with which His Majesty has fortified Malta's spirit was in the consciousness of every one yesterday: as the ship carrying the King entered the Grand Harbour to the cheers of the enthusiastic and delighted onlookers; as His Majesty landed at the Customs House, at the unforgettable scene in Valletta and the unsurpassed welcome accorded His Majesty as he toured the towns and villages of Malta.'[3]

London. Rear-Admiral Sir Edward Neville Syfret has been promoted to Vice-Admiral. Sir Edward, who is 53, has been one of the war's outstanding naval personalities and received the knighthood

3 HM first visited Malta as a midshipman on HMS *Collingwood* in 1913. He was then Prince Albert; he commemorated his visit by planting a tree at San Anton Gardens. His last visit to Malta was in 1927, as a young naval officer in company with Her Majesty the Queen (then the Duke and Duchess of York) aboard HMS *Renown*.

for bravery in getting important convoys through to Malta while commanding cruisers in the Mediterranean.

Algiers. The first Maltese Battalions raised by the British in Tunis parade through the streets of the city.

Malta Spitfires continue to harass the enemy in Sicily. Tue 22 Jun

The public is reminded of the possibility of chemical warfare and gas attacks being adopted by the enemy. A house to house inspection of respirators is carried out.

As from today the sounding of the sirens and the hoisting of the red-and white checked flag will mean the presence of enemy aircraft. The red flag will only be hoisted to notify the possibility of heavy bombing. Thu 24 Jun

Bombs, AA shells, and other missiles which are proving to be fatal to people tampering with them are on view at the Qrendi Police Station today and tomorrow.

Malta Mosquitoes continue their widespread attacks on Sicilian and Italian railways.

Sir Archibald Sinclair, Secretary of State for Air, visits Malta and tours aerodromes. In a short speech to air crews, Sir Archibald said: 'The magnificent defence of Malta was mainly a matter for the Royal Air Force, helped by the fine work of the Army's anti-aircraft gunners. The Army, too, had helped on the aerodrome, while the Royal Navy brought in the supplies and petrol which enabled Sir Hugh Lloyd and Sir Keith Park to sustain the defence. It is my privilege to thank you.'

Exhibitions of bombs, AA shells, and other missiles today at Mqabba Police Station. Sat 26 Jun

A small formation of enemy aircraft over Malta. Barrage.

Exhibition of bombs, AA shells, and other missiles today and tomorrow at Siġġiewi Police Station. Sun 27 Jun

London. A British Liner which survived the famous Malta convoy saga is home after ten months' hazards at sea. The crew are greeted by a message from the Minister for War Transport, Lord Leathers: 'I am most anxious you should realize how much the courage and determination of you and your fellows who sailed in that particular Malta convoy have been admired throughout this country and the Empire.'

Mon 28 Jun

Military exercises over Grand Harbour and Marsamxetto Harbour, Marsaxlokk, and St Paul's Bay. Missiles dropped from aircraft.

Governor Gort visits Bugeja Hospital and Cini Hospital, both at Ħamrun.

5.30 p.m. The rally of the Home Guard of Valletta and Floriana was held opposite the Camerata, Merchants Street, Valletta.

London. Operating from Malta, four minesweepers, the *Speedy*, *Hythe*,

Hebe, and *Rye* are chasing Axis mines. This flotilla helped to clear the mines around Malta to allow the first convoy to pass through.

Tue 29 Jun

Exhibition of bombs, AA shells, and other missiles on view today and tomorrow at Żebbuġ Police Station.

A small formation of enemy fighters flew over Malta. Heavy barrage. Casualty: *Żebbuġ*: Catherine Vella (17).

Thu 1 Jul

Exhibition of bombs, AA shells, and other missiles today and tomorrow at Qormi Police Station.

Malta Spitfire-bombers over Sicily. A Macchi and a number of Messerschmitt 109s are destroyed.

Fri 2 Jul

Our fighter bombers attack Biscari aerodrome.

London. The *London Gazette* announces the award of the British Empire Medal (Civil Division) to Faustino Pace, master of the victualling yard craft at HM Dockyard in Malta. The citation says that by the courage and devotion of the crews of the victualling yard craft the watering and provisioning of HM's ships and merchant vessels have been carried out despite the many severe air-raids Malta has experienced. As master of one of the craft primarily concerned on this work; Mr Pace has shown 'a devotion to duty under extremely trying conditions and has rendered exceptional service'.

London. From 1939 to end of June 1943 Axis aircraft lost as against RAF aircraft in various war zones are:

	Axis	RAF
Great Britain	4,201	900
Europe	1,857	5,357
Middle East (incl. Malta)	3,500	1,977

Losses in Tunisia in 1942–43 amounted to 2,231 Axis aircraft against 795 of the North West African air forces; losses in the Far East, India, and Burma during the same period were 4,042 Axis against 149 RAF aircraft.

Bastions scarred by bombs.

Sat 3 Jul

Exhibition of bombs, AA shells, and other missiles from today to next Monday at Rabat Police Station.

Sun 4 Jul

One alert sounded when a small formation of unidentified aircraft approached the island.

Our Spitfires escorted bombers of the USAAF on bombing missions over Sicily.

Tue 6 Jul

Five enemy fighters – Macchi, Messerschmitts, and Focke-Wulf 190s – destroyed by Malta's Spitfires over Sicily.

Wed 7 Jul

Exhibition of bombs, AA shells, and other missiles today at Dingli Police Station.

a.m. At a specially convened sitting of the Council of Government held at the Palace, Governor Gort announces the policy of His Majesty's Government to restore Responsible Government to Malta, as early as possible after the cessation of hostilities. In his address, the Governor said: 'It is my honour to read to the Council an announcement which is being made simultaneously by the Secretary of State for the Colonies to the House of Commons … Since the present Constitution of Malta was inaugurated in 1939 the Fortress has successfully withstood a siege of two-and-a-half years. During the siege, the island was subject to heavy and sustained attacks from the air and to a good shortage of increasing gravity. By their steadfastness and fortitude under the severe hardships thus occasioned, the people of Malta, together with its gallant garrison, rendered service of incalculable value to the Allied cause. His Majesty's Government has noted with particular satisfaction that throughout the whole of this period the Council of Government continued to discharge its normal functions in relation to legislation and the discussion of public affairs. For more than ten years, between 1921 and 1933, the people of Malta enjoyed full legislative and administrative responsibility under the Crown in the conduct of their internal affairs, but the control of Naval and Military Services and of all matter appertaining to the position of Malta as an Imperial Fortress or otherwise affecting Imperial interest or policy were reserved to the Imperial Government. It is the policy of His Majesty's Government that Responsible Government in the same sphere should again be granted to Malta after the war.'

Malta Spitfires escorted American bombers on missions over Sicily. One Messerschmitt 109 was destroyed.

Mr C. Micallef, who was missing on 16 February 1942, is now reported to be a prisoner-of-war interned in Java Camp.

Today's editorial of the *Times of Malta* is entitled 'Self-Government'. – 'The new Constitution will embody Responsible Government in the same sphere as that enjoyed between 1921 and 1933, thereby granting to the Maltese people full legislative and administrative responsibility under the Crown in the conduct of their internal affairs. Lord Gort's announcement is an outstanding landmark in Malta's constitutional history, and reminiscent of that made by Lord Plumer some 23 years ago, when the Milner-Amery Constitution was announced in 1921.' Thu 8 Jul

Exhibition of bombs, AA shells, and other missiles today and tomorrow at Għaxaq Police Station.

Sicily is invaded by Allied troops. The first stage in battle of Europe. Sat 10 Jul

Today's leader of the *Sunday Times of Malta* is entitled 'Battle for Sicily'.– 'The battle for the liberation of Europe has commenced with troops from the United Kingdom, the United States, and Canada invading Sicily.' Sun 11 Jul

Following are the Senior Officers commanding the present combined operations in the Mediterranean:

Admiral of the Fleet Sir Andrew Cunningham Bart, C-in-C Mediterranean; Admiral Sir Bertram Ramsey, Naval Commander; Gen. Sir Harold Alexander, Deputy C-in-C Allied Forces; Gen. Sir Bernard Montgomery, GOC British Forces; Air Chief Marshal Sir Arthur Tedder, Air C-in-C Mediterranean Air Command; Vice-Admiral Henry K. Hewitt, Naval Commander, commanding US Naval Forces, Mediterranean; Lieut. Gen. George S. Patton Jr., Commanding General American Force; Lieut. Gen. Carl

Clearing away heavy masonry after bomb hits.

Spaatz, Commanding General NW, AAF; Air Marshal Sir Arthur Conningham, NW Africa, Tactical Air Force; Major Gen. James Doolittle, Commanding General, Strategical Air Force; Air Vice-Marshal Sir Hugh P. Lloyd, AOC, NW Africa Coastal Air Force.

Exhibition of bombs, AA shells, and other missiles today and tomorrow at Kirkop Police Station.

Tue 13 Jul

Exhibition of bombs, AA shells, and missiles between today and Thursday at Tarxien Police Station.

Wed 14 Jul

Mr Carmelo Borg is reported prisoner-of-war at La Grande Caserne, St Denis (Seine), France.

Thu 15 Jul

Malta Mosquitoes and Beaufighters engage enemy aircraft. A Junker 88 which was carrying torpedoes, exploded after receiving one burst from a Mosquito. A Heinkel 111 was also reported destroyed.

Exhibition of bombs, AA shells, and missiles between today and Sunday at Żejtun Police Station. Fri 16 Jul

Exhibition of bombs, AA shells, and missiles today at Kalkara Police Station. Tue 20 Jul

Enemy aircraft made a concentrated attack today. HAA and LAA batteries engaged. Bombs fell in widespread areas causing considerable civilian damage.

Casualties: *Qormi*: Philip Bonnici (38), Carmel Borg (27), John Borg (53), Carmel Cauchi (38), Lewis Psaila (45), Carmel Ellul (18), Joseph Pullicino (27), Jane Scerri (19), Carmel Vella (28), Peter Paul Zahra (54); *Sliema*: Ramiro Floridia (66), Joseph Galea (62), Joseph Vella (53), Lino Vella (1 1); *Valletta*: Carmela Canavaugh (24), Mary Canavaugh (46), Marguerite Scerri (75).

Alert sounded. Heavy barrage put up. Mon 21 Jul

Exhibition of bombs, AA shells, and missiles between today and Sunday at Ħamrun Police Station. Fri 23 Jul

Palermo, one of the principal ports of Sicily, falls to the Allies.

Enemy aircraft make sharp raids on the island. Heavy barrage of fire. Three enemy JU 88s and a HE 111 shot down. Sun 25 Jul

Casualty: *Żabbar*: Vincent Attard (86).

Exhibition of bombs, AA shells, and missiles today and tomorrow at Marsa Police Station.

Rome. Proclamation by King Vittorio Emmanuele: 'His Majesty the King Emperor has accepted the resignation of the Duce as Head of the Government, Prime Minister, and Secretary of State, tendered by His Excellency Benito Mussolini. He has appointed as Head of the Government, Prime Minister, and Secretary of State His Excellency, Marshal of ltaly, Pietro Badoglio.'

Tue 27 Jul

Malta-based Boston and Baltimore bombers of the Tactical Air Force give close support to army operations in Sicily.

Fri 30 Jul

Exhibition of bombs, AA shells, and missiles today and tomorrow at Gżira Police Station.

A raid sounded when a large formation of aircraft approached the island.

Heavy barrage put up.

The Pope has sent the sum of £5,000 to the Archbishop of Malta as a contribution towards the relief of the war victims of Malta. In January of this year His Holiness had already sent a contribution of £5,000 for the reconstruction of blitzed churches in Malta.

The public is advised that the smoke screen which is put up over target areas may cause irritation to the nose, eyes or throat, in which case the best thing to do is to cover the face with a moistened handkerchief. The smoke can be dispersed by waving a blanket or a jacket.

Sun 1 Aug

Exhibition of bombs, AA shells, and other missiles between today and Tuesday at Sliema Police Station.

Eisenhower, the Allied C-in-C Mediterranean, arrives in Malta for talks with Field-Marshal Viscount Gort and the Admiral of the Fleet, Sir Andrew Cunningham. Eisenhower's statement: 'The Epic of Malta is symbolic of the experience of the United Nations in this war. Malta has passed successively through the stages of woeful unpreparedness, tenacious endurance, intensive preparation, and the initiations of a fierce offensive. It is resolutely determined to maintain a rising crescendo of attack until the whole task is complete. For this inspiring example the United Nations will be forever indebted to Field-Marshal Lord Gort, the fighting services under his command and to every citizen of the heroic Island.'

Mon 2 Aug

Night fighters from Malta over Sicily. A Junkers 88 and a Messerschmitt 109 are shot down.

FOR SECURITY REASONS THIS COPY MUST NOT BE TAKEN OUTSIDE MALTA

TIMES OF MALTA

The "GEORGE CROSS"

No. 2,478 PRICE 2d. THURSDAY AUGUST 5, 1943 1,433 DAY OF WAR AGAINST NAZISM

EISENHOWER TO GORT'S MALTA

From "Woeful Unpreparedness" To "Fierce Offensive"

GENERAL DWIGHT EISENHOWER, ALLIED COMMANDER-IN-CHIEF, MEDITERRANEAN

THE FOLLOWING HISTORIC STATEMENT WAS MADE IN MALTA ON AUGUST [illegible] BY GENERAL EISENHOWER, THE ALLIED COMMANDER-IN-CHIEF MEDITERRANEAN, WHEN HE ARRIVED HERE FOR TALKS WITH FIELD MARSHAL THE VISCOUNT GORT V.C., AND ADMIRAL OF THE FLEET SIR ANDREW CUNNINGHAM.

JOHN GUNTHER'S EXCLUSIVE STORY OF THE HISTORIC OCCASION UPON WHICH THIS STATEMENT WAS MADE APPEARS ON PAGE 4 OF THIS ISSUE

Eisenhower's Statement

"THE EPIC OF MALTA IS SYMBOLIC OF THE EXPERIENCE OF THE UNITED NATIONS IN THIS WAR. MALTA HAS PASSED SUCCESIVELY THROUGH THE STAGES OF WOEFUL UNPREPAREDNESS, TENACIOUS ENDURANCE, INTENSIVE PREPARATION, AND THE INITIATION OF A FIERCE OFFENSIVE.

"IT IS RESOLUTELY DETERMINED TO MAINTAIN A RISING CRESCENDO OF ATTACK UNTIL THE WHOLE TASK IS COMPLETE. FOR THIS INSPIRING EXAMPLE THE UNITED NATIONS WILL BE FOREVER INDEBTED TO FIELD MARSHAL LORD GORT, THE FIGHTING SERVICES UNDER HIS COMMAND, AND TO EVERY CITIZEN OF THE HEROIC ISLAND."

FIELD MARSHAL THE VISCOUNT GORT, V.C., GOVERNOR AND COMMANDER-IN-CHIEF, MALTA

UNITED STATES AIR OFFENSIVE
FIGURES FOR FOUR WEEKS OVER SICILY

(Reuter's Service)

WASHINGTON [illegible] ... dropped [illegible] tons of bombs, destroyed 342 planes and probably destroyed 94 others, probably sank three ships and damaged ten more with the loss of 100 United States aircraft.

The raid on Rome on July 19 was the heaviest daylight bombing attack of the war. [illegible] heavy bombers and [illegible] medium bombers reached their targets and dropped 1,[illegible] tons of bombs.

Only eight transport planes were lost out of hundreds used for dropping parachute troops and releasing gliders, shortly before dawn on July 10.

General Eisenhower, accompanied by Major-General Oxley, G.O.C. Troops, Malta, inspecting a Guard of Honour at Verdala Palace, shortly after his arrival in Malta.

Fascist Purge
BADOGLIO INVESTIGATING PARTY FORTUNES

(Reuter's Service)

LONDON, August 4.

Rome radio announced today that Marshal Badoglio had ordered an enquiry into the fortunes amassed by the Fascists under the Mussolini regime.

• • •

The Italian news agency says that the Italian Ministry of Education today issued instructions to purge all school books of Fascist propaganda. All University examinations held in Italy in April have been declared invalid "because the examiners were required to belong to the Fascist Party".

Other Rome News - Page 2

THE MALTA FRONT:
LONE RAIDER OVER ISLAND

The following communique was [illegible] ... Heavy Anti-Aircraft Artillery engaged the raider.

FIERCE BATTLE BENEATH ETNA
Inch By Inch Allied Advance
AXIS HAMMERED FROM LAND, SEA AND AIR

(Reuter's Service) ALLIED HEADQUARTERS, NORTH AFRICA, August 4

WITH the Axis given no time to bury their dead, a [illegible] battle is tonight raging along half of the 60-mile front in Sicily from Catania to the [illegible], with 8th. Army artillery literally blasting the Germans from one defended position after another. The Hermann Goering Grenadiers, the 15th. Panzer Division and German parachute units are fighting harder than they have ever fought before and are contesting every step of the Allied advance as British and Canadian troops press steadily towards the Etna foothills. On the 8th Army's left British troops sweeping through Centuripe have substantially [illegible] their bridgehead, opening up an [illegible] threat to Axis lateral communications with Catania round the southern slope of Mount Etna although Catania itself is still held by the Axis in great strength. Following the capture of Troina by the Americans, the whole of the northern wing of the German line [illegible] and the American spearhead has driven deep into the Axis flank between Troina and Mistretta.

ALL-OUT AIR OFFENSIVE:

While Allied warships are [illegible] a non-stop barrage on the [illegible] along the coast and are maintaining a [illegible] Messina Straits, Allied aircraft without [illegible] are maintaining their continuous and deadly [illegible] and strafing of Axis positions dug into the rocky slopes and concealed in lava crevices around the base of Mount Etna.

David [illegible], Reuter's air correspondent at Allied H.Q. [illegible] that the attacks are much determined and are being carried out in greater numbers than any since the [illegible] stages of the Sicilian campaign. In one spot where heavy concentrations of Axis vehicles were located, 80 trucks were destroyed and 100 others were damaged. Every branch of the North-west African Air Forces is taking part in this heavy Sicilian offensive. Coastal Beaufighters have kept up their recent record of getting at least one Axis vessel daily.

WE MAY TRAP 100,000 MEN

An Allied spokesman today said: "If we can cut off the Axis troops before they can make a dash across the Straits of Messina we shall capture about 100,000 men — the Nazi [illegible] and divisions, one Panzer division, one Italian division and units of the toughest fighters in the Nazi army — the parachutists."

(Continued on Page 2, col 2)

STOP PRESS

MOSCOW, August 5. — OFFICIALLY ANNOUNCED RUSSIANS BROKEN INTO OREL. (Reuter).

LONDON, AUGUST 5. — GERMAN NEWS AGENCY ANNOUNCED OREL EVACUATED BY GERMANS. (REUTER).

General Dwight Eisenhower, Allied Commander-in-Chief, Mediterranean, visits Malta.

Wed 4 Aug

The ferry service between Valletta and Senglea and vice-versa resumes today from 6.30 a.m. to 6.30 p.m. The fare will be 1½ d. each way and the public is requested to tender the exact fare. Booklets containing 20 tickets at 2s. 6d. each are obtainable from the cashiers at both land stages. These booklets are also valid for the ferries in Marsamxett Harbour.

Exhibition of bombs, AA shells, and other missiles today at St Julian's Police Station.

Thu 5 Aug

Exhibition of bombs, AA shells, and missiles today at Mġarr Police Station.

Fri 6 Aug

Bombs, AA shells, and missiles on view today and tomorrow at Floriana Police Station.

Weekend mid-day Bus Service is announced as a result of slightly improved stock position of petrol, tyres, etc.

Sun 8 Aug

Bombs, AA shells, and missiles on view between today and Tuesday at Valletta Police Station.

Tue 10 Aug

Malta Mosquitoes over Southern Italy.

London. Field-Marshal Gort is appointed Colonial Commandant of the Honourable Artillery Company in succession to the late Viscount Galway.

Wed 11 Aug

Bombs, AA shells, and missiles on view today at St Paul's Bay Police Station.

Thu 12 Aug

Bombs on view today at Birżebbuġa Police Station.

Mro Paolo Nani has composed a *Requiem Mass* for solos, chorus, and orchestra dedicated to the parishioners of the church of St Paul Shipwrecked, killed during the Valletta blitz.

Fri 13 Aug

Exhibition of bombs, AA shells, and missiles today at Marsaxlokk Police Station.

Sat 14 Aug

Exhibition of bombs today at Żurrieq Police Station.

Sun 15 Aug

Bombs, AA shells, and missiles on view today at Mellieħa Police Station.

Thu 19 Aug

Alert sounded.

With Sicily in Allied hands, the danger of enemy action against Malta has become more remote. In view of this, the ban on the ringing of church bells and also the relaxation of restrictions on the holding of processions are removed.

p.m. General Giraud, the leader of the Fighting Forces of France, in Malta on a private visit to Viscount Gort. Giraud landed at Luqa airfield. The scene at Luqa was one of ceaseless activities; British and American warplanes of every type were landing or taking-off in waves. Air ViceMarshal Sir Keith Park personally supervised the eleventh hour arrangements for Gen. Giraud's reception at the aerodrome. Giraud's plane, an American Mitchell bearing the name 'Baby Alice', made a perfect landing and Giraud took the salute. After the inspection of the Guard, Sir Keith Park introduced to Giraud, M. Xavier Gauthier, *Chevalier de la Legion d'Honneur, Croix de Guerre,* French Consul and Delegate in Malta of the French Committee of the National Liberation, and other personalities. Accompanied by Major Gen. Oxley, Giraud then drove to Verdala Palace, his car flying the French *Tricolor*. He is staying at Verdala as Lord Gort's guest.

Fri 20 Aug

Today's leader of the *Times of Malta* is dedicated to 'General Giraud'. – 'Malta has had the privilege of welcoming many illustrious statesmen and soldiers of the United Nations, but not the least spontaneous and real welcome is that which is extended to General Giraud on his visit to this wartime – and now triumphant – island. Gen. Giraud is welcomed both for the esteem with which he himself is regarded personally, and as Chief of all the French armed forces outside Nazi-occupied Europe. Symbolic of the spirit of the Entente Cordiale are the old bonds of comradeship between Gen. Giraud and Viscount Gort. Both are soldiers of the previous war against Germany, while in the days which preceded the 1940 break-through Gen. Giraud commanded the French Seventh Army on the left of Lord Gort's command.'

Sun 22 Aug

The Stella Maris Band of Sliema performs a set of new marches on the occasion of the feast of Our Lady of the Sea (Stella Maris): *Invasion of Sicily*, *Great Little Island*, *Great Warriors*, all by M. Zammit; *Coronation March*, *Eighth Army on the Move*, by C. Ciappara; *Għal Noto* by F. Camilleri; and *Mare Nostrum* by C. Grech.

Fri 27 Aug

Air-raid alert sounded. Heavy barrage.

Tue 31 Aug

New York. Veterans from the Battle of Malta and the Middle East are among the 350 British officers and men, of a composite anti-aircraft group who paraded up Broadway today for a civic welcome.

AD 1943

September – December

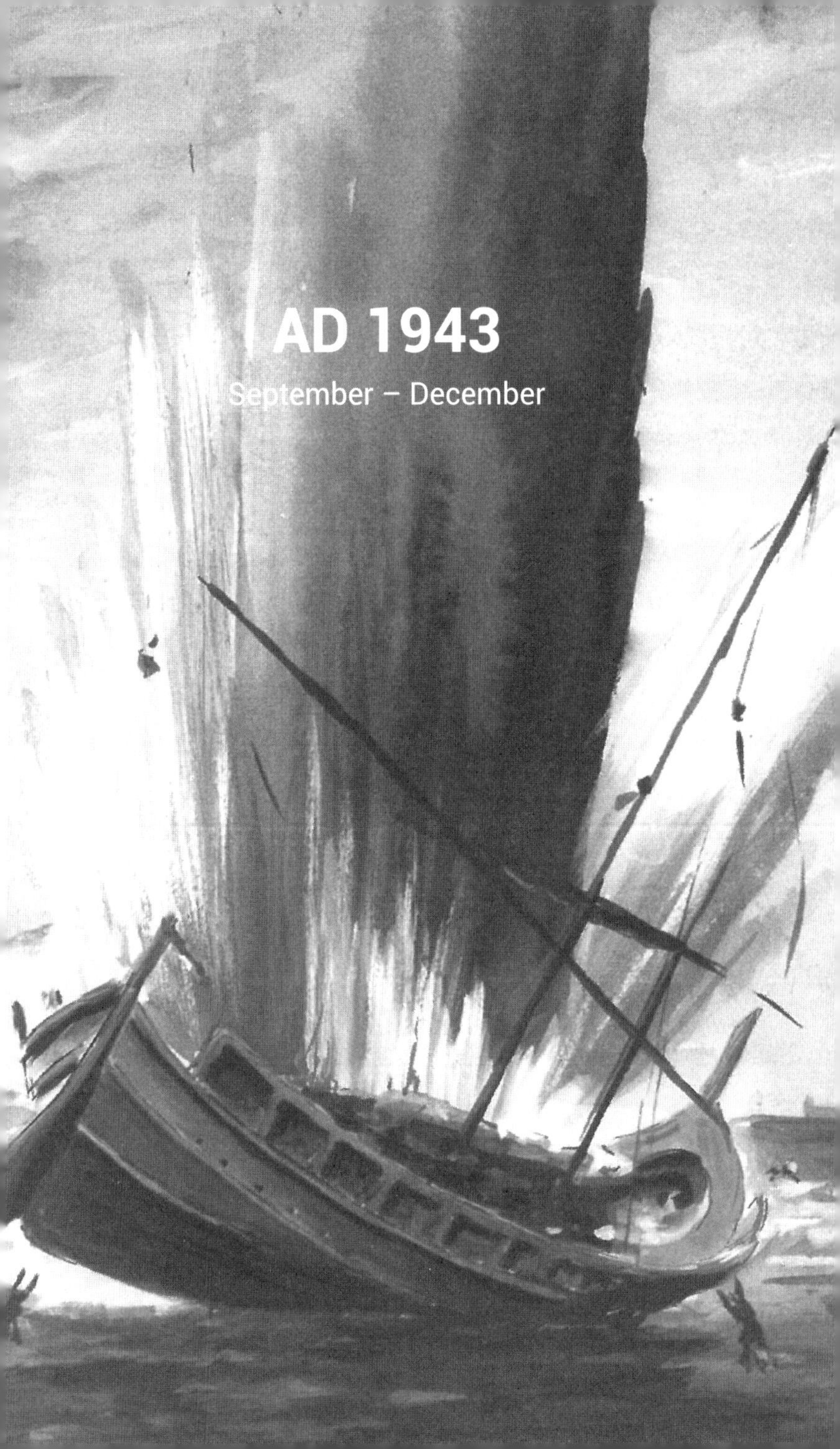

Wed 1 Sep

As from today stevedores, lightermen, and other labourers engaged on the unloading of convoys will no more be issued with tea, since shops around the Grand Harbour will be supplied with coffee and will be able to supply cups of coffee to convoy workers.

London. Flight Lieutenant George Beurling, known as 'Screw Ball' of Malta fame, who has been acting as an instructor at the RAF Air Gunnery School in Britain, has been sworn in as a member of the Royal Canadian Air Force.

Fri 3 Sep

Today's leader of the *Times of Malta* is entitled 'RAF Gift to Malta'. – 'This evening *Faith,* the sole survivor of the Gladiators which met and engaged the full onslaught of the *Regia Aeronautica* in the initial Italian bombing onslaught against Malta, will pass to her rightful place in repository of so much of the island's military history – the Armoury at the Palace, Valletta ... The story of *Faith, Hope,* and *Charity* is one that will never die. It will always rank high among tales of high courage, determination, and battle against seemingly impossible odds. Their very names were at first jokingly applied, but now pass into the island's battle story. They were the three Gladiator aircraft – there was another used as a reserve machine from which spare parts could be drawn – which were kept perpetually in fighting trim and which continually took to the air in the first days of the war. They were flown by volunteer pilots from Air Headquarters and RAF stations, and competition for the honour of flying them was always very keen. The pilots sat in the cockpits during every minute of daylight, even while the aircraft were being refuelled and minor repairs were being made. The Gladiators were always ready to take-off at a moment's notice, and to keep them always in fighting trim required the most intensive efforts by the ground staff. Much ingenuity in improvisation was necessary. In one case, when all spare parts had been used, the airframe of one Gladiator was repaired by modifying parts made for a Swordfish naval aircraft – instantly to be dubbed 'Gladfish' by its ground crew. *Faith, Hope,* and *Charity* had an astonishing number of victories against the enemy, despite the extremely heavy and unfavourable odds. And the triumphs and the vicissitudes of Malta's defending Gladiators were followed and discussed with intense pride and

The presentation ceremony of the Gladiator *Faith*.

anxiety by Malta's people, who, during the first shock of war, and in the subsequent period of Fascist air attacks had their spirits uplifted by the indomitable example of this RAF gallantry constantly before their eyes. Malta will always be grateful to the men who flew the early Gladiators and will always cherish *Faith*, the survivor of the gallant trio.'

This afternoon units of the RAF Regiment and the Malta Police, accompanied by the RA (Malta) Band and escorted by Mounted Police, marched down to Palace Square. There was enthusiastic applause as Lord Gort appeared on the Palace balcony, accompanied by the Archbishop, and other leading personalities. In a commemorative speech Air Vice-Marshal Sir Keith Park said: 'In May 1940 Malta possessed no fighter defences and the AOC obtained from the C-in-C Mediterranean four Gladiators belonging to the Fleet Air Arm which were lying in store at Kalafrana. As there were no fighter pilots in Malta, six RAF pilots volunteered to form a small fighter flight, which was formed at Hal Far on 4 June 1940.

Now Italy declared war on 11 June 1940 and at 0645 hours on that day a flight of three Gladiators took off to intercept a formation of ten Italian bombers that attempted to attack the Dockyard and Hal Far aerodrome. The enemy formation was driven off, and during the evening the Gladiators were again despatched to intercept a formation of 25 enemy bombers and shot down one of the enemy without loss to themselves. Three of the Gladiators were christened *Faith, Hope,* and *Charity,* and the aircraft on parade is *Faith,* the sole survivor. For 18 days following the Italian declaration of war, these Gladiators were air-borne daily and intercepted a total of 144 Italian bombers and fighter escort. During that period the Gladiators destroyed or badly damaged five enemy aircraft without loss to themselves and succeeded in turning away many formations of bombers. By 28 June, the Malta fighter defences had been increased by the addition of four Hurricanes. The Gladiators, however, continued to operate, and on 10 July our small fighter force shot down three out of 20 enemy aircraft, which had up till that time not succeeded in achieving any damage by their bombers. During the first five months of the war against Italy, and her ally, *Faith, Hope,* and *Charity,* supported by a handful of Hurricanes, intercepted 72 enemy formations and destroyed or seriously damaged 37 enemy bombers and fighters. From these small beginnings was built the fighter defence of Malta which in July 1942 put a stop to the daylight bomber raids by intercepting the enemy and smashing up his formations before they could reach Malta. In this month of July, our Spitfires destroyed 137 enemy aircraft for a loss of only 18 fighter pilots … The defence of Malta can justifiably be included among the epics of this war, and *Faith* has earned a place of honour in the armoury of Malta. The part played by *Faith, Hope,* and *Charity* is symbolic of the courage and endurance displayed by the people of Malta during the long struggle against vastly superior Axis Air Forces. I now have great pleasure to hand over this famous old fighter, *Faith,* as a gift to the people of Malta.' The Maltese anthem was then played.

Giuseppe Cordina of Ħamrun is reported to be a prisoner-of-war at Campo di Concentramento, Corropoli, Teramo, Italy.

Sat 4 Sep

The British Comedian George Formby appears in person on the stage at the Coliseum Theatre, Valletta, today. He entertains the public with his famous banjo, after the special show of his latest successful film, *Get Cracking*.

Sun 5 Sep

Some 200 men of the United State Coast Artillery Battalion now manning a sector of the Maltese defences made a pilgrimage to the Islet of St Paul (Selmunett), the traditional site of the shipwreck of the Apostle Paul. They were ferried across the mile-wide bay in the picturesque fishing boats and gathered at the foot of a huge statue of St Paul.[1] Their chaplain, Lee Pridgen of Atlanta (Georgia) addressed the gathering: 'It is a privilege to be able to turn aside in the midst of the war, and visit this quiet, sacred spot. It is a prerogative not given to many; an opportunity for which each one of us should be grateful. Here on this spot, on this little island separated from the island of Malta by a few hundred feet, St Paul was shipwrecked. We are strangers here, our homes are far away, but each of us, whether Christian or Jewish, feels akin to this place, because the man to whose honour yonder monument was erected was first of all a noble Jew then a Christian ... and departing, leave behind us footprints on the sands of time.'

Wed 8 Sep

Valletta, like the rest of the island, will be beflagged for four days to mark the Victory celebrations as from today.

The feast of the Nativity of Our Lady (*Il-Bambina*) – also known as Our Lady of Victories – is celebrated at Senglea. The blitzed sacristy of the parish church has been turned into a chapel, since the parish church proper has not yet been restored. The venerated statue of Our Lady had been taken for safety to Birkirkara but this year it was brought to this temporary chapel at Senglea. It was taken in procession to the church of St Philip which, though facing the harbour at the edge of Senglea, luckily escaped the Blitz. Mgr Emanuel Galea, Auxiliary Bishop of Malta, performed the religious service; the congregation included Rear-Admiral and Mrs Kenneth Mackenzie. The people of Senglea, now scattered all over the island,

1 The stone statue of St Paul is the work of the Maltese sculptor Sigismondo Dimech and was erected on the site in 1845.

and of the other two Dockyard cities of Vittoriosa and Cospicua, assembled among the ruins of Senglea to celebrate this traditional feast of Our Lady. The Beland Band of Żejtun, the Maria Mater Gratia Band of Żabbar, and the De Paule Band of Paola played marches, whilst flowers were strewn in the patch of the religious procession as it wound its way through street which had been carefully cleared of the rubble. As the statue of Our Lady, which was being carried shoulder-high reached the Marina, a megaphone from on board a naval vessel in the creek 'bawled out the news' of the unconditional surrender of Italy. Returning to St Philip's church, Can. Emanuel Brincat, Archpriest of Senglea, who was conducting the procession, was handed a note by Rear-Admiral Mackenzie, Admiral Superintendent HM Dockyard, informing him of the surrender of Italy. Can. Brincat went up the pulpit and told the congregation of the grace which Our Lady had that day obtained for them. A hymn to Our Lady was then sung, followed by Benediction. The text of the note read as follows: 'The Admiral Superintendent would like you to know that the Italian Armed Forces have surrendered unconditionally today and he feels that it is a great tribute to Malta that this has taken place on the occasion of the feast of Our Lady of Victories.'

An enemy Junker 88 that flew over Malta was destroyed by the land defences.

Italy surrenders unconditionally.

Editorial comment of the *Times of Malta* dedicated to 'Victory Day'. – 'The bells of the Three Unconquered Cities of Vittoriosa, Cospicua, and Invicta were ringing their joyous peals to celebrate the victory of 1565, and they were still ringing to commemorate that conspicuous anniversary, when the news was announced of the unconditional surrender of the Italian Armed Forces.' Thu 9 Sep

Allied troops land at Salerno in Italy.

After the unconditional surrender of Italy, units of the Italian Navy at anchor in Maltese water.

Italian warships surrender in Malta. Sat 11 Sep

From Taranto: battleships *Andrea Doria*[2] and *Giulio Cesare*;[3] cruisers *Luigi Cadorna* and *Pompeo Magno*; destroyer *Dareco*.

From Spezia: battleships *Eugenio di Savoia* and *Vittorio Veneto*;[4] 5 cruisers, including *Italia* (formerly *Littorio*),[5] and 5 destroyers.

Large crowds gather in Valletta to celebrate Victory. In his speech from the Palace Balcony Lord Gort says: 'Who would have prophesied that the Statue of Our Lady of Victories would again be carried in procession through the ruined streets of Senglea Invicta.' Sun 12 Sep

More Italian naval units arrive.

From Taranto: battleship *Caio Duilio* (flagship Admiral Da Zara).[6]

From Spezia: cruisers *Duca degli Abruzzi, Giuseppe Garibaldi, Emmanuele Duca d'Aosta,* and *Raimondo Montecuccoli*; destroyers *Alfredo Oriani, Velite, Artigliere, Fuciliere, Gregale, Legionario,* Legnano, *Nicolo Ricci,* and *Riboti.*

Today's leader of the *Times of Malta* entitled 'Fruits of Victory'. – 'The presence of 22 vessels of the Italian battle fleet in Maltese waters turns public attention to the immediate fruits of the Italian capitulation. According to the terms of the armistice accepted by the Italian Government, all Italian naval and merchant shipping is to be placed at the disposal of the Allies, and harbours and airfields are to Mon 13 Sep

2 *Andrea Doria* the sister ship of the *Caio Duilio*, was launched in 1913 and completed in 1916.

3 *Giulio Cesare*, 2,500 tons, was reconstructed in 1933–37; armament of ten 2.6-inch guns and carries four aircraft; complement of 1,200 officers and men.

4 *Vittorio Veneto*, 35,000-ton battleship, was launched in Genoa in 1937; her main armament consists of nine 15-inch guns.

5 *Italia*, which is the sister ship to *Vittorio Veneto*, was formerly the battleship *Littorio*. She changed name when Badoglio took over.

6 The battleship *Caio Duilio* 23,622 tons, was launched in 1913 and completed in 1915; main armament of thirteen 12-inch guns, sixteen 6-inch; smaller armament revised to cope with air attack; fitted with a catapult and carries one aircraft; also armed with two submerged 18-inch torpedo tubes.

be held for their use irrespective of whether the German troops are in occupation or not.'

More arrivals of the Italian Navy at Malta; torpedo boats *Libra* and *Orione*; submarines *Giro Monetti, Atropono, Julea,* and *Fratelli Bandiera*; and the seaplane carrier *Giuseppe Miraglia*.[7] The first Italian merchant vessel to arrive is the *Nettuno* (5,000 tons).

A personal message from the King to Admiral of the Fleet, Sir Andrew Cunningham, C-in-C Mediterranean: 'On the occasion of the arrival of the Italian ships at Malta I wish to send you and to all under your command my heartfelt congratulations on this triumphant results of three years of war in the Mediterranean, in which the Navy in conjunction with the other Services has played so distinguished part.'

Tue 14 Sep

Casualties: *Gozo* **(***Nadur***):** Coronato Azzopardi (9), Joseph Azzopardi (7).

Wed 15 Sep

The following Italian merchant ships have arrived at Malta from Bari: *Luana* (1,140 tons), *Celia* (525), *Monte Bello* (570), *Constanti C* (1,000), *Lucrino* (5,636), *Renucci* (1,800), *Bellagosa* (669), and *Atimia* (282).

Thu 16 Sep

Maltese volunteers are wanted for service as clerks with Allied Military Government as Occupied Territory (AMGOT) in Italy.

Sun 19 Sep

Squadron Leader John Pudney has published his third wartime book of verse, entitled 'South of Forty', which contains the following poem called 'Malta in blitz days':

So they trampled in Three Cities
about the port,
And Valletta built by gentlemen for
gentlemen, and quays

7 *Miraglia,* 5,000-ton seaplane carrier, with a main armament of four 4-inch guns and antiaircraft armament.

And the garnished churches, and the
alleys of stairs
Where noble quarterins passed which
could not be bought,

And rooms where parchment faded
with the family trees.
So that the carven limestone of the
little houses

Clogs the fair prospects, stumbles on
the squares,
Wind in an elegian chandelier
carouses

A brocaded remnant curdles upon
the breeze.

As a result of the improved situation in the Mediterranean, it has been decided as from today to close the Victory Kitchens. Tue 21 Sep

The ban on the export of newspapers from Malta is relaxed. This censure had been imposed for security reasons. Tue 28 Sep

Restrictions on curfew are lifted. Sat 2 Oct

73-year-old Prime Minister and Commander-in-Chief of the Union of South Africa, Field-Marshal Ian Christian Smuts, *en route* for Britain, visits Malta as the guest of Governor Gort and stayed at San Anton. The great statesman and soldier was accompanied by his two sons. He left Malta in a fourengined plane of Transport Command escorted by ten of the latest type Spitfires. Sun 3 Oct

As from today the Historical Research Branch at 382, High Street, Ħamrun, is transferred to the Information Office, 85, Queen Adelaide Square, Valletta. Thu 14 Oct

The first field-gun captured by the Allies in the Sicilian Campaign was presented to the People of Valletta by the 51st Highland Division, who wished in this manner to commemorate their brief stay in Malta prior to the Sicilian invasion.

Fri 22 Oct **p.m. The historic** Italian field-gun, the first to be captured by the Allies in the Sicilian Campaign, was formally presented to a Committee representing the Citizens of Valletta by Major Gen. W.H. Oxley, General Officer Commanding Troops Malta, on behalf of the 51st Highland Division, who wished in this way to commemorate their brief stay in Malta prior to the Sicilian invasion. The presentation was made in the presence of Mrs D. Campbell, wife of the Lieutenant Governor; Vice-Admiral J. Hamilton, Vice-Admiral Malta; Major Gen. C. Christie, Commanding Royal Artillery, Malta; and members of the Government and of the Nobility of Malta. The legend inscribed on the brass reads: 'Presented to the People of Valletta by the 51st Highland Division, The First Italian Gun captured in the Sicilian Campaign, July 1943.'

Sat 23 Oct **The Archbishop announces** that Pope Pius XII has appointed as his Coadjutor with right of succession, Mgr Michele Gonzi, Bishop of Gozo, who is nominated at the same time Titular Bishop of Lirbe and Apostolic Administrator *ad nutum S. Sedis* of the Diocese of Gozo with powers of a residential Bishop. Mgr Gonzi was born in Vittoriosa on 13 May 1885; studied at the Royal University of Malta; ordained priest in 1908; graduated Doctor of Sacred Theology in 1910; and graduated in Rome in Canon Law. On his return to Malta, he filled the chair of Professor in the Seminary of Malta and Professor of Sacred Scripture and Hebrew at the Royal University of Malta. Mgr Gonzi made his solemn entry in the Cathedral Church of Gozo on 10 August 1924.

As from today clubs, restaurants, and snack bars will re-open for the sale of light meals between the hours of noon and 8 p.m. daily. However, it is not yet possible to remove completely restrictions upon the provision of meals in those establishments, as the supply, especially of fresh foodstuffs, is not yet sufficient to satisfy all needs. Thu 28 Oct

The Barracca Lifts start running again from 8 a.m. to 7 p.m. daily. Buskett Gardens are no longer a prohibited area.

Speech by the Governor on the occasion of the opening of the Fourth Session of the Council of Government: 'One of the gauges of the progress we have made since those [blitz] days has been the abolition of the Communal Feeding Department. Nobody is more aware than I am how unpopular the Victory Kitchens were with the public, and, indeed, I believe they were also unpopular with Hon. Members. Nevertheless, when history records the full story of the Siege, everyone will then appreciate how much the Communal Feeding Department contributed in our survival. We will always remember Victory Kitchens in retrospect but, perhaps with the passage of time, these memories will mellow … We shall always be thankful for our survival and for the part these islands have played during the war years, but now that the tide of war has receded from our shores we must realize that we are entering a new phase of our wartime life. The irksome restrictions are being gradually lifted … But the day will come when the weapons of war are stilled in Europe and then these islands will once again move forward to the status of a self-governing community within the British Commonwealth of Nations. It will carry with it heavy burdens of responsibility for Tue 2 Nov

Maltese Statesmen and it will demand from the peoples of these islands a fund of moral courage and resolution, of patience and good will, equal to the physical courage and endurance which brought the Maltese Nation through the arbitrament of war.'

Thu 11 Nov

This morning on the occasion of the 25th anniversary of the 1918 Armistice, the Lieutenant Governor D. Campbell acting on behalf of Governor Gort, unveiled a memorial to Malta's civilian war victims in the Addolorata Cemetery.[8] Mgr Emanuel Galea, Titular Bishop of the Tralles and Vicar General, represented the Archbishop. On arrival, Mr Campbell and Mgr Galea headed a procession of distinguished representatives of Malta's Civilian Front and advanced to the foot of the memorial. His Honour then unveiled the grey marble cross on its granite base, bearing the words: 'To the Memory of Civilian Casualties of the War 1939–19…'. There was a word of poignancy in that unfinished inscription. Mgr Galea then performed the ceremony of the Blessing of the Memorial and gave the Absolution to those it commemorates. Mr Campbell placed a wreath of poppies and roses at the foot of the Memorial: 'From the Government and People of Malta', and Prof. A.V. Bernard, Chief Government Medical Officer, placed a wreath of poppies: 'From the members of the Medical and Health Department'. Prof. Bernard called for the observance of two minutes' silence and the gathering bowed their heads in prayer and remembrance.

Fri 12 Nov

Today's leader of the *Times of Malta* is dedicated to the 'Civilian War Memorial'. – 'A grey marble cross was unveiled yesterday at the Addolorata Cemetery … Henceforth this memorial stands to perpetuate the memory of the civilian casualties of Malta during the war. It was His Excellency who, recently visiting the Addolorata Cemetery, expressed the wish that a memorial should be erected over the graves of those civilians, men, women, and children, who lost their lives through enemy action. It was fitting that the memorial to the Civilian War Dead of Malta should have been unveiled on Poppy Day – the Day of Remembrance for the fallen Servicemen of

8 The erection of the Cemetery commenced in 1869, on plans and designs of architect Emanuel Aloisius Galizia.

TO THE MEMORY
OF
CIVILIAN CASUALTIES
OF THE WAR
1939 — 19

the Empire ... The memorial itself is a simple but dignified monument, austerity symbolizing wartime grief and bereavement and eternal faith in the Cross. Mercifully Malta's civilian casualties have not been so high as they might well have been – had the German attacks developed earlier. As it was, vital months were gained between the onset of the initial Italian attacks and the German blitzes for the then Government to make up its mind to construct deep rock shelters. Had these shelters not been available when the *Luftwaffe* moved down in force to Sicily, there would have been a catastrophic price to pay in lives – a veritable massacre of the innocents. Malta's civilian war casualties to date number 1,495 killed. Not a large total number but each a personal tragedy. Proportionally, however, it constitutes a high death roll; it means that one person in every two hundred of the total population of Malta and Gozo have lost their lives through enemy action. Over one-half per cent of the total population killed by air attack constitutes a much higher percentage rate of casualties than that suffered by Britain and therefore is probably greater than in any other country in the world – with the possible exception of Germany.'

Governor Gort has left Malta for a few days. During his absence Vice Admiral L. Hamilton, CB, DSO, Vice-Admiral, Malta, will act as the Governor's Deputy.

Mon 15 Nov

Governor Gort returns to Malta after a short visit to Gen. Alexander's headquarters.

As from today the Lieutenant Governor's office and the Attorney General's office will move to the Palace, Valletta.

Thu 18 Nov

There are rumours that Churchill is in Malta.

Fri 19 Nov

Exchange of messages: 'To Cardinal Maglione – Vatican City – Please convey Holy Father respectful congratulations from clergy and people safety His Holiness recent aerial bombardment Vatican City. Assurance of prayers.'

Field-Marshal Lord Gort, Prime Minister Winston Churchill and Vice-Admiral L. Hamilton visit the Dockyard inside the Grand Harbour.

'Città del Vaticano – Archbishop Caruana, La Valletta, Malta – His Holiness gratefully acknowledges kind message assurance of prayers. Your Grace Imparts Paternal Blessing.'

p.m. Winston Churchill wearing the peaked cap and seaman's jacket and with his familiar cigar visits the Dockyard. At one point there was a lively rush for a cigar butt dropped by the Prime Minister. From the Dockyard Gates, Lord Gort took Churchill on a brief drive through the shattered city of Senglea. The people came out from their shacks and shelters to cheer and wave. He then drove to Valletta through Victoria Gate and on to the Palace. At Palace Square, a cheering crowd gathered. Inside the Palace he was shown round the State Rooms. Churchill then appeared from the balcony and saluted the crowds below.

Wed 1 Dec

An official communiqué released today says: 'The Prime Minister, the Rt. Hon. Winston Churchill, visited Malta on his way to a conference with President Roosevelt and Generalissimo Chiang Kai-Shek, and stayed two days in the island as the guest of HE the Governor at San Anton Palace. The British Chiefs of Staff also visited Malta at the same time, and with Mr Churchill, took part in discussions with Lord Gort, Gen. Eisenhower, Gen. Sir Harold Alexander, Air Chief Marshal Sir Arthur Tedder and Admiral Sir Andrew Cunningham. Mr Churchill was accompanied by his daughter, Section Officer Sarah Oliver, and his personal staff. Mr Churchill visited HM Dockyard and drove through the streets of Valletta to the Palace.'

Thu 2 Dec

Today's editorial of the *Times of Malta* is dedicated to 'Churchill in Malta'. – 'Malta would have liked to have had the opportunity of prior announcement in order to see and greet Mr Churchill but the impossibility of this is understood and the overriding feeling is that of delight that Mr Churchill has paid Malta a visit during wartime.'

Sat 4 Dec

The feast of St Barbara, the patron saint of gunners.

The feast is celebrated at the church of St Barbara[9] in Kingsway, which has been re-opened after having been closed for some time because of damages suffered in the blitz.

Mon 6 Dec

The President of the United States of America, the Prime Minister of Great Britain, and the Premier of the Soviet Union (Roosevelt–Churchill–Stalin) meet at Teheran, the capital of Iran, to confirm their common policy.

Wed 8 Dec

President Roosevelt arrives at Luqa aerodrome in a C54 Douglas Transport plane, escorted by twenty Lightnings and Spitfires. Awaiting the President's arrival were Viscount Gort, Lieut. Col V. Micallef, ADC, His Lordship Mgr Gonzi, attended by his chaplain, and other personalities. A Guard of Honour, drawn up in a hollow

9 This church dates back to 1739 and was built at the expense of the Langue of Provence, the senior Langue of the Order of the Knights of St John.

square three deep, was formed by detachments from the Royal Navy, and Marines, the Army, and Royal Air Force. The Army detachment comprised men from infantry units of the United Kingdom and Malta. The Band of the Royal Malta Artillery was in attendance. Accompanying President Roosevelt were Gen. Eisenhower, Supreme Allied Commander-in-Chief Mediterranean, Rear Admiral Ross Macintire, the President's personal physician, Major John Boettiger, the President's son-in-law, and others. A jeep was waiting on the President; it was one of the American jeeps presented last July by Gen. Eisenhower to the Governor at the time of the invasion of Sicily and that had been subsequently allotted to Air Vice-Marshal Sir Keith Park. It has been newly painted. 'Husky' (as the AOC's jeep is known throughout the island) came to a standstill facing the Guard of Honour as the President took the salute and the Band of the RMA played the Star-Spangled Banner and the Stars and Stripes broke the masthead. In a short address to the gathering, President Roosevelt said: 'Nearly a year ago the Prime Minister and I were in Casablanca, shortly after landings by British and American troops in North Africa, and at that time I told the

President Roosevelt in Malta.

Prime Minister "some day we would control once more the whole of the Mediterranean and that then I would go to Malta". For many many months I have wanted on behalf of the American people to pay some little tribute to this island and to all the people, Civil and Military, who during these years have contributed so much to democracy, not just here, but all over the civilized world, and so at last we have been able to come… I have here a little token, a scroll, a citation from the President of the United States speaking on behalf of all the people and may I read it to you: "In the name of the people of the United States of America I salute the Island of Malta, its People and defenders, who in the cause of freedom and justice and decency throughout the world have rendered valorous services far above and beyond the call of duty. Under repeated fire from the skies, Malta stood alone but unafraid in the centre of the sea, one tiny bright flame in the darkness, a beacon of hope for the clearer days which have come. Malta's bright story of human fortitude and courage will be read by posterity with wonder and gratitude throughout all the ages. What was done in this Island maintains all highest traditions of gallant men and women who from the beginning of time have lived and died to preserve civilization for all mankind – Franklin D. Roosevelt, December 7, 1943." I have signed it at the bottom and I wrote on it not today, but yesterday, 7 December, because that was the second anniversary of the entry into the war of the American People. We will proceed until that war is won, but more than that, we will stand shoulder to shoulder with the British Empire and our other Allies in making it a victory worthwhile.' President Roosevelt then handed the case containing the scroll to Major Boettiger who placed it in the hands of the Governor. The citation is written in illuminated letters on a scroll of parchment. The scroll reposes on a velvet backing in a beautiful leather case, the cover of which is embossed with the national white-and-red shield of Malta edged with gold. At the top of the scroll are the Malta Arms backed by the crossed flags of Britain and the United States. The whole is contained in a mahogany case which Lord Gort handed to Major Gordon Duff, his Military Secretary. In thanking the President, Gort said: 'We are very sensible of the greatness of this occasion and of the important place which 7 December 1943, will occupy in our history … May I be permitted, on behalf of the

Armed Forces and Peoples of Malta, to thank you, Mr President, most respectfully, most sincerely, and most gratefully for the sentiments it expresses and for the great gesture of friendship which inspired you to undertake this special journey. Malta is, perhaps, not unjustifiably proud that she has been able to play her part in the Mediterranean war, but the language in which the Citation is couched and, if I may be permitted to say so, Mr President, the moving phrases which you have so generously used in making this presentation impress upon us how highly you rate such services as our Island Fortress has been able to render to the cause of the United Nations. No one can be asked to do more in war than to fulfil his or her duty – no one can do less, and that you, Sir, and the Citizens of the United States of America should feel, that the Armed Forces and Peoples of these Islands have not failed the United Nations, is in itself a full reward … I can assure you, Sir, that this Citation will be a treasured and highly-prized addition to the historic archives of Malta … I therefore have it in mind, Mr President, with your consent to reproduce the Citation in bronze and to place it in the Palace Square in Valletta where it will stand, in all weathers, as a permanent monument to a great and unique occasion.'

The President decided to make an impromptu visit to the Cottonera side of the island. Roosevelt entered Lord Gort's car and, accompanied by the Governor and escorted by his personal guard (an armed guard), the President drove through Marsa, Paola, Żabbar, Ricasoli, Kalkara, Vittoriosa, Cospicua, the Dockyard, and Senglea back to Luqa airfield. President Roosevelt's unscheduled tour was greeted with cheers by the people all along the way.

The feast of the Immaculate Conception was celebrated today. The ceremony of the Consecration of Malta and Gozo to the Immaculate Heart of Mary is held at St John's Co-Cathedral following the votive procession with the icon of Our Lady of Carafa from St John's to Sarria church[10] in Floriana and back. The Act of Consecration which is that used by Pope Pius XII on 30 October 1942, when he consecrated the Church and the World to the Immaculate Heart of Mary, is read by Mgr Gonzi.

10 The chapel dates back to 1585 and is dedicated to the Immaculate Heart of Mary, though it is commonly known after its founder Fra Martino De Sarria Navarra. The architecture and paintings are by Mattia Preti.

Exchange of telegrams:

'Cardinal Maglione – Vatican City – Occasion Consecration of Malta and Gozo Immaculate Heart Mary we beg assure HH filial devotion Clergy and Laity two Dioceses fervent prayers His August Person and Peace He desires – Archbishop Caruana, Bishop Gonzi.'

'Archbishop Caruana – Malta – Holy Father acknowledging kind message paternally blesses Pastors Clergy Faithful Dioceses Malta and Gozo – Cardinal Maglione.'

Sat 11 Dec

Today's editorial comment of the *Times of Malta* is dedicated to 'Roosevelt's Visit'. – 'The President of the United States has made a special journey to Malta in order to present a citation on behalf of the American People to the people civil and military of the island. This act has deeply moved all in Malta and the news of it is echoing around the world. The honour is a signal one. It takes its place with the red-letter occasions in this memorable year of 1943 – the occasion of His Majesty the King's visit to Malta on 20 June, and that of Mr Churchill on 17 November. Malta has ever made and lived through history … Few could have foreseen here in Malta. in 1940, 1941, and 1942, when the battle for the Mediterranean and for the island's survival was being fought at heavy odds that so soon a triumphant Malta would be welcoming this great man, three times elected President of the United States; carrying with him a tribute to the people and garrison in the form of the citation which President Roosevelt had had prepared for him in Washington – from where in the past he had followed the island's stand amid the wrack of war then being waged in the Mediterranean and North Africa. President Roosevelt's determination to visit Malta caused him to carry the citation with him on his journey to the epoch-making conferences at Cairo and Teheran; conferences at which complete agreement was reached by the leaders of the United Nations as to the scope and timing of military operations, which will be undertaken from the East, West, and South to bring the war to a victorious end.'

Sun 12 Dec

The illuminated citation presented to the people of Malta and Gozo by President Roosevelt will be on view in Palace Square today.

In the event of rain, the citation will be exhibited inside the Main Gateway of the Palace, Valletta.

Fri 17 Dec

9.15 a.m. HG the Archbishop of Malta, Mgr Maurus Caruana, OSB, KBE, GCOJ, passed peacefully away at the Blue Sisters' Hospital, Sliema, at the age of 76. He was attended by Fr Carmel Farrugia, Parish Priest of St Gregory church, from whom he received the Viaticum; Extreme Unction was administered to His Grace by Bishop Gonzi. He was attended by his physician, Prof. J. Debono while his nearest relatives were at the bedside.

Governor Gort sent the following message to His Lordship: 'It is with sadness in my heart that I write to express my very real sorrow at the death of our beloved Archbishop. For myself, I am conscious that I have lost a personal friend and I am also conscious of the sadness his death must evoke in the hearts of the Maltese people after all the years he has devoted to watching over and guiding their spiritual welfare. While I have long appreciated the grief it has been to him to be in failing health latterly, I know what joy it gave him to be spared long enough to see the Maltese people triumph over those who sought to break their will ...'

The Most Revd Dom Sir Lewis Maurus Caruana was born at Floriana on 16 November 1867. He studied at St Ignatius College, St Julian's, and continued his studies in Scotland in 1882 at the monastery of Fort Augustus. He made his vows in the Benedictine Order in 1885 and was ordained priest in 1891. For some time he was the parish priest of Fort Augustus. In 1905 he accompanied Mgr Ambrose Agius, an eminent Maltese prelate, as secretary, on the latter's mission as Apostolic Delegate to Manila in the Philippines. Dom Maurus established a reputation as an orator and in 1908 preached a course of Lenten Sermons at Westminster Cathedral. In January 1915 he succeeded as Archbishop of Malta, His Lordship Bishop Pietro Pace. The solemn consecration of Dom Maurus as Archbishop of Malta took place in Rome on 10 February 1915. The consecration was conducted by Cardinal Merry del Val at the Basilica of Santa Maria in Trastevere, one of the co-consecrators being Mgr Macintyre, the rector of the English College. One of his first public functions as Archbishop of Malta was the unveiling and blessing

H.M. KING GEORGE VI AWARDED TO MALTA The "GEORGE CROSS" ON THE 906th. DAY OF THE WAR APRIL 15th., 1942

TIMES OF MALTA

No. 2,588 | Price 2d. | SATURDAY DECEMBER 11 1943 | 1,560 DAY OF WAR AGAINST NAZISM

ROOSEVELT VISITS MALTA

America's Tribute to Island's People and Defenders

HISTORIC CEREMONY AT LUQA AERODROME

LUQA aerodrome was the scene of an historic occasion in the annals of Malta when last Wednesday President Roosevelt arrived there in a C. 54 Douglas Transport plane escorted by twenty Lightnings and Spitfires.

It was a perfect December morning with a blue sky lightly flecked with white clouds and brilliant sunshine. All was peace on the aerodrome on which in the past hordes of Junkers and Stukas had for months concentrated their efforts making it the most bombed airfield in the world. On the 8th. December 1943 the once crater-pocked airfield stretched without a ripple to the sky-line.

FRANKLIN D. ROOSEVELT PRESIDENT OF THE UNITED STATES OF AMERICA

AT THE AERODROME

Awaiting the President's arrival were H.E. Field Marshal Viscount Gort V.C. Governor and Commander-in-Chief, attended by Major Gordon Duff, Military Secretary, Lieutenant Colonel V. Micallef, A.D.C., Captain Holland, Major Geddes, and Major Woodford. There were also His Lordship Mgr. Gonzi attended by his chaplain, the Rev. John Vella Galea B.A.; the Lieutenant Governor Mr. D. C. Campbell, the three Service Chiefs, Vice Admiral Hamilton, Major General Oxley and Air Vice Marshal Sir Keith Park, along with Lieutenant Templeton R.N.V.R., Lt. H. A. F. Radley A.D.C. and Fl/Lt. H.C.C. Carver in attendance. Together with the Service Chiefs were Sir George Borg Chief Justice of Malta, and the members of the Executive Council including Lt. Colonel Strickland leader of the elected majority and Mr. E. Valenzia L.P.

PRESIDENT'S ARRIVAL

A Guard of Honour drawn up in a hollow square, three deep was formed by detachments from the Royal Navy and Marines, the Army and R.A.F. The Army detachment comprised men from infantry units of the United Kingdom and Malta. The band of the Royal Malta Artillery was in attendance.

At [illegible] the President's 'plane and its escort were to be seen circling over the aerodrome

Then the great moment arrived as the President's 'plane piloted by Major Otis Bryant of the U.S.A.A.F. touched ground and made a perfect landing ten minutes later.

HIS EXCELLENCY'S GREETING

The 'plane taxied to its allotted position as the escort 'planes hovered over the aerodrome and then landed, taking up alignment while His Excellency Lord Gort was welcoming the President of the United States and Mr. Roosevelt's distinguished companions.

They were General Eisenhower, Supreme Allied C-in-C Mediterranean; Admiral Leahy; Mr. Harry Hopkins; General Spaatz; Major General Bedell Smith, Chief of Staff to General Eisenhower; Rear Admiral Wilson Brown, Naval A.D.C. to the President; Rear Admiral Ross Macintire, the President's personal physician; Major General Edwin Wilson, Secretary and Military A.D.C. to the President; Major John Boettiger, the President's son-in-law. While Lord Gort remained by the 'plane with President Roosevelt the other distinguished visitors moved forward to greet the Service Chiefs and their companions. General Eisenhower was heard to say "Delighted to see you all again."

INSPECTION OF GUARD OF HONOUR

Meanwhile President Roosevelt had entered the waiting jeep. It was one of the American jeeps presented last July by General Eisenhower at the time of the invasion of Sicily to the Governor and that had been allotted by him to Air Vice Marshal Sir Keith Park. It had been newly painted. "Husky" as the A.O.C.'s jeep is known throughout Malta came to a standstill facing the Guard of Honour where the President took the salute as the Band of the R.M.A. played the Star Spangled Banner and the Stars and Stripes broke at the mast-head. History was made without precedent—the flag of the United States of America waved over Luqa aerodrome and the President of that great country proceeded to inspect the Guard of Honour together with Field Marshal Lord Gort.

PRESENTATION TO THE PRESIDENT

At the conclusion of the inspection His Excellency presented the following to President Roosevelt:—His Hon. the Lieutenant Governor Mr. D. C. Campbell; His Lordship Mgr. Michael Gonzi, Bishop of [illegible], Administrator of Gozo and Coadjutor of His Grace

the Archbishop of Malta; the Air Officer Commanding Mediterranean Air Vice Marshal Sir Keith Park, the Vice Admiral Malta, Vice Admiral Hamilton; General Officer Commanding the Troops Major General Oxley; His Honour the Chief Justice Sir George Borg, the Attorney General the Hon. Mr. L. Galea LL.D.; the Hon. Mr. G. N. N. Nunn and the Hon. Mr. T. V. Scrivenor Assistants to His Honour the Lieutenant Governor, the Treasurer to the Government, the Hon. Mr. E. Cuschieri; the Hon. Mr. P. Bell, Legal Secretary, the Hon. Mr. R. Castillo, Secretary to the Government; the Hon. Lieutenant Colonel R. Strickland leader of the Elected Majority and the Hon. Mr. E. Valenzia, L.P.

As President Roosevelt shook hands with Air Vice Marshal Park he was heard to say: "I have heard about you from my boys."

PRESIDENT DELIVERS CITATION

After the presentation Lord Gort attended by Major Gordon Duff and Lieutenant Colonel Micallef took up a position in the centre of the square formed by the Guard of Honour facing President Roosevelt. Behind Lord Gort, were Bishop Gonzi, the Service Chiefs, the Chief Justice and members of the Executive Council. President Roosevelt, a powerful and commanding figure, remained seated in the jeep and standing alongside were two members of his staff. At a distance of a few yards in a line were the distinguished visitors who had accompanied President Roosevelt; and behind them again were their personal staff and the aides-de-camp of the Service chiefs.

In the firm resonant tone which the radio has made familiar to all freedom-loving peoples, President Roosevelt addressed the assembled gathering:

Lord Gort, Officers and Men, good People of Malta,

"Nearly a year ago the Prime Minister and I were in Casablanca shortly after the landings by British and American troops in North Africa and at that time I told the Prime Minister some day we would control once more the whole of the Mediterranean and that then I would go to Malta.

For many many months I have wanted on behalf of the American people to pay some little tribute to this Island and to all the people civil and military, who during these years have contributed so much to democracy, not just here but all over the civilised world and so at last we have been able to come. At last I have been able to see something of the historic land and I wish I could stay for I have many things to do. May I tell you though that during these past three weeks the Prime Minister and I feel that we two have struck strong blows

for the future of the human race and so in this simple way I am taking opportunity to do what all the American people would join with me in doing. I have here a little token a scroll, a citation from the President of the United States speaking on behalf of all the people and may I read it to you:—

"In the name of the people of the United States of America I salute the Island of Malta, its People and defenders who in the cause of freedom and justice and decency throughout the world have rendered valourous service far above and beyond the call of duty.

Under repeated fire from the skies, Malta stood alone but unafraid in the centre of the sea, one tiny bright flame in the darkness, a beacon of hope for the clearer days which have come.

Malta's bright story of human fortitude and courage will be read by posterity with wonder and gratitude throughout all the ages.

What was done in this Island maintains all highest traditions of gallant men and women who from the beginning of time have lived and died to preserve civilisation for all mankind."

FRANKLIN D. ROOSEVELT
President

DECEMBER 7, 1943.

"I have signed it at the bottom and I wrote on it not today, but yesterday, December 7, because that was the second anniversary of the entry into the war of the American people. We will proceed until that war is won but more than that we will stand shoulder to shoulder with the British Empire and our other Allies in making it a victory worth while."

Concluding President Roosevelt handed the case containing the scroll to Major Boettiger who placed it in the hands of His Excellency.

The citation is written in illuminated letters on a scroll of parchment. The scroll reposes on a velvet backing in a beautiful leather case, the cover of which is embossed with the national white and red shield of Malta edged with gold. At the top of the scroll are the Malta arms backed by the crossed flags of Britain and the United States. The whole is contained in a mahogany case which Lord Gort handed to Major Gordon Duff.

LORD GORT'S THANKS

His Excellency in thanking the President, said:—

"Mr. President,

"We are very sensible of the greatness of this occasion and of the important place which December 7, 1943 will occupy in our history. It is a day which Malta will never forget and I can assure you Sir, that this Citation presented in person by the President of the United States of America, has moved us very deeply. May I be permitted on behalf of the Armed Forces and Peoples of Malta to thank you, Mr. President, most respectfully, most sincerely and most gratefully for the sentiments it expresses and for the great gesture of friendship which inspired you to undertake this special journey.

Malta is, perhaps not unjustifiably proud that she has been able to play her part in the Mediterranean war, but the language in which the Citation is couched and, if I may be permitted to say so, Mr. President, the moving phrases which you have so generously used in making this presentation impress upon us how highly you rate such services as our Island Fortress has been able to

(Continued on Page 4).

H.E. THE VISCOUNT GORT, V.C., RECEIVES FROM MAJOR JOHN BOETTIGER, MR. ROOSEVELT'S SON-IN-LAW, THE MAHOGANY CASE CONTAINING THE ILLUMINATED SCROLL, IMMEDIATELY AFTER THE PRESIDENT HAD DELIVERED THE CITATION.

President Roosevelt in Malta.

of the monument of Christ the King, outside Kingsgate, which monument commemorates the XXIV International Eucharistic Congress held in Malta in 1913.

Today's editorial comment of the *Times of Malta* is dedicated to 'Archbishop Caruana'. – 'The death of His Grace the Most Reverend Monsignor Dom Sir Maurus Caruana … which occurred yesterday, has come unexpectedly and Malta, as a Catholic Nation now mourns the passing away of her pastor after an episcopate of twenty-eight years. His Grace's tenure of office started in 1915, when the nations of the world were locked in conflict, and it has terminated in the midst of another bitter struggle. It must have been a great consolation to His Grace that the Divine Providence should have ordained that he should have lived to see the United Nations on the sure path of victory, for his health had been uncertain for very many years.' Sat 18 Dec

Noon. A test is carried out of the Air-Raid Sirens, which have now remained idle for some time, with a view to ensuring that they are ready for use in an emergency. The sirens sounded in the following order: the 'All Clear' for 15 seconds, followed by the 'Warning', and finally the 'All Clear' for similar periods with a break of 15 seconds between each signal.

In the afternoon the body of Mgr Caruana was taken by private cortege from the Blue Sisters' Hospital to the Bishop's Palace, Valletta. In the hearse at the head of the coffin was the Archbishop's green hat. The body was borne into the Palace where the body in full episcopal vestments and mitre was laid on the pall-covered catafalque.

Lying-in-state at the Bishop's Palace of His Grace the late Mgr Caruana. Throughout the day an uninterrupted stream of people filed past the catafalque. NCOs of the King's Own Malta Regiment with arms reversed guarded the coffin. Members of religious Orders intoned the Office for the Dead. Sun 19 Dec

This morning the solemn obsequies of His Grace Mgr Caruana, were conducted in St John's Co-Cathedral, Valletta. Thousands of Tue 21 Dec

The funeral of Archbishop Dom Maurus Caruana.

people filled the streets through which the funeral cortege passed on its way from the Bishop's Palace up Bishop Street, down Kingsway, round into Merchants Street, and then to St John Street. The route was lined by officers, NCOs and men of the Royal Malta Artillery and the King's Own Malta Regiment, and there was a Guard of Honour at the Merchants Street approaches to St John Square, as well as mounted and foot police. Church bells tolled and flags fluttered at half-mast. The cortege was headed by representatives of the confraternities of Valletta and after them came the Capuchins, the Franciscan Conventuals, the Carmelites, the Augustinians, the Friars Minor, and the Dominicans. The Seminarists, the Canons of the Collegiate Church of St Paul Shipwrecked, the Cathedral Chapter of Gozo, and the Cathedral Chapter of Malta followed. After them came His Lordship Mgr Emanuel Galea, Bishop of Tralles, and His Lordship Mgr Michele Gonzi, Bishop of Malta. Their Lordships walked in. front of the bier on which Archbishop Caruana was carried. The body was arrayed in full episcopal vestments with the green hat hung at the foot of the bier, behind which were carried, on crepe covered cushions, the late Archbishop's regalia and decorations.

At the wish of His Lordship the Bishop of Malta and his deputies no wreaths were carried in the cortege and there were no flowers in the CoCathedral. Midway down the aisle, ablaze with candles, was the *chapelle ardente,* in which was laid the catafalque, bearing the coat-of-arms of His Grace, and carrying the motto '*Fortis et Ardens*'. Bishop Gonzi was assisted in the celebration of Pontificial High Requiem Mass by Mgr R. Capurro and Mgr Camilleri. The Presbyter Assistant was Mgr G. Apap Bologna, Archdeacon of the Cathedral Chapter, assisted by Mgr Vella and Mgr Cavendish. The Mass was sung in Gregorian Chant by a *schola cantorum* composed of members of the secular and regular clergy. After Mass, His Lordship Mgr Galea delivered the funeral oration in Maltese, paying tribute to His Grace the Archbishop. After Mgr Galea had descended from the pulpit, absolutions were given. The Last Post was sounded by trumpeters of the Royal Malta Artillery outside the church.

In the afternoon the burial took place in private at St Gregory church where His Grace had the tomb prepared. The parish priest Fr Farrugia received the body. Psalms were chanted by the choir and the grave was blessed by the Archdeacon of the Cathedral Chapter. The late Archbishop's hat was· removed from the coffin before the burial and will be hung in the church of St Gregory.

Fri 24 Dec **Christmas Eve.**

Christmas message by the Governor: 'The victories in North Africa and the opening of the Western Mediterranean, the visit of His Majesty the King in June, the invasion of Sicily and Italy, the surrender of the Italian Fleet, and the presentation of the Citation by the President of the United States of America, all combine to make 1943 a year which the peoples of Malta and Gozo will long recall with gratitude in their prayers. We can look forward with confidence to the final overthrow of Nazi Germany and I send to the Civil Government and the people of these islands my greetings for Christmas and my good wishes for their continued happiness and ever increasing well-being in the New Year.'

Tue 28 Dec **Bishop Gonzi has** been elevated to the rank of Archbishop by the Pope.

Wed 29 Dec **Today's leader of** the *Times of Malta* is dedicated to 'Malta's Archbishop'. – 'HG Archbishop Gonzi who has just recently taken over the diocese of Malta and the burden of this important See is to be congratulated on the signal distinction that has been bestowed upon him by the Holy Father and through him on the island of Malta. The late Archbishop Caruana was Archbishop of Rhodes and Bishop of Malta, and the Holy Father has been pleased to ordain that the present holder of the See of Malta shall have the rank and dignity of Archbishop.'

Thu 30 Dec **This morning in** the church of the University in Valletta, the Royal University of Malta conferred on HE the Governor Viscount Gort the degree of Doctor of Laws (LL.D.) *Honoris Causa*. This was the first time, since the outbreak of war, that the Royal University of Malta succeeded in holding a graduation ceremony on a peacetime scale. During the ceremony Fr Seraphim M. Zarb, OP, Professor of Dogmatic Theology, delivered the oration in Latin. Then came the highlight of the day: the conferment itself. HE left his seat and stood on the step below the dais, while the Rector of the University, having read the introductory part of the formula, proceeded to vest him with the trappings of honour; the four-cornered hat, as a symbol given to victors after the contest, the gown, belonging to the college of lawyers, the book of wisdom, and the ring, given to those who merit highly of their country. Lastly, the Rector embraced HE as a mark of congratulation. HE then took the oath at the hands of the Bishop Galea, signed his name in the *Liber Aurens* (Golden Book) and waited while the Secretary of the University read a translation of the Diploma conferred upon HE. The diploma was then presented to HE by the Rector.

AD 1944

Today's leader of the *Times of Malta* is entitled 'A New Year 1944'. – 'A momentous and ever memorable year lies in the past as the threshold is crossed into 1944. The fifth wartime New Year opens with news of further triumph from all war zones.' Sat 1 Jan

Among the New Year's honours awards, the Very Revd Can. Emanuel Brincat, Archpriest of Senglea, has been awarded the title of Member of the British Empire (MBE).

One alert is sounded. The AA guns were engaged but no bombs were dropped. Mon 10 Jan

This morning one enemy aircraft which flew over Malta was shot down in the sea. HAA artillery was engaged. Sun 23 Jan

The Congress composed of representatives of all the constituted bodies and set up to convene a National Assembly for the purpose of drafting a new Constitution for Malta meets for the first time. The sitting is held at De La Salle Palace, Valletta. Prof. Contino Luigi Preziosi and Prof. Giuseppe De Giorgio were elected President and Secretary respectively. They will retain their posts until such time as the National Assembly has been convened. Thu 10 Feb

London. Acting Air Vice-Marshal Archibald Herbert Wann, one of the airship pioneers of the RAF, has been appointed Air Officer Commanding RAF in Malta. He succeeds Air Marshal Sir Keith Rodney Park who was recently appointed Air Officer Commanding-in-Chief Middle East. Fri 11 Feb

Inoculation against typhoid and paratyphoid. Wed 23 Feb

HM the King, by Royal Warrant addressed to the Duke of Norfolk, Earl Marshal, assigns to the Island Fortress of Malta the following Armorial Bearings: 'Per Pale argent and gules on a canton azure a representation of the George Cross proper.' The Warrant is dated 28 December 1943. The historic document is recorded in the College of Arms.

HE the Governor has received the following message from Gen. Sir William Dobbie: 'I am glad to know that the signal honour conferred upon the people of Malta by HM in the award of the George Cross is being incorporated in the Arms of Malta. It will thus provide a lasting reminder to the people of Malta, to the British Empire, and the World, of the trials bravely borne and of the great contribution which Malta with God's help was able to render to the British Empire in the hour of its great need.'

An appeal is published in the Press for books in Maltese to provide reading to troops stationed in isolated areas.

Thu 2 Mar

During today's sitting of the Council of Government the Nationalist member, Dr Giorgio Borg Olivier, delivered a stirring speech calling for the repatriation of Maltese internees.

Mon 6 Mar

As from today the Department of Imposts and Lotto and the Land Valuation Office have moved from Lija to Valletta.

The following area will receive supplies of freshly-made fruit cake during this week:

Monday	6th	–	Marsa
Tuesday	7th	–	Qrendi
Wednesday	8th	–	Birkirkara
Thursday	9th	–	Attard and Lija
Friday	10th	–	Naxxar and Għargħur
Saturday	11th	–	Dingli, Rabat, Mtarfa, and Mdina.

The ration will be ¼ *ratal* per head and the price will be 2s. per *ratal*.

Wed 8 Mar

An alert is sounded when a small formation of enemy aircraft approached the island. This was Malta's 3338th alert.

Washington. President Roosevelt received a delegation from the Maltese community of New York, which comprises some 12,000 Malta-born citizens. The delegation presented him with a scroll in

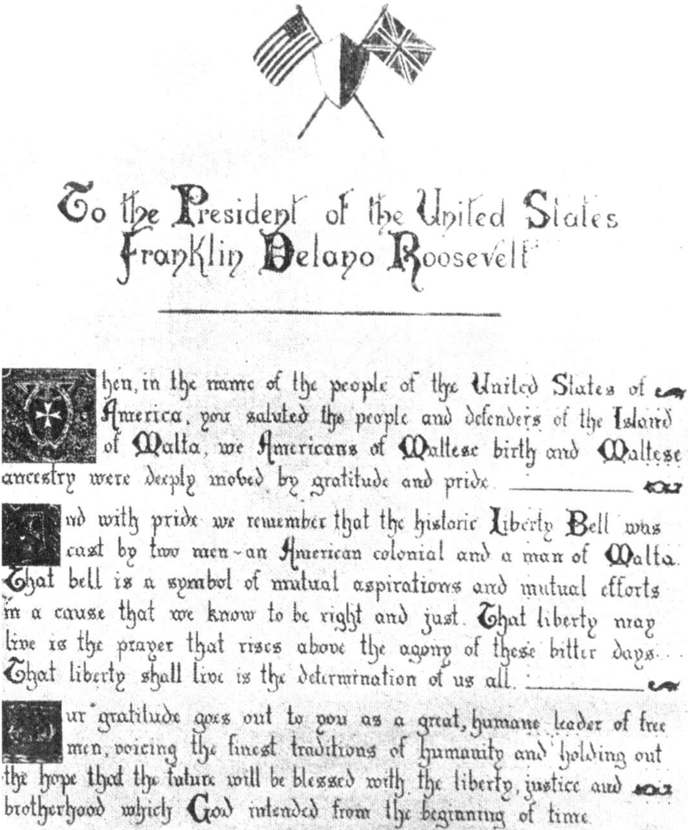

To the President of the United States
Franklin Delano Roosevelt

When, in the name of the people of the United States of America, you saluted the people and defenders of the Island of Malta, we Americans of Maltese birth and Maltese ancestry were deeply moved by gratitude and pride.

And with pride we remember that the historic Liberty Bell was cast by two men - an American colonial and a man of Malta. That bell is a symbol of mutual aspirations and mutual efforts in a cause that we know to be right and just. That liberty may live is the prayer that rises above the agony of these bitter days. That liberty shall live is the determination of us all.

Our gratitude goes out to you as a great, humane leader of free men, voicing the finest traditions of humanity and holding out the hope that the future will be blessed with the liberty, justice and brotherhood which God intended from the beginning of time.

The Maltese Community of Metropolitan New York

President - Maltese Union Club

President - Malta Association of [illegible]

President - Maltese American [illegible]

The Eighth day of March, Nineteen Hundred and Forty Four

Scroll presented to President Roosevelt by the Maltese Community of New York.

appreciation of the scroll he presented to the People of Malta during his visit last December.

Thu 9 Mar

The Governor congratulates the People of Malta on the manner in which the black-out regulations were observed when the air-raid warning was sounded today.

Sat 11 Mar

The National Congress holds its second sitting.

Sun 12 Mar

The ceremony of the presentation of the Sword of Honour to Lord Gort is held at Żebbuġ. The main square (St Philip Square) fronting the old parish church was beflagged with the banners of the Allied Band Clubs. The car in which Viscount Gort was seated was drawn by the crowd. Troops from the Royal Malta Artillery and the King's Own Malta Regiment lined the approaches to the Square. The Governor walked to the dais under a canopy formed by banners and flags of different band clubs. Revd Loreto Callus, President of St Philip Band Club, delivered a commemorative speech: 'The timely arrival of Your Excellency was an augury of calm and sunshine, peace and glory! Your Excellency could not have taken over the reins of our Island Fortress at a more critical stage, the time of that supreme crisis, when the enemy having mercilessly assaulted her, was straining his muscles in a desperate attempt to strangle her by a tight blockade. May 8 [1942] saw the beginning of our Crispin's Battle.' Then amidst the applause of the people, Prof. Philip Farrugia representing all the Clubs presented the Sword of Honour to Lord Gort. HE replied: 'I shall never cease to regard this sword with affectionate pride all my life and I shall do so, not only because men have always regarded the sword as the symbol of military honour, but also on account of the many memories of wartime Malta and Gozo with which I shall always associate it. As the years pass by it will never fail to remind me of the many dangers and the many trials which we mutually suffered and mutually surmounted, many kindnesses and, in particular, the wonderful gesture of spontaneous generosity and good will which prompted the Maltese People to honour me as they have honoured me today… It has been a delightful and yet moving experience for me this afternoon to have the opportunity of speaking not only to the St Philip Band Club, but also to the representatives of well over sixty other Band and Allied Clubs. I am deeply conscious that these clubs, who have made this magnificent presentation to me today, constitute an integral and characteristic part of the national life of Malta and Gozo, and that they are truly representative of these islands and their proud citizens. It is a unique assembly and I cannot express adequately in words how highly I appreciate the intimacy of this occasion and the closeness of the bond which for all time will unite us.'

At the close of His Excellency's speech, the band played a special march 'Sword of Honour', sung by the Żebbuġ school children. Revd P. Galea Archpriest of Żebbuġ, then unveiled a marble tablet commemorating the event.

The sword, forged by 83-year-old Tom Beasley, who has been making swords for the Wilkinson Sword Company for 60 years, measures 38 inches. The scabbard is made of silver and with an embossed silver-gilt cross guard. There is a Field-Marshal's badge on the show side and the arms of Malta on the reverse. The ivory

The scene at Żebbuġ on the occasion of the Sword of Honour to Lord Gort.

Żebbuġ – Lord Gort holding the Sword of Honour during the presentation ceremony.

The blade of the 'Sword of Honour' presented to Viscount Gort carries a floral design with the inscription: '*Presented by the Band and Allied Clubs in Malta and Għawdex, interpreters of the People's Admiration, Gratitude, Devotion, and Love to HE Field-Marshal The Viscount Gort, VC, their Great Leader and Governor during the Second Siege of Malta*'.

grip is held by four Tudor roses and a laurel wreath eyelet for the gold bullion sword knot. The blade carries a floral design with an inscription and the George Cross on one side and the arms of Lord Gort and the Royal Cipher on the reverse.

The inscription on the sword reads: 'Presented by the Band and Allied Clubs in Malta and Għawdex, interpreters of the People's admiration, gratitude, devotion, and love, to HE Field-Marshal the Viscount Gort, VC, their great leader and Governor during the Second Siege of Malta.'

Today's leader of the Times of Malta is dedicated to the 'Sword of Honour'. – 'Occasions such as yesterday's at Żebbuġ, when the Sword of Honour was presented to HE the Viscount Gort, VC are few and far between. The scene in the village square was a memorable one ... Yesterday's happy intermingling of the people and all the dignitaries of Church, Services, and Civil Government, rejoicing together in the simple ceremony that was held, was a living example of democratic traditions which have been preserved in the island.' Mon 13 Mar

As from today cigarettes are derationed. The maximum retail price of cigarettes remains at 7d. per packet of 10. Tue 21 Mar

The large Crucifix of the church of St Mary of Jesus (*Ta' Ġieżu*) of Valletta which was taken to Gozo during the blitz is brought back to Malta. Sun 26 Mar

Good Friday processions are again held in Valletta, Rabat, and Qormi. Fri 7 Apr

Casualties: *Sliema*: **George** Debono (7), Eric Frendo (15), Albert Giorgio (11), John Giorgio (9). Tue 11 Apr

One hostile aircraft over Malta. Land defences engaged. No bombs dropped. Fri 28 Apr

Wed 10 May

London. Air Minister Sir Archibald Sinclair told the House of Commons that members of the Royal Air Force who were in Malta during the bombing period were being returned to a home station, provided they had been two years on that station. He added that the posting home must be subject to the availability of shipping and the exigencies of the Service.

Mon 15 May

The Office of the Protection Officer in Valletta has been transferred to the Old Railway Station in Ordnance Street, Valletta.

Wed 17 May

The Diocese of Malta has been elevated to an Archdiocese and the Diocese of Gozo has become a Suffragan Metropolitan of Malta. Archbishop Gonzi is raised to the dignity of a Metropolitan and becomes the first Archbishop of Malta and Metropolitan of the Province of Malta.

Mon 22 May

Archbishop Gonzi makes his solemn entry in the Cathedral, Mdina.

Fri 26 May

General Giraud and General Georges, two distinguished French soldiers, arrive on a short visit to Malta as the guests of Governor Gort.

Fri 2 Jun

Vatican City. Pope Piux XII broadcasts a stirring appeal today, his name day. The Pope's voice from the heart of the battle-ringed city came clearly, calmly, and forcefully, over the radio. The Pope said, 'In this world conflict of human tragedy developing around us, events in the past year have reached grave and atrocious proportions which horrify all Christian and human feelings. Once more we feel it our duty to share your anguish of soul and to deplore the increasing tragedies, destruction, ruin, and death which only a year ago would have appeared impossible, but which have nevertheless become a stark reality. The very sacred soil round St Peter's Eternal City and the Mother of Civilization has had to experience present day methods of war.'

The American Fifth Army under General Mark Clark enters Rome. Sun 4 Jun

Rome is captured by the Armies of the United Nations under the command of Gen. Sir Harold Alexander. Mon 5 Jun

Today's editorial comment of the *Times of Malta* is entitled 'Rome Victory'. – 'With the fall of Rome the evil roots of Fascism have been uprooted from the Eternal City. All rejoice that this has been accomplished without the city meeting the fate of Naples and the destruction of those religious and cultural monuments which are the world's heritage. The Pope's broadcast on the eve of the fall of Rome was a memorable appeal to all belligerents.' Tue 6 Jun

This morning a second Front has opened. Allied troops – British, American, and Canadian – under Gen. Sir Bernard Montgomery opened their attack against Hitler's fortress on the northern coast of France. Large-scale landings on Normandy coast are reported.

Priority is given to the repairing of Government property damaged by enemy action, especially hospitals and schools. Tue 20 Jun

Vice-Admiral L.H. Hamilton, Vice-Admiral Malta, unveils a commemorative tablet on the Customs House steps, marking the scene of disembarkation of King George VI a year ago. A Guard of Honour was formed by the St Angelo Royal Marines and paraded near the Customs House steps. HMS *Aurora*, which had brought the King from North Africa on his Malta visit, is back in the Grand Harbour. Her captain was present during the ceremony and her band formed part of the Royal Marine detachment on parade. Admiral Hamilton's speech: 'At this place, one year ago today, the King landed in a Victorious Malta. His visit was the first that he had paid to the island as King and the first visit of the Sovereign since 1912 when King George V landed on his way back from the Coronation Durbar. Malta has received many royal visits in the past. King Edward VII came twice to the island as Prince of Wales before he came as King in 1907. His brother, the Duke of Edinburgh, commanded the Mediterranean fleet from 1886 to 1889, and his daughter Melita was born at the Palace of San Antonio. The last

Bilingual poster in English and Maltese to mark the capture of Rome.

Prince of Wales came to open Parliament in 1921. The present King came as Duke of York in 1927, during his Empire tour to Australia, and when he arrived last year, however much he might have found the face of Malta changed, he found the spirit as it has always been. Coming, as he did, by sea, he emphasized the close connection that

Malta has with the Royal Navy. It is a happy coincidence, too, that the ship which brought the King from North Africa should be back in Grand Harbour today. I am very glad to see *Aurora* here, and more especially because I have a special connection with the ship having had the honour to command her myself at Narvik in 1940. Today, as a year ago, she is playing a part in the ceremony. Her Captain is present and her band is part of the Royal Marine detachment on parade. The royal visit that we are here to commemorate was a more significant affair than those which had been paid to the island in times of peace. His Majesty arrived in the triumphant fortress at a time when victory was in the air.' At the conclusion of the address, the band of the Aurora played the God Save the King. Then Admiral Hamilton removed the flags of Britain and Malta, thereby unveiling the tablet, which reads:

His Majesty King George VI
landed here from HMS Aurora
on
20th June 1943
shortly after the raising
of the Siege.

Marble tablet at the Customs House indicating the site where King George VI landed during his Malta visit.

Thu 22 Jun **The public is** reminded of the existing possibility of chemical warfare and of gas attacks being adopted by the enemy. As from today house to house inspection of respirators commences in several localities.

Thu 29 Jun **The aerodromes at** Ħal Far, Ta' Qali, and Luqa have been declared to be protected areas and access thereto is prohibited to the public.

Wed 26 Jul **Street lighting is** being gradually restored in Valletta and in other localities.

Malta-based fighters score successes against enemy reconnaissance aircraft.

London. The Colonial Secretary stated in the House of Commons that 25 Maltese British subjects are at present held in detention in Uganda on behalf of the Government of Malta; of the original party of 44, 17 were repatriated last year. The others are at present again under review by the Governor with a view to possible repatriation and release.

Sat 5 Aug **Today's leader of** the *Times of Malta* is dedicated to 'Lord Gort, VC'. – 'Never, an age, When God has need of him, Shall want its Man, predestined by that need. – This evening, with pride and sadness, the People of Malta will bid godspeed to HE Field-Marshal the Viscount Gort … No Governor of Malta has held office during such a dramatic period of the Island's history as that which it has been Lord Gort's destiny to shape, and his victory, over almost insuperable odds which existed when he came to Malta 27 months ago, ·has won him the island's gratitude and affection for all time. Lord Gort's departure brings vividly to mind the days of his arrival when the *Luftwaffe* was dominant over the skies of Malta battering unceasingly the worn and besieged garrison and people. Lord Gort has shared with the People of Malta the zenith of the island's trials and the zenith of the island's triumph. He guided the destinies of the people from the darkness of war's night, and the hunger of the Siege, into the brilliance of the day of victory and plenty.'

p.m. Viscount Gort was accorded an enthusiastic send-off as he drove triumphantly through Kingsway.

Lord Gort left Malta for the United Kingdom. Vice-Admiral Sir Louis Hamilton, KCB, DSO, has assumed the duties of Officer Administering the Government. Sun 6 Aug

The annual festivities celebrating the martyrdom of St Laurence are this year (after a lapse of four years) held at Vittoriosa again. Although the old conventual church has been severely damaged through enemy action, the damage has now been temporarily repaired and the statue of the Patron Saint, which had been taken to the nunnery of St Benedict at Mdina for safety, has now been brought back to Vittoriosa in pilgrimage. Tue 10 Aug

Paris liberated. The French Delegate in Malta to the Provisional Government of France has issued a message: 'After four years' temporary occupation Paris is again free… France has fought and resisted from the very beginning both from outside through her Fighting Forces and from within through the heroic incessant Resistance Movement. Her faith and grim stubborness have not been in vain. Just as France in 1914-18 did not give up, so France of 1940 did not despair. *La France a perdu une bataille mais non la guerre* (France has lost a battle but not the war) .*Vive la France*!' Wed 23 Aug

Malta's National Day is this year marked by the unveiling of HM the King's message bestowing the George Cross to Malta [15.4.1942] and President Roosevelt's Citation commemorating his visit to Malta [8.12.1943], both of which have been reproduced in bronze lettering on two tablets,[1] now fixed on either side of the main entrance of the Palace, Valletta. Vice-Admiral Sir Louis Hamilton, the Officer Administering the Government, unveiled the tablets to the playing of the Stars and Stripes, the Maltese Anthem and God Save the King by the Band of the King's Own Malta Regiment. During the ceremony HE delivered a speech: 'The 8th September is a date of deep historical significance in the history of Malta. It is the date on which, in 1565, the Knights of St John – the heirs of the Fri 8 Sep

1 The tablets were made in the engineering department of Malta Dockyard.

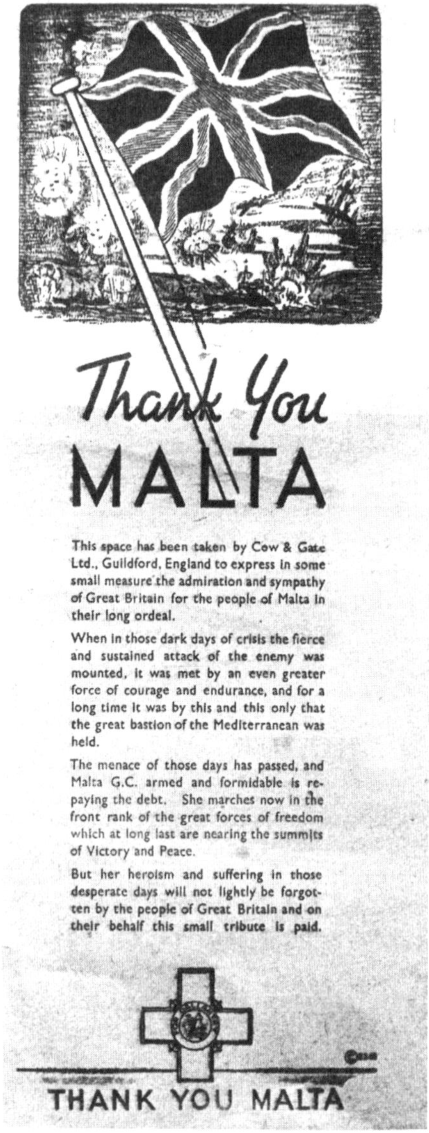

An expression of admiration and sympathy for the People of Malta by Cow & Gate of Guildford, England.

BUCKINGHAM PALACE

THE GOVERNOR,
MALTA

TO HONOUR HER BRAVE PEOPLE I AWARD THE GEORGE CROSS TO THE ISLAND FORTRESS OF MALTA TO BEAR WITNESS TO A HEROISM AND DEVOTION THAT WILL LONG BE FAMOUS IN HISTORY.

GEORGE R.I.

APRIL 15TH. 1942.

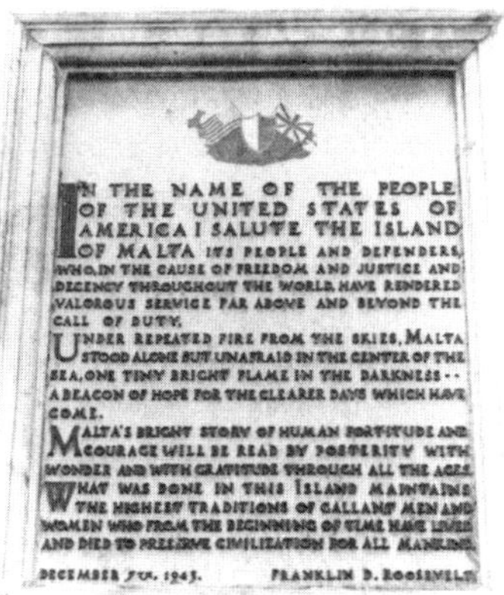

IN THE NAME OF THE PEOPLE OF THE UNITED STATES OF AMERICA I SALUTE THE ISLAND OF MALTA ITS PEOPLE AND DEFENDERS, WHO, IN THE CAUSE OF FREEDOM AND JUSTICE AND DECENCY THROUGHOUT THE WORLD, HAVE RENDERED VALOROUS SERVICE FAR ABOVE AND BEYOND THE CALL OF DUTY.

UNDER REPEATED FIRE FROM THE SKIES, MALTA STOOD ALONE BUT UNAFRAID IN THE CENTER OF THE SEA, ONE TINY BRIGHT FLAME IN THE DARKNESS -- A BEACON OF HOPE FOR THE CLEARER DAYS WHICH HAVE COME.

MALTA'S BRIGHT STORY OF HUMAN FORTITUDE AND COURAGE WILL BE READ BY POSTERITY WITH WONDER AND WITH GRATITUDE THROUGH ALL THE AGES.

WHAT WAS DONE IN THIS ISLAND MAINTAINS THE HIGHEST TRADITIONS OF GALLANT MEN AND WOMEN WHO FROM THE BEGINNING OF TIME HAVE LIVED AND DIED TO PRESERVE CIVILIZATION FOR ALL MANKIND.

DECEMBER 7TH. 1943. FRANKLIN D. ROOSEVELT.

King George VI's message bestowing the George Cross to Malta and President Roosevelt's Citation commemorating his visit to Malta are reproduced in bronze lettering on two tablets, now fixed on one side of the main entrance of the Palace, Valletta.

chivalry of Europe – and the people of Malta finally defeated and drove off the Turkish invaders after a siege of six months and preserved Malta from the Infidel. It is also the date on which, one year ago, Fascist Italy surrendered unconditionally.'

Fri 15 Sep

Lieutenant General Sir Edmond Charles Acton Schreiber, KCB, DSO, has been appointed Governor and C-in-C Malta in succession to the FieldMarshal Viscount Gort.

Mon 25 Sep

The new Governor Sir Edmond Schreiber arrives in Malta.

Tue 26 Sep

The ceremony of the swearing-in of Sir Edmond Schreiber as Governor of Malta is held in the Hall of St Michael and St George at the Palace, Valletta. In a speech Sir Edmond said: 'Though I have never visited Malta before and I have not had the fortune to have been able to share with the people of Malta their trials of the siege, this does give me the advantage of approaching your problems with an open mind. I realize that there must be many problems of reconstruction and improvement of conditions to be faced up to here in Malta. I am sure we can solve them together, if we tackle them in the unselfish spirit for the common good which has brought the peoples of the British Empire through the dark days of the war to the victories our magnificent forces are now winning at sea, on land and in the air.'

Fri 6 Oct

A plan showing the reconstruction scheme for Valletta and Floriana has been prepared and is on view at the Office of the Public Works, the Palace, Valletta.

Sat 7 Oct

Meeting of the National Congress.

Sun 15 Oct

The German News Agency has announced the death of Gen. Field-Marshal Rommel. He died from injuries in his head received in a motor-car accident while Commander-in-Chief of the Army Group in the West. The news bulletin says: 'With the death of Gen. Field-Marshal Rommel, the soldierly life of one of our most successful commanders has reached its fulfilment. His name will be for ever linked with the two years heroic fight of the German Afrika Korps. Hitler has ordered a State Funeral.'

Wed 18 Oct

Today's editorial comment of the *Times of Malta* is dedicated to 'Rommel and Malta'. – 'With the Berlin announcement of the death of Rommel the Germans have lost one of the most publicized of their military leaders. Rommel undoubtedly had a forceful personality, but this and his leadership on the field of battle were played up to fantastic height by Goebbels' propaganda ... Kesselring, in Sicily, wanted to eliminate Malta first, while Rommel – one of the earliest Nazis with power of access to Hitler himself, and newly created Field-Marshal after a flying trip home to Berlin – was eager to concentrate on the drive to Alexandria and the Nile. Rommel was able to override Kesselring ... If Kesselring's plan of campaign had been adhered to instead of altered to attune with Rommel's strategy, Malta's acquaintance with war would have been all the more intense, and would doubtless have included an invasion bid. Gun for gun Malta's small area constituted the strongest defended fortress anywhere and there would have been slaughter of German paratroops and gliders; or both. Kesselring thought the prize was worth the effort and sacrifice. Rommel thought otherwise. Rommel's impatience and its effect upon Nazi strategy spared Malta the ordeal of attempted invasion. Because ordeal it would have been, particularly for the civilian population while the battle was being fought out, probably over the course of a dozen days or so, prior to the defeat of the enemy bid. There could have been no evacuation for civilians and German civilians' experience in their own town of Aachen now under attack provides some indication of what the war picture might have been in Malta in 1942. There is no question that the garrison of Malta comprised the finest troops ever. The fight would have been unparalleled. Rommel's death recalls this period, but only the verdict of history will put it into its proper military perspective.'

Owners of chapels situated in the Addolorata Cemetery and in other government cemeteries are advised to ensure that such chapels, especially those that were damaged through enemy action, are made secure against trespassers. Sat 21 Oct

Pope Pius XII receives in private audience the new Governor of Malta, Sir Edmond Schreiber. Mon 23 Oct

Whilst clearing debris, workmen discovered a small-sized bomb lying in a heap of stones in the upper storey of Messrs Richard Ellis in Kingsway,[2] Valletta. The bomb is reckoned to have been dropped three years ago. It has been removed by members of the Royal Engineers Bomb Disposal Squad. Thu 26 Oct

The National Congress holds a sitting. Sat 28 Oct

2 Richard Ellis, photographer and photographic goods dealer, established in 1871 was photographer by special appointment to King George V, the Duke of Edinburgh, the Duke of Hesse, Queen Alexandra, King Edward VII, Prince Louis of Battenberg, and other members of royal families.

Solemn pilgrimage from Birkirkara to Cospicua in fulfillment of the blitz-time vow made by the Rev. Chapter of the Collegiate church of the Immaculate Conception of Cospicua.

Mon 30 Oct

Members of the Demolition Squads have cleared the last traces of the historic Clock Tower at Vittoriosa which was extensively damaged during the blitz. The Clock Tower was built by Grand Master D'Omedes in 1549 to serve as a vedette or observation tower. It proved of paramount strategic importance during the siege of

1565. Quadrilateral in form and decadent Norman in style, the Tower was a special landmark of Vittoriosa.

Sat 11 Nov

Mgr Giuseppe Pace DD, JCD, Ph.D., Archdeacon of the Cathedral Church of Gozo and Vicar General, has been appointed Bishop of Gozo.

Mgr Emanuel Galea, DD, JCD, B.Litt, Bishop of Tralles and Vicar General of Malta, has been appointed Auxiliary Bishop of Malta.

Mon 13 Nov

An Air Ministry communiqué issued in London announces that the 45,000- ton German battleship *Tirpitz* has been sunk in Trimsoe Fjord, Norway, by 29 RAF Lancasters.

Sun 19 Nov

This evening some 30,000 people from all the towns and villages of Malta took part in a solemn pilgrimage when the statue of Our Lady of the Immaculate Conception was brought back to the Collegiate Parish Church of Cospicua.

TIFKIRA TAL-PELLEGRINAGG MINN B'KARA
GHAL BORMLA FID-19 TA' NOV. 1944.

Kwadru ta' Marija Immakulata
Miqjuma fil-Perins. Coll. u Parr.
Knisja-Santwarju ta' Bormla.

TIFKIRA TAL-PELLEGRINAGG MINN B'KARA
GHAL BORMLA FID-19 TA' NOV. 1944.

Statwa ta' Marija Immakulata
Miqjuma fil-Perins. Coll. u Parr.
Knisja Santwarju ta' Bormla.

Leaflet printed on the occasion of the pilgrimage which brought back the statue of Our Lady from Birkirkara to the parish church of Cospicua.

Cheers and the chanting of hymns and of the Te Deum characterized the procession. The procession passed through Birkirkara, Ħamrun, Marsa, Paola, and Cospicua.

Fri 24 Nov **Tempering with signals'** equipment and the removal of wire or cables are declared a serious offence, as such tempering interferes with the war effort.

Thu 30 Nov **A plan of** the re-planning scheme for the Three Cities is on view at the Public Works Department, the Palace, Valletta.

Sun 10 Dec **The church of** St Publius, parish church of Floriana, is re-opened for its normal functions now that it has been considerably repaired.

Wed 13 Dec **London. The Secretary** of State for the Colonies announces in the House of Commons that 25 Maltese internees in Uganda have now been released and that steps are being taken for their repatriation in Malta.

Sun 31 Dec **New Year Message** by Governor Sir Edmond Schreiber: 'We have now entered in the sixth year of the war. 1944 has been a year of great achievement by the Allies. We have been the greatest combined operation of all time in the invasion of Normandy, culminating in the great victory, which freed nearly the whole of France and Belgium. There have also been great victories in Italy, including the liberation of Rome, and the Germans have been driven out of nearly all the Balkans. Our armies, after a most arduous campaign, have had a series of victories over the Japanese in Burma, and in the Pacific great advances have been made towards the heart of Japan. The Royal Navy has regained dominion of the seas, and we now see the Mediterranean – almost completely free of any enemy shipping. In the air the Allied air forces have achieved overwhelming superiority. Germany is hemmed in all sides and suffering a gigantic aerial bombardment, while the ring about the Japanese forces is daily closing in … All this shows that 1945 will be yet another year of endeavour and sacrifice. The final defeat of Germany may take some time … Let our New Year resolution be: In 1945 we will be worthy of our glorious past.'

AD 1945

Today's editorial comment of the *Times of Malta* is dedicated to the 'New Year 1945'. – 'Another leaf in the calendar of the years has been turned and the world embarks upon the passage through 1945. There is a solemnity about the beginning of a new year, traditionally associated with resolutions to make the new better than the old, to fashion the future to a better shape than the past. That resolution is necessary today as ever, albeit that this is the sixth occasion when a new year has opened in time of war and that there is more cause than ever before for sober confidence that complete triumph over the Nazi challenge to civilization will be achieved during the ensuing twelve months. There is much suffering still.' Mon 1 Jan

It is learned from official sources that Fr Maurus Inguanez, a Maltese member of the religious community of Monte Cassino Abbey, saved from destruction the famous Keats and Shelley relics that were there preserved and restored them to the Memorial House in Rome. Fr Inguanez smuggled the relics through the Nazi lines and hitch-hiked with them to Rome. Mon 8 Jan

The National Assembly held its first sitting in the Hall of St Michael and St George, the Palace, Valletta. Prof. Contino Luigi Preziosi is elected President. During the sitting a message sent to the Assembly by the Governor is read. Mgr Michele Gonzi also addressed a message to the Assembly on this historic occasion: 'May God will that the Assembly will succeed in drafting and winning for our Malta a Constitution, that, while safeguarding the rights and interests of all social classes, will be a Constitution truly worthy of a courageous people, wholly loyal and Catholic.' Sat 20 Jan

The traditional ceremony of the presentation of candles to the Governor by the Parish Priests of Malta and Gozo is held in the Hall of St Michael and St George, the Palace, Valletta – the historic frescoes[1] embellishing the hall and representing episodes of the Siege of 1565 are gradually having their wartime 'bandages' taken Tue 6 Feb

1 The frieze frescoes were painted by Matteo Perez d'Aleccio (1547–1616) a pupil of Michelangelo.

off The Governor's speech: 'It is great pleasure for me to take part for the first time in this ancient ceremony of Candlemas. The ceremony was reinstated last year, when the Allied victories made it clear that action by the enemy was no longer likely against Malta. 1944 has been another year of victorious advances by the Allies … The path before us leading up to final victory, and into the peace after victory, is a steep and stony one. Our progress along it may be slow and painful, but we are moving steadily up it. Malta has left behind the dangers and hunger of the Siege, the complete blocking of the streets, and many of the heavier restrictions on its daily life. The obstacles in the path ahead are many, but they must be overcome, and they can be overcome by our united efforts. The first steps have already been taken towards achieving Self-Government. The National Assembly has started its task of working out a form of Constitution … The task of reconstruction is slowly taking shape. The Report of the Town Planning Consultant has now been completed… It forms a framework on which the people of Malta will be able to plan the future of the built-up areas round the harbour … Here in Malta you have the heritage of the original crusaders. This war is a crusade against the evils of Nazism and Fascism. We shall need the crusading spirit more than ever, if we are to win the Peace.'

Mon 12 Feb

A joint statement officially released in London, Washington and Moscow, reveals that the 'Big Three' – Prime Minister Winston Churchill, President Franklin Roosevelt, and Marshal Joseph Stalin – have met at Yalta, the Crimean seaside resort thirty miles south-west of Sebastopol. Among the major decisions taken at an eight-day conference were comprehensive plans for the final defeat of Germany and the break up of the German war machine. It is also officially disclosed that Mr Churchill and Mr Roosevelt visited Malta on their way to the conference. The meeting was preceded by an Anglo-American conference in Malta, where Mr Anthony Eden and Mr Stettinius conferred. Also taking part in the Anglo-American conference held in Malta (at Montgomery House, Floriana) were Major Gen. E. Jacob, Gen. Sir Hastings Ismay, Admiral Sir James Somerville, Admiral of the Fleet Sir Andrew B. Cunningham, Bart., Field-Marshal Sir Alan Brooke, Marshal of the RAF Sir Charles

IN THIS ISSUE

	Page
FOREIGN NEWS	2, 3 & 5
ANGLO-AMERICANS MEET IN MALTA	1
SPORTS	4
BRITAIN'S 10-YEAR PLAN	5
TRANSITION IN MALTA	7
PICTURES	10 & 12

TIMES OF MALTA

No. 2,851. TUESDAY, FEBRUARY 13, 1945 Price 2d.

CHURCHILL-ROOSEVELT MEET IN MALTA

Anglo-American preliminary to "Big Three" Meeting

THE PRESIDENT

MARSHAL STALIN

The meeting of the "Big Three" was preceded by an Anglo-American meeting in Malta, where Mr. Churchill and Mr. Roosevelt met, and where Mr. Anthony Eden and Mr. Stettinius conferred. Mr. Churchill and Mr. Roosevelt met Marshal Stalin at the Crimean seaside resort of Yalta.

THE PRIME MINISTER

MALTA AND YALTA

A JOINT statement, officially released tonight in London, Washington and Moscow, reveals that the "Big Three" — Prime Minister Winston Churchill, President Franklin Roosevelt and Marshal Joseph Stalin, have met at Yalta, Crimean seaside resort 30 miles south-west of Sebastopol.

Among the major decisions taken at an eight-day conference were comprehensive plans for the final defeat of Germany and the "break up for all time of the German war machine." It is also officially disclosed that Mr. Churchill and Mr. Roosevelt visited Malta on their way to the conference.

The Joint Statement of the Three Powers is published on Page 2.

(Right) Anglo-American Conference in session in Malta's "Montgomery House"; (Reading from right to left) Major-General E.I.C. Jacob; General Sir Hastings L. Ismay; Admiral Sir James Somerville; Admiral of the Fleet Sir Andrew B. Cunningham, Bart.; Field Marshal Sir Alan F. Brooke; Marshal of the R.A.F., Sir Charles Portal; Field Marshal Sir Henry Maitland-Wilson; Major-General R.E. Laycock; Commander R.D. Coleridge, R.N. and Air Marshal Robb.

Among the American representatives at the Joint Anglo-American conference were: (reading from left to right) Rear-Admiral L.D. McCormick, U.S.N.; Vice-Admiral C.N. Cooke, U.S.N.; Fleet Admiral E.J. King, U.S.N.; General of the Army General George Marshall, U.S.A.; Brigadier-General A.C. McFarland, U.S.A.; Major-General L.S. Kuter, U.S.A., and Lieutenant-General B.B. Somervell, U.S.A.

VICTORY ATMOSPHERE IN THE MALTA CONFERENCE ROOM: Marshal of the R.A.F. Sir Charles Portal with Field Marshal Sir Alan Brooke, Chief of Imperial General Staff and Admiral of the Fleet Sir Andrew B. Cunningham, Bart.

Churchill-Roosevelt meeting in Malta.

Portal, Field Marshal Sir Henry Maitland Wilson, Major Gen. R. Laycock, Cdr. R. Coleridge, RN, Air Marshal Robb, Admiral King, Chief of US Navy, and Field-Marshal Sir Harold Alexander.

The Anglo-American Service Chiefs toured Valletta and did not fail to visit the church of St John's.

Sat 17 Feb

National Assembly holds second sitting.

Wed 28 Feb

A grim relic of the blitz days: the body of a serviceman – believed to be a victim of an air-raid in April 1942 – is unearthed by men engaged at work on a bombed site on the corner of Britannia Street and Old Bakery Street, Valletta, formerly the site of St Andrew's Hotel.

Thu 1 Mar

Today's leader of the *Times of Malta* is dedicated to 'Yalta and Malta' – 'All in these islands have read with pride and appreciation the Prime Minister's references to the historic conference held in Malta and its "battle-scarred harbour" … The Yalta conference and the Malta talks will go down in history as epoch-making events.'

Fri 2 Mar

Third sitting of the National Assembly.

Thu 8 Mar

The last of the Maltese internees who had been deported to Uganda in 1942 land at the Customs House, where they are received by their relatives and friends. The group of internees include Dr Enrico Mizzi, Sir Arturo Mercieca, former Chief Justice, and Mgr Albert Pantalleresco, Dean of the Cathedral Chapter of Malta.

Sun 11 Mar

London Press reviews the official publication *The Air Battle of Malta*, which has been prepared for the Air Ministry by the Ministry of Information and printed at His Majesty's Stationery Office.

Fri 16 Mar

Fourth sitting of the National Assembly. In his Annual Report Gust published) on the work and activity of the Medical and Health Department relating to 1943, Prof. A.V. Bernard, CBE, MD, DPH, DTM&H, Chief Government Medical Officer, says: 'The number of civilian casualties due to operations of war was relatively small this year. It came to 101 injured of whom 63 required detention in hospital. Six died. 2l persons were killed outright bringing the total dead to 27. The following is a summary of war casualties from 11 June 1940 to 31 December 1943: Seriously injured 1,846, slightly injured 1,932, died of wounds 296, killed outright 1,190, missing presumed dead 54. Total dead 1,540; of which 703 were men, 433 women, and 404 children. The fatal cases represent 5.7 per thousand of the population. Sea traffic with other countries was re-established during the year. In spite of the dangers which this represented as regards the importation of infection, no exotic diseases occurred. The prevalence of rat infestation gave us some anxious moments. The large accumulation of debris in the devastated areas afforded safe harbourage and ample breeding facilities for these vermin. Conditions were worsened by the dastardly habit of some people of throwing kitchen garbage on these accumulations. As soon as red squill and other necessaries were obtained, the anti-rat campaign was intensified and the larger accumulations of debris were treated with cyanogen and sulphur fumigation. Rat-proofing of buildings was practically impossible owing to lack of materials. In spite of the great disturbance of our normal hospital arrangements, accommodation was provided for a number of patients above the average of pre-war times and it was found possible to hospitalize the majority of the patients during the infantile paralysis and the typhoid fever outbreaks. Owing to the severe damages sustained by the Central Hospital, its several Departments have remained dispersed in emergency establishments. It was only possible to bring back the female medical patients during this year. Repairs and rebuilding of the demolished parts have been taken in hand and it is hoped that some other Departments will be returned here in the near future. This building, however, will never again suffice for the purpose of a complete general hospital for the population of Malta. In pre-war years the state of overcrowding was already acute and similar condition\ can never again be tolerated. What is more, more bed space is required as more people must, under present conditions, be hospitalized both because many patients cannot be treated at home on account of the overcrowding of dwellings and because the

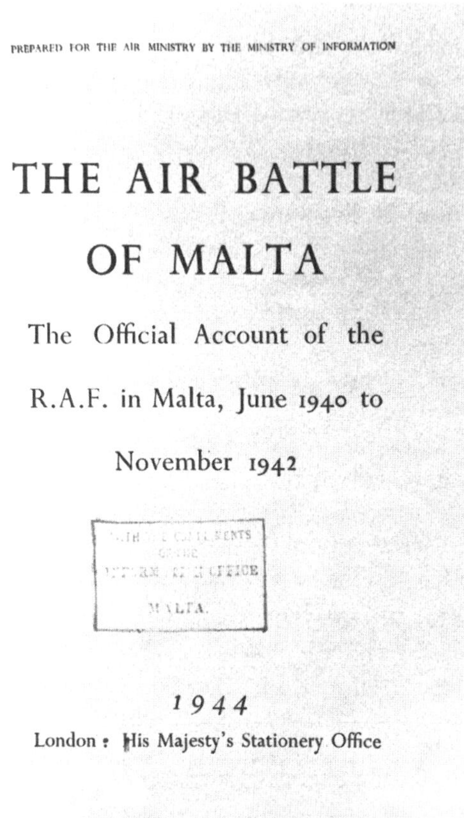

PREPARED FOR THE AIR MINISTRY BY THE MINISTRY OF INFORMATION

THE AIR BATTLE OF MALTA

The Official Account of the R.A.F. in Malta, June 1940 to November 1942

1944

London: His Majesty's Stationery Office

Frontispiece of the book entitled *The Air Battle of Malta*, being the Official Account of the RAF in Malta (June, 1940 – Number, 1942), prepared for the Air Ministry and published by His Majesty's Stationery Office (1944).

people have now become more hospital-minded and have learnt to appreciate the excellent service which they obtain in our hospitals.'

Sun 8 Apr **Solemn entry of** Bishop Giuseppe Pace into the Cathedral Church of Gozo.

Thu 12 Apr

New York. The White House announces the sudden death of President Roosevelt. The President died suddenly of cerebral haemorrhage at Warm Springs, Georgia. Senator Harry Truman, Vice-President, takes office as President of the United States of America.

Sat 14 Apr

Telegram sent by His Honour the Governor's Deputy to Mrs Roosevelt: 'On behalf of the garrison and the people of the Island Fortress of Malta, I convey to you and the people of the United States our deepest sympathy in your most grievous loss. The recent visits to Malta of the late President will ever be remembered and cherished and his inspiring citation will live long in the minds of the people of these islands.'

Mon 16 Apr

A motor truck unloading stone rubble from bombed areas at the Chalet Għar-id-Dud, Sliema, overshot the mark and fell into the sea

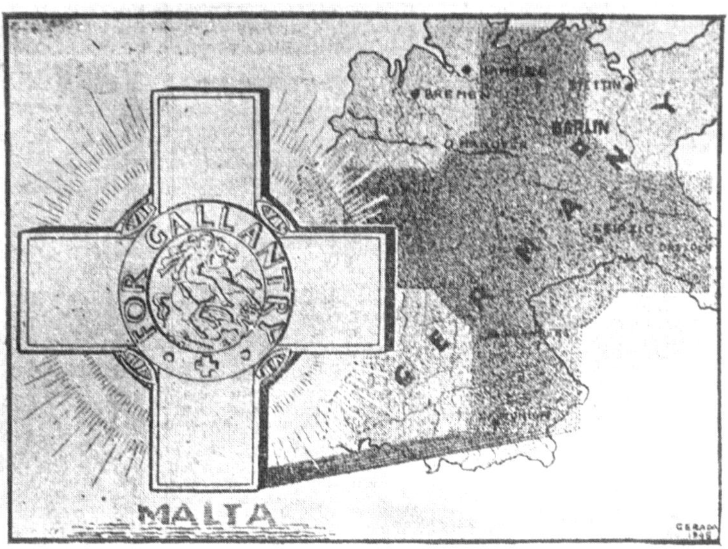

The Glow of Victory casts the Shadow of Defeat. *(Sunday Times of Malta)*

TIMES OF MALTA

No. 3,016 WEDNESDAY, MAY 2, 1945

AWARDED TO MALTA APRIL 15, 1942

HITLER DEAD

(Reuter's Service)

LONDON, May 1.

THE GERMAN RADIO ANNOUNCED TONIGHT THAT HITLER IS DEAD. "OUR FUEHRER", THE RADIO SAID, "FELL AT HIS BATTLE POST IN THE REICH CHANCELLERY IN BERLIN THIS AFTERNOON. TRUE TO HIS GREAT IDEAL TO SAVE THE PEOPLES OF EUROPE FROM BOLSHEVISM HE HAS RISKED HIS LIFE AND MET WITH A HERO'S DEATH. THE GREATEST HEAD OF GERMAN HISTORY HAS LEFT THE STAGE."

Hitler's death was preceded by the playing of solemn Wagnerian music including "Twilight of the Gods".

Then came "Achtung! Achtung! In a few minutes you will hear a serious and important message to the German people. We are now going to play a slow movement of Bruckner's 7th Symphony."

Finally came the report of Hitler's death. All this time the southern German radio network went on broadcasting light music.

A CORRESPONDENT'S ACCOUNT OF MUSSOLINI'S LAST HOURS APPEARS IN PAGE 2

"I HAVE NOT SEEN HIMMLER" — BERNADOTTE

(Reuter's Service)

STOCKHOLM, May 1.

Count Bernadotte stated at a press conference today: "I have not seen Himmler during my last visit to Germany and Denmark. I have not forwarded any message from Himmler or any other authoritative German."

He added that during his latest visit to Copenhagen, from which he returned today, he met Werner Best, German Minister to Denmark.

LIST AND LEEB CAPTURED

(Reuter's Service)

S.H.A.E.F., May 1.

Marshall Yarrow, Reuter's special correspondent, cables:

Field Marshals Sigmund List and Wilhelm Ritter von Leeb have been captured by the U.S. 7th Army.

List was found at his home at Partenkirchen. He was wearing civilian clothes and stated he was relieved of his command in 1942 when he refused to lead a suicide attack on Stalingrad.

Leeb was taken near Fuessen while digging in his garden.

Tito Link With Allies

DRIVE FOR BRENNER OPENED

(Reuter's Service)

ALLIED H.Q., MED., May 1.

NEW Zealand troops today linked up with Marshal Tito's army. No details of the link up are yet available, although it is known that Tito's men yesterday broke into the big Italian naval base of Trieste. The British 13th Corps then had 50 miles to go for the link-up.

Desmond Tighe, Reuter's special correspondent at Allied Headquarters, Italy, cables:

The drive for the Brenner Pass, vital mountain gateway into Southern Bavaria has opened. 5th Army troops are pushing towards Trento, the Alpine city 70 miles south of the pass. Men of the U.S. 10th Mountain Division spearheading the drive, have captured Torbole and two other towns on the shores of Lake Garda.

STIFF RESISTANCE

German remnants, which the German C-in-C Vietinghoff is trying to gather in the mountains, are putting up a stiff resistance.

MILAN PLAINS

On the Milan plains front the U.S. 4th Corps has pushed on to the line of the Ticino river which flows from Lake Maggiore into the Po, forestalling any move by German troops trapped in Western Italy to break out into the Alps.

The 8th Army are pressing on well towards Trieste and in the last 24 hours captured over 10,000 prisoners.

M.A.A.F. Fortresses, operating for the first time in five days, bombed railway targets at Salzburg in Austria, vital communication centre for Hitler's "southern redoubt".

'TANK BUSTERS' RECORD

An official announcement today from Allied H.Q. said that about half the German tank strength in Italy has been destroyed during the past month by the Desert Air Force.

Doenitz Takes Over

"STRUGGLE WILL CONTINUE"

The German radio added that the former Commander-in-Chief Admiral Doenitz is Hitler's successor.

Admiral Doenitz, speaking over radio said: "Our Fuehrer has fallen at his command post. My first task is to save the German people from destruction by Bolshevism. If only for this task, the struggle will continue. Against the British and Americans I shall have to pursue the fight so far and so long as they hamper my struggle against the Bolsheviks."

"V" DAY PLANS

POSSIBILITY OF ANNOUNCEMENT THIS WEEK

(Reuter's Service)

LONDON, May 1.

THE Prime Minister, Mr. Churchill, answering questions in the House of Commons today by Mr. Greenwood (Lab.) said: "I have no special statement to make about the war position in Europe except that it is definitely more satisfactory than it was this time five years ago (laughter)."

PRIME MINISTER'S RADIO ANNOUNCEMENT

H.M. THE KING TO BROADCAST

Battle Of The Ports

MONTGOMERY MOVING IN FOR KILL

(Reuter's Service) SUPREME HEADQUARTERS A.E.F., May 1.

Marshall Yarrow, Reuter's special correspondent in Paris, cables:

ALLIED TROOPS — BELIEVING IN THE GERMAN SURRENDER ONLY WHEN IT COMES — CONTINUE TO SMASH HARD AT BOTH THE NORTH AND SOUTH POCKETS OF TRUNCATED GERMANY. FIELD MARSHAL SIR BERNARD MONTGOMERY'S ARMIES ARE MOVING IN FOR THE KILL AND THE BIG PORTS OF HAMBURG, BREMERHAVEN, WILHELSHAVEN AND EMDEN ARE ENTERING THEIR LAST DAYS OF LIFE.

– Probing Towards Hamburg:

While General Sir Miles Dempsey's troops swarmed across the Elbe south-east of Hamburg, the British and Americans under British command have joined up their bridgehead into a solid foothold 20 miles long and 12 miles deep and from this springboard armoured elements are probing towards Hamburg, Germany's second largest city and biggest port. West of the port Allied units have entered Stade, practically clamping Hamburg in the tightening jaws of a vice.

Leading tanks of the 11th Armoured Division, pushing on from the Elbe bridgehead, are tonight within 18 miles of the big German Baltic port of Luebeck. A link-up with Russian forces to the east is possible any day now.

BREMERHAVEN:

EMDEN:

WILHELMSHAVEN:

ROKOSSOVSKY SWEEPING WEST FOR LINK-UP

New Gains on Wide Front

(Reuter's Service) MOSCOW, May 1.

MAKING sweeping gains on a 60-mile front, Marshal Rokossovsky's armies sweeping forward for the link-up with Field Marshal Montgomery's forces, today captured Stralsund, on the Baltic coast opposite the island naval base of Ruegen, announces Marshal Stalin in one of two special Orders-of-the-Day.

The Order also announces the capture of Grimmen, Malchin, Waren and Wesenberg, important communication centres and strongpoints in the German defences.

A second Order-of-the-Day announces the capture of Brandenburg, capital of the province of the same name, and taken by Marshal Zhukov's men.

BERLIN

Duncan Hooper, Reuter's special correspondent in Moscow, cables:

The Berlin battle — now well behind the main Soviet front line — has developed into a gigantic mopping-up operation. The German defence is disorganised and broken, although some German ... still fight on fanatically.

... times are lining the streets with white surrender flags. Against this some S.S. battalions have made suicide pacts to go down with the buildings they are defending.

Colonel-General Berzarin, Soviet Commander in Berlin, is already getting some sort of normal life re-established in the occupied areas. Some factories have been re-opened, power stations and water works will be in operation by Thursday and 20 hospitals have been opened for German wounded.

Announcement of Hitler's death.

from a height of about 25 feet. The driver, who went down with the truck, escaped unhurt.

Wed 18 Apr

A copy of *The Air Battle of Malta* has been presented to the Royal Malta Library. The copy is signed by Air Vice-Marshal F.H. Maynard, CB, AFC, 1940/41; Air Vice-Marshal Sir Hugh P. Lloyd KBE, CB, MC, DFC, 1941/42; and Air Marshal Sir Keith Park, KCB, KBE, MC, 1942/43, each of whom was in turn Air Officer Commanding, Royal Air Force, at Malta, during the period covered by the official RAF story.

Fri 20 Apr

Sixth sitting of the National Assembly.

Fri 27 Apr

Allied troops stand shoulder to shoulder in Germany – the Russians after fighting back, 2,000 miles across Europe from Stalingrad, the British and Americans after crossing the English Channel and advancing 1,000 miles.

A communiqué from No. 10 Downing Street, announces: 'General Eisenhower reports firm contact has been established between his ground forces and those of our Soviet Allies.'

Sun 29 Apr

Mussolini, dressed as a German soldier, tried to escape to Switzerland, but was recognized by Italian partisans.

Crowds of people filed past the bullet-riddled body of Benito Mussolini. It lay in the Piazza Loreto, Milan, from where Mussolini began his '*Marcia su Roma*' (March on Rome) 23 years ago.

Tue 1 May

Hitler is dead.

The German radio announces that Hitler is dead. 'Our Fuhrer fell at his battle post in the Reich Chancellery in Berlin. True to his great ideal to save the peoples of Europe from Bolshevism, he has risked his life and met with a hero's death. The greatest head of German history has left the stage.'

The former Commander-in-Chief Admiral Karl Doenitz is Hitler's successor.[2]

Wed 2 May

Circular by Archbishop Gonzi: 'By the Grace of God, the end of the war in Europe is very imminent ... His Grace the Archbishop orders that as soon as the news is given, the bells in the Cathedral, the Co-Cathedral, the Collegiate, the Parochial and the Conventual Churches (also in the others; if so desired) will ring for half an hour without any delay. If this news comes after 9 p.m., the bells will ring at 8 a.m. on the following morning.'

Goebbels, Hitler's propaganda minister, commits suicide.

Mon 7 May

Germany surrenders unconditionally. The signing took place at a little red school-house, which is Gen. Eisenhower's Headquarters. Gen. Alfred Jodl, the new German Army Chief-of-Staff signed for Germany, Gen. Bidell Smith, Gen. Eisenhower's Chief-of-Staff, signed for the Supreme Allied Command. Gen. Ivan Susloparoff signed for Russia and Gen. François Sevez for France.

Poem entitled 'Victory', written by the Gozitan poetess, Mary Meilak:

Victory came with heavy slow wheels
Dragged by heroic, sturdy, mind,
Waving flags, proclaiming freedom
To long-tried, tortured mankind.

Now that Victory bells do ring,
Thanks to God, in union sing.
Victory came dressed like an angel
When the sky kissed Europe's face,

One May morning, one fine morning,
The long-for, great Day of Days.
Now that Victory bells do ring,
Blessings, we, in duty sing!

2 Admiral Doenitz had been brought to Malta during World War One (1914–18) as a prisoner after his U-boat had been sunk in the central Mediterranean. It was his first command.

VICTORY NUMBER

TIMES OF MALTA

No. 3,021 TUESDAY, MAY 8, 1945

GERMANY OUT!

UNCONDITIONAL SURRENDER

TODAY 'VE' DAY IN EUROPE

TODAY IS "VICTORY IN EUROPE DAY" IT IS OFFICIALLY ANNOUNCED, IN ACCORDANCE WITH ARRANGEMENTS BETWEEN THE THREE GREAT POWERS.

AN OFFICIAL ANNOUNCEMENT IS TO BE BROADCAST BY THE PRIME MINISTER, MR WINSTON CHURCHILL TODAY AT 1 P.M. G.M.T., (3 P.M. MALTA TIME) AND THE DAY WILL BE REGARDED AS A HOLIDAY. THE DAY FOLLOWING (WEDNESDAY) WILL ALSO BE A HOLIDAY.

"GOD SAVE THE KING"

HIS MAJESTY THE KING IS TO BROADCAST TODAY TO THE PEOPLES OF THE BRITISH EMPIRE AND COMMONWEALTH AT 7 P.M. G.M.T. (9 P.M. MALTA TIME). PARLIAMENT, IT IS STATED, WILL MEET AT THE USUAL TIME.

Britain's Gratitude To Fighting Men

H.M. THE KING'S MESSAGE TO GENERAL EISENHOWER

THE GRATITUDE OF THE BRITISH PEOPLE FOR THE "COMPLETE AND CRUSHING VICTORY" OVER GERMANY IS EXPRESSED BY HIS MAJESTY THE KING IN A TELEGRAM SENT TO GENERAL EISENHOWER, SUPREME ALLIED COMMANDER.

"Eleven months ago you led the Allied Expeditionary Force across the English Channel, carrying with you the hopes and prayers of millions of men and women of many nations," it said. "To it was entrusted the task of annihilating the German armies in Western Europe and thus liberating the peoples whom they had enslaved."

MISSION ACCOMPLISHED

"All the world now knows that after fierce and continuous warfare this force has accomplished its mission with a finality achieved by no other such expedition in history.

"On behalf of all my peoples I ask that you, its Supreme Commander will tell its members how deeply grateful we are to them and how unbounded is our admiration for the courage and determination which, under your wise leadership, has brought them to their goal of complete and crushing victory.

"I would ask you also to convey a special message of congratulations to my own forces now under your command. Throughout the campaign they have acquitted themselves in all services with valour and distinction for which their fellow countrymen will forever hold them in honour."

MAY 7, 1945 Germans Laid Down Arms

SURRENDER SIGNED IN EISENHOWER'S HEADQUARTERS

(Reuter's Service)

RHEIMS, MAY 7.

THE ALLIES ANNOUNCE THAT GERMANY SURRENDERED UNCONDITIONALLY TODAY (MONDAY). THE SURRENDER TOOK PLACE AT 2.40 A.M. (FRENCH TIME), AT A LITTLE RED SCHOOL-HOUSE WHICH IS GENERAL EISENHOWER'S HEADQUARTERS.

Colonel-General Gustav Jodl, the new German Army Chief-of-Staff, signed for Germany.

The New York Radio giving an account of the signing ceremony, says that General Bidell Smith, General Eisenhower's Chief-of-Staff, signed for the Supreme Allied Command, General Ivan Susloparoff signed for Russia and General Francois Sevez for France.

The American broadcaster, speaking over the European service from London in German, told the Germans that General Eisenhower was not present at the signing.

He afterwards received General-Admiral von Friedeberg.

(Continued on Page 2)

Churchill On The Rhine

CHURCHILL ON THE RHINE: The Prime Minister, accompanied by Field Marshal Montgomery, Field Marshal Sir Alan Brooke, and (behind the Premier) General Simpson, photographed on the bank of the Rhine on March 26.

BRITISH SECOND ARMY

27 Divisions Smashed 79

Don Campbell, Reuter's special correspondent with the British 2nd Army cables

TWENTY-SEVEN BRITISH AND AMERICAN DIVISIONS WHICH FOUGHT UNDER THE COMMAND OF THE BRITISH 2nd ARMY, HAVE DESTROYED 79 GERMAN DIVISIONS—AT THE RATE OF ONE PER DAY OVER ONE PERIOD. THEY HAVE LIBERATED 11,000 SQUARE MILES OF EUROPE AND CONQUERED 70,000 SQUARE MILES OF GERMANY, INCLUDING 110 GERMAN TOWNS.

FROM "D" DAY TO "V" DAY:

These figures are included in what may be termed the official statistical story of the British 2nd Army from "D" day to its own Victory Day — May 5 — a total of 333 days.

In those 11 months of battle General Sir Miles Dempsey's men have opened and maintained 11,000 miles of road, constructed 76 airfields and built 676 bridges which, placed end to end, would stretch 116 and a half miles.

Unconditional surrender of Germany.

Victory came laden with glory,
Passed the gates' triumphal arch,
Sprinkling joy in Allies' Quarters,
Strewing bliss along her march.

Now that Victory bells do ring,
Palm and laurel with us sing!
Victory came as a Death's Conqueror
As Soul's Agent, killing strife

Promising crown to Peace dethroned
And in Europe bringing life.
Now that Victory bells do ring,
Grateful hearts in chorus sing!

Tue 8 May

Following the unconditional surrender by German Plenipotentiaries of all German land, sea, and air forces to the Allies, the surrender agreement is ratified and confirmed at Berlin today. The Ratification is signed by Air Chief-Marshal Sir Arthur Tedder, Deputy Supreme Commander, and General De Lattre Tassyny on behalf of the Supreme Commander, and Marshal Zukhov on behalf of the Soviet Union. The German representatives are Field-Marshal Keitel, Chief of the German High Command, and Commander-in-Chief of the German Army, Navy and Air Forces.

Today is 'Victory in Europe Day' in accordance with arrangements between the three Great Powers.

Malta proclaims in flowers the end of the war in Europe.

Kingsway in Valletta decorated to mark the end of hostilities.

The leader of the *Times of Malta* (*Victory Number*) is dedicated to 'Victory Day'. – 'On May 8, 1943, the bells of Malta pealed to celebrate the fall of Tunis and to herald the German surrender in Africa. The peals of victory bells today ring out to hail the unconditional surrender of all German fighting forces in Europe, land, sea, and air … While all rejoice at the liberation of all peoples of Europe let all give thanks to Almighty God who gave strength and power to the leaders of the peoples of the British Commonwealth and Empire and of the United Nations to smite the power of evil and to vanquish it. Let us rejoice and return thanks with the knowledge that after thanksgiving for victory in Europe we must pull together for the further task of finishing the war in the world.'

A second V-Day Edition of the *Times of Malta* is published. To mark Victory Day in Valletta, large crowds thronged into Kingsway and the Palace Square. The King's Own Band and the La Valette Band, supported by the banners and standards of the bands of the suburbs and villages, paraded. Archbishop Gonzi appeared on the balcony and was given a rousing reception. Further applause marked the appearance of the Governor and the Services Chiefs. In his address to the gathering on the piazza, His Excellency said: 'Let us honour the magnificent men who have fought, endured, and finally conquered the enemy by sea, land, and air; the people in the home lands throughout the Empire who have worked, sacrificed, and suffered; and our Allies who gathered so mightily to our support. Freedom and peace are once more possible for Europe. Pray God we do not cast these prizes away by internal strife within nations, or by external rivalry between them. Do not let us forget in our joy the sorrow and misery the war in Europe has left in its trail. Our work for the deliverance of the world is not yet over, much sacrifice will be demanded of us to alleviate the sufferings of Europe.'

To mark the cessation of hostilities, HE has extended a measure of clemency and amnesty to a number of civil prisoners detained in the Civil Prisons. Others have had their prison sentence reduced by varying periods. Eight boys are released from the Approved School.

Vice-Admiral Sir F.H. Dalrymple-Hamilton, KCB, relieves Vice-Admiral Sir Louis Hamilton, KCB, DSO, as Vice-Admiral, Malta. Dalrymple-Hamilton commanded HMS *Rodney* (1939–41), was Admiral Commanding Iceland (1941–42) and Naval Secretary to the First Lord of the Admiralty (1942–44).

Sir Wilfred Woods, KCMG, KBE is in Malta to advise the Colonial Secretary on the present and prospective financial position of the Malta Government.

Wed 9 May

Malta V-Day message to the King: 'On the conclusion of hostilities and the utter defeat of the enemies of Your Majesty in Europe, the Garrison and people of Malta desire to offer their heart-felt congratulations to Your Majesty at the triumph of our Arms and the successful outcome of the War with Germany, fully confident that it will lead to a lasting peace guaranteeing the freedom of the peoples of Your Empire and those of the United Nations. Malta is determined to continue to render every assistance and co-operation in the Empire's war against Japan.'

TIMES OF MALTA

No. 3,022 WEDNESDAY, MAY 9, 1945

IN THIS HOUR OF VICTORY WE TURN TO REMAINING FOE

STRONG IN FAITH AND UNITY

H. M. THE KING'S "VE" DAY BROADCAST TO THE NATION AND EMPIRE

(Reuter's Service) LONDON, May 8.

KING GEORGE VI IN HIS VICTORY DAY BROADCAST TO THE NATION AND EMPIRE TONIGHT, WARNED THE BRITISH PEOPLE THEY STILL HAD TO DEAL WITH THE JAPANESE — A DETERMINED AND CRUEL FOE — "AND TO THIS WE SHALL TURN WITH THE UTMOST RESOLVE AND WITH ALL OUR RESOURCES."

HIS MAJESTY THE KING SAID: "TODAY WE GIVE THANKS TO GOD FOR OUR GREAT DELIVERANCE. SPEAKING FROM OUR EMPIRE'S OLDEST CAPITAL CITY, WAR BATTERED BUT NEVER FOR ONE MOMENT DAUNTED OR DISMAYED — SPEAKING FROM LONDON, I ASK YOU TO JOIN ME IN THAT ACT OF THANKSGIVING.

"GERMANY, WHO DROVE ALL EUROPE INTO WAR HAS BEEN FINALLY OVERCOME. IN THE FAR EAST WE HAVE YET TO DEAL WITH THE JAPANESE, A DETERMINED AND CRUEL FOE. TO THIS WE SHALL TURN WITH THE UTMOST RESOLVE AND ALL OUR RESOURCES."

One Pause For Thanksgiving:

"But at this hour, when the dreadful shadow of war has passed far from our hearths and homes in these islands, we may at least make one pause for thanksgiving and then we must turn our thoughts to tasks all over the world which the peace in Europe brings with it.

THE FALLEN:

"First let us remember those who will not come back: their constancy and courage in battle, their sacrifices and endurance in the face of a merciless enemy; let us remember the men in all the Services, the women in all the Services who have laid down their lives. We have come to the end of our tribulation and they are not with us at the moment of our rejoicing.

THE VICTORIOUS

"Next, let us salute in proud gratitude the great host of the living who brought us to victory.

"I cannot praise them to the measure of each one's service, for in total war efforts all rise to the same noble height and all are devoted to the common purpose. Armed or unarmed, men and women, you have fought and striven to your utmost.

"None knows that better than I do and as your King I thank with a full heart those who bore arms so valiantly on land, sea or in the air and all civilians who, shouldering their many burdens, carried them unflinchingly and without complaint.

OUR FAITH AND UNITY:

"With those memories in our minds let us think what

(Continued on page 8)

"VE" DAY IN MALTA

"VE" crowd in Kingsway yesterday ... towards Palace Square. (Other pictures: Page 8).

A MINUTE PAST MIDNIGHT

Jon Kimche, Reuter's military correspondent in London, cables:

AT one minute past midnight with the formal "Cease Fire" on all the fronts — after five years, eight months and four days — the Third German Reich ceases its legal existence and its Government ceases to function. Germany and her Government will have become a subjugated, conquered and occupied country without further independent existence. There will be no armistice as in 1918. As from one minute past midnight tonight the whole of German man-power and all German military and private property is at the disposal of the Allies.

GERMANS SIGN CAPITULATION IN PRAGUE

(Reuter's Service) PRAGUE, May 8.

Prague radio tonight (Tuesday) said that an agreement for the German capitulation in Prague and surrounding areas starting at 8 p.m. (local time) tonight has been signed.

CAPITULATION IN NORWAY

(Reuter's Service) STOCKHOLM, May 8.

The Swedish radio announced tonight that Allied delegates arrived in Oslo tonight to receive the German capitulation.

Sven Aagee Nielsen, Reuter's special correspondent inside Norway cables:

Allied naval units which are reported to have arrived in Oslo Fjord will, it is believed, form the nucleus of the British mission in Norway.

Formations of the German army are marching towards the Swedish frontier. It is believed they will be interned in Sweden.

Detachments of quislings are on their way northwards where, it is believed, they will be forced to build roads as part of their punishment.

—The 3rd. Army Fought On

(Reuter's Service) U.S. 3rd ARMY, H.Q., May 8.

Frontline troops of the United States 3rd Army, rolling through Czechoslovakia, did not know of the "Cease Fire" ordered for 8 a.m. today until four hours later.

The war still went on and there was fighting along the road from Pilsen to Prague and at the southern end of General Patton's 150-mile front stretching from Czechoslovakia to Austria.

GERMAN CAPITULATION

The Surrender Terms

— SUPREME HEADQUARTERS, A.E.F.

(Reuter's Service) PARIS, May 8.

The following is the text of the German military unconditional surrender to the Allies:

"FIRSTLY, we, the undersigned, acting by the authority of the German High Command, hereby surrender unconditionally to the Supreme Commander of the Allied Expeditionary Force, and simultaneously to the Soviet High Command, all forces on land, sea and in the air who are, at this date, under German control.

"Secondly, the German High Command will at once issue orders to all German military, naval and air authorities and to all forces under German control to cease active operations at 23.01 hours (Central European Time) on May 8, and to remain in positions occupied at that time. No ship, vessel or aircraft is to be scuttled or any damage done to their hull, machinery or equipment.

"Thirdly, the German High Command will at once issue these orders to the appropriate commanders and ensure the carrying out of any further orders issued by the Supreme Commander of the Allied Expeditionary Force and by the Soviet High Command.

"Fourthly, this act of military surrender is without prejudice and will be superseded by any general instrument of surrender imposed by, or on behalf of the United Nations and applicable to Germany and the German armed forces as a whole."

German Fleet

ADMIRALTY ORDERS

The Admiralty announces that the following orders have been issued for the surrender of the German fleet:

"All German and German-controlled warships, auxiliaries, merchant ships and other craft at sea are being ordered to report their position in plain language to the nearest Allied Wireless Telegraphy Station and are being given orders to proceed to such Allied ports as directed. They will remain in

(Continued on Page 2)

King George VI broadcasts a Victory Day speech.

Sun 13 May

Leader of today's *Sunday Times of Malta* is entitled 'Day of Thanksgiving'. – 'Today, Sunday May 13, has been dedicated .at the wish of His Majesty the King as a Day of Thanksgiving in Britain for the great victory which has been vouchsafed to the champions of Christian democracy after nearly six years of unprecedented effort and sacrifice. His Grace the Archbishop had directed that a Te Deum is to be sung today in the Cathedral Churches, Collegiate and Parish Churches of the Diocese ... It is fitting that all should unite on this solemn occasion to give thanks and render homage to the Almighty.'

Tue 15 May

p.m. Pilgrimage held by the Reverend Chapter of St Paul Shipwrecked of Valletta in thanksgiving for the deliverance from war and for the protection which the Apostle has extended to the whole island and in particular to the church dedicated to him in Valletta. The holy relic of the wristbone of St Paul is carried in procession from St Paul's Church in Valletta to the church of St Publius, Floriana, and back. Mgr Emanuel Galea, Vicar General, conducted the pilgrimage. The Metropolitan Archbishop participated. Canon J. Mifsud made a moving and patriotic address at St Publius Church.

Fri 18 May

Eighth sitting of the National Assembly.

Wed 23 May

Britain's National Government comes to an end as Prime Minister Churchill resigns.

Thu 24 May

Heinrich Himmler, German SS Chief, commits suicide.

Fri 25 May

Ninth sitting of the National Assembly.

Wed 20 Jun

Some 500 German prisoners-of-war arrive in Malta; they will be under the direct control of the local Military Authorities, who will employ these prisoners on works detailed by the War Department. This arrangement will render possible the release of local masons now working with the Services and thereby have them engaged on reconstruction projects. No person is allowed within 50 yards of the perimeter of any prisoner-of-war camp.

The fiercest and bloodiest 82-day-long battle in the Pacific has ended with the fall of Okinawa. Thu 21 Jun

Feast of St Peter and St Paul – the *Mnarja*. The Agrarian Society holds a 'Victory Year' agricultural show at Boschetto Gardens. Tue 29 Jun

The bronze monument commemorating the Great Siege of Malta of 1565 is being restored to its old site at Great Siege Square in Valletta. The central figure symbolizes Maltese unity, while the figures on either side symbolize Religion and Civilization.[3]

London. Among six promotions to the rank of Rear-Admiral announced today is that of Capt. E.G. Russbrooks who, while in command of HMS *Eagle*, helped to save Malta by flying off fighter reinforcements to the island, and Capt. G.S. Russell who was naval liaison officer at Gibraltar and to the Governor of Malta Lord Gort. Fri 6 Jul

Guam. Air Marshal Sir Hugh Lloyd, AOC Malta at the time of the heaviest attacks by the *Luftwaffe*, has been appointed Commander of the British Air Forces in the Pacific. Wed 18 Jul

Speech by the Governor on the occasion of the opening of the Fifth Session of the Council of Government: 'Much has happened since my predecessor, Lord Gort, addressed this Council, nearly twenty-one months ago. The tide of victory has already turned in favour of the Allies, and it continued to mount relentlessly until finally on 8 May 1945, it submerged all Germany. Now that tide is mounting on the other side of the world. Thankful for their deliverance from the hands of the enemy, I know that the people of Malta have watched and will watch with admiration the fighting forces of the Allies in their stupendous task of ridding the world of the aggressors. Malta Thu 19 Jul

3 The memorial which was unveiled on 8 May 1927 is the work of Antonio Sciortino. In the early days of the war it was removed to a safe place as a precaution against air attacks.

is proud to have played her part in active operations … The recovery from acute battle conditions in a world at war must inevitably be a slow process, especially when that recovery depends, as it must do in these islands, which have so few natural resources, on so many factors beyond our control. On the other hand, when we contrast the conditions in these islands twenty-one months ago with those of today, the improvement in them is most marked.'

Fri 20 Jul **Tenth sitting of** the National Assembly.

Fri 27 Jul **Eleventh sitting of** the National Assembly.

The Labour Party wins the General Elections in Britain.

Sat 28 Jul **As from today** demolition and clearance work is taken in hand at Floriana – St Calcedonius Street and Granaries Square.

Mon 6 Aug **The first Atomic** Bomb, the bomb with a blast effect of 20,000 tons of TNT, has been dropped on the Japanese army base at Hiroshima.

Wed 8 Aug **Today's leader of** the *Times of Malta* is dedicated to the 'Atomic Bomb'. – 'The dropping of an atomic bomb upon a target in Japan marks a new era wherein strategic concepts of the past are out-of-date. The blast power of this new bomb is more than two thousand times greater than the previous largest, the British ten-tonner. The immense force of the new bomb is released by atomic energy – which marks the attainment of a decades-old scientific objective.'

Tokyo. Two days after the first atom-bombing in history, Tokyo Radio says that all living things, human and animal, were 'literally seared to death' in Monday's atom attack on the fortress city of Hiroshima with a population of 318,000 inhabitants.

Sun 12 Aug **Special Order of** the day by the Governor to the Three Services: 'I congratulate All Ranks of the Royal Navy, the Army, and the Royal Air Force serving in Malta on the part they have played in winning the war. One of the outstanding features of this Great War has been the close co-operation between the Three Fighting Services. Nowhere has this been better exemplified than in Malta. May the comradeship and mutual confidence so created be preserved in the years that lie ahead. All ranks may well feel proud that through six long years they have outfought one enemy after another. This achievement is due fundamentally to their morale and discipline.'

Archbishop's circular: 'Thanks to God, the war has come to a definite close and the long wished-for announcement of Peace has been made.' Tue 14 Aug

Feast of the Assumption of Our Lady into Heaven (*Festa ta' Santa Marija*). Wed 15 Aug

Japan has surrendered.

V(J)-Day.

Today's leader of the *Times of Malta* entitled 'Victory Day'. – 'The announcement of Victory has come and with a nation-wide thanksgiving to God. The celebration of Victory will reach its climax today, when the peals of Victory bells will ring out to hail the unconditional surrender of the Japanese, while the sirens throughout Malta and Gozo will wail their last "All Clear" signal … Today we give most humble and hearty thanks to the Almighty for deliverance. While paying loyal and humble tribute to the fallen, we render thanks to God that the days of peril are over for our gallant sailors, soldiers, and airmen, among them thousands of our own countrymen are to be found in every theatre of war on sea and land and in the air.'

The announcement of Japan's capitulation reaches Malta at 1 a.m. today. But Victory was announced officially to the People of Malta at 6 a.m. by the sounding of the sirens, the ringing of bells.

Message addressed to HM the King by the Governor: 'These Islands, which even in the darkest days of air attacks and siege never lost confidence in final victory, are proud of the part which they played in its attainment.'

Message addressed to all Colonies, Protectorates, and Mandated Territories by the Secretary of State for the Colonies: 'Final victory

TIMES OF MALTA

No. 3,197. WEDNESDAY, AUGUST 15, 1945

VICTORY AND PEACE ON EARTH

JAPAN ACCEPTS ALLIED SURRENDER TERMS

(Reuter's Service)

"Japan has today surrendered. The last of our enemies has been laid low....." with these words Britain's Prime Minister, Clement Attlee, gave the nation the news it had waited for the past 24 hours, at 2300 hrs. G.M.T. tonight. (1 a.m. Malta time).

Giving the full text, the Prime Minister said

"WITH REFERENCE TO THE ANNOUNCEMENT ON AUGUST 10 REGARDING THE ACCEPTANCE OF THE PROVISIONS OF THE POTSDAM DECLARATION AND THE REPLY OF THE GOVERNMENTS OF THE UNITED STATES, GREAT BRITAIN, THE SOVIET UNION AND CHINA, SENT BY THE SECRETARY OF STATE MR. J. BYRNES ON AUGUST 11, THE JAPANESE GOVERNMENT HAS THE HONOUR TO REPLY TO THE GOVERNMENTS OF THE FOUR POWERS AS FOLLOWS:

"(1) His Majesty the Emperor has issued an Imperial rescript regarding Japan's acceptance of the Potsdam Declaration.

"(2) The Emperor is prepared to authorize and ensure the signature by his Government and the Imperial H.Q. of the necessary terms for carrying out the provisions of the Potsdam Declaration.

(3) His Majesty is also prepared to issue this communication to all military, naval and air authorities to issue to all forces under their control wherever located, to cease active resistance and to surrender arms.

Signed Togo
Foreign Minister"

General MacArthur has been appointed Allied Commander to receive the surrender.

EMPEROR HIROHITO

YOUR NEWSPAPERS

No Publication Tomorrow

There will be no publication tomorrow of either the "Times of Malta" or "Il-Berqa".

Both newspapers will re-appear on Friday, as usual, as will "The Sunday Times of Malta".

The "Big Four"

It was President Truman, the then Prime Minister Winston Churchill and Generalissimo Chiang Kai-shek that on July 26, 1945, formulated the Potsdam Declaration to Japan. The Declaration has since been adhered to by Generalissimo Stalin.

RT. HON. CLEMENT ATTLEE

V(J)-DAY

H.M. THE KING'S BROADCAST

The following notice has been received from the Information Office, Malta:

HIS MAJESTY THE KING WILL BROADCAST TO THE NATION AT [illegible] HRS. G.M.T. ([illegible] P.M. MALTA TIME) ON V(J)-DAY

CHIANG KAI-SHEK (China)

MARSHAL STALIN (Soviet Union)

WINSTON CHURCHILL (Great Britain)

PRESIDENT TRUMAN (United States)

Surrender of Japan and the end of hostilities.

over the Forces of Aggression has been achieved. It is a source of great pride to me that one of my first tasks in office should he to send you such a message. Let us thank God in all humility that the task has been so quickly completed; that this horrible slaughter and destruction are now ended and that the efforts of mankind can once more he devoted to the happiness of mankind … Let us hope, pray, and work together to build from the desolation of War a new and prosperous era of Peace and Good Will among Nations.'

This evening large crowds flocked into Valletta when they were addressed by the Governor's Deputy, Vice-Admiral Sir Frederick Dalrymple-Hamilton, from the Palace balcony: 'The Maltese people will, I know, have a feeling of satisfaction that they have taken their part in the building up of this mighty power … Malta has also given up a number of her much-needed houses and allotted a large proportion of her building labour to provide the accommodation so essential for a large Naval and Air Staging Station. We can well he proud of this mighty power of the Empire and her allies which has been forged to bring freedom back into the world, but let us never

A silent tribute to the heroes of the Malta Convoy. *(Sunday Times of Malta)*

forget that no material power in ships, tanks, aircraft, or guns is of any avail, but for the spirit of the men who work and fight them. As it was in Europe, so it was in the Far East. It has been the indomitable fortitude and morale of plain men, which has withstood and finally conquered a fanatical enemy, often in unimaginable conditions of hardships due to country and climate. Let us now humbly honour these men, so many of whom have undergone untold suffering or have made the supreme sacrifice. War in the world is now over, and we give thanks to Almighty God that He has given us the final victory over the aggressor nations. We rejoice that the slaughter is over. We can now turn all our attention to the building up again of a ravaged world. It always takes longer to build than to destroy. There is much to be rebuilt, both material and moral, but with the high example before us of the men and women who have worked, fought, suffered, and died for the cause of freedom, we can but set about our task of rebuilding with the same spirit of unselfishness and high endeavour. In this spirit let us now rejoice and go forward.'[4]

Fri 17 Aug

Today's editorial comment of the *Times of Malta* is dedicated to 'Our Lady of Victories'. – 'And so it was that Malta on August 15, 1945, came to celebrate Victory and the religious festival of Santa Marija. There was no spectacular gathering in the city, but Victory and Santa Marija were celebrated together, most fervently throughout the island, and in the night the towns and villages were lighted up, giving Malta, together with the ships in the harbour, a Victory glow perhaps unique on that night in the Mediterranean.'

Sun 19 Aug

This morning His Grace Archbishop Gonzi intoned the Te Deum, the Catholic hymn of thanksgiving to the Almighty, during a special Thanksgiving Service for Victory held in St John's Church. During the ceremony His Grace delivered a stirring address: '*Exultemus*. Let us rejoice. This was the cry that came out spontaneously from the bottom of our hearts, when at the dawn of last Wednesday [15 August] the Feast of the Assumption of the Blessed Virgin Mary all the bells of Malta announced to us the end of hostilities in the

4 The Governor had left for England. The speech was prepared by His Excellency and read by his Deputy.

world … Let us also show our gratitude to those who are injured and incapacitated perhaps for life, victims of battles on land, on sea and in the air.' The Archbishop was given a rousing ovation as he left the church after the ceremony. The bells of St John's accompanied by those of all the other churches in Valletta and Floriana again pealed out a joyous note.

Victory horse races were held this afternoon at Rabat (Malta).

Broadcast by the Governor, Sir Edmond Schreiber, to the people of Malta: 'His Majesty's Government recognizes Malta's great services to the Allied cause during the war and is most anxious to implement the promise made in 1943 to restore to the Maltese people Responsible Government in the same sphere as they enjoyed between 1921 and 1933. It feels that it is indeed fitting that the Maltese should assume their former responsibility for the management of their own affairs. It is a matter of concern to His Majesty's Government that there should be no cause or excuse for avoidable delay in making good that promise … Not only is our aim to launch the ship of Responsible Government, but we must all take our part in ensuring that the waters into which it is launched are as untroubled as we can make them.' Sun 31 Aug

Index

B

C

D

F

G

T